JESUS
AND THE
FORCES
OF DEATH

JESUS
AND THE
FORCES
OF DEATH

THE GOSPELS' PORTRAYAL
OF RITUAL IMPURITY WITHIN
FIRST-CENTURY JUDAISM

MATTHEW THIESSEN

Baker Academic
a division of Baker Publishing Group
Grand Rapids, Michigan

Published by Baker Academic
a division of Baker Publishing Group
PO Box 6287, Grand Rapids, MI 49516-6287
www.bakeracademic.com

Paperback edition published 2021
ISBN 978-1-5409-6487-8

Printed in the United States of America

The Library of Congress has cataloged the hardcover edition as follows:
Names: Thiessen, Matthew, 1977– author.
Title: Jesus and the forces of death : the gospels' portrayal of ritual impurity within first-century Judaism / Matthew Thiessen.
Description: Grand Rapids, Michigan : Baker Academic, a division of Baker Publishing Group, 2020. | Includes bibliographical references and index.
Identifiers: LCCN 2019039575 | ISBN 9781540961945 (cloth)
Subjects: LCSH: Purity, Ritual—Christianity—Biblical teaching. | Purity, Ritual—Judaism—Biblical teaching. | Jewish law. | Bible. Gospels—Criticism, interpretation, etc. | Christianity and other religions—Judaism. | Judaism—Relations—Christianity.
Classification: LCC BS2545.P95 T45 2020 | DDC 226/.06—dc23
LC record available at https://lccn.loc.gov/2019039575

With Love,
For Peter and Agnes Thiessen

Contents

Preface

Back when I should have been writing my doctoral dissertation on circumcision, I became obsessed with ritual purity systems. Apart from the inevitable compulsion of a doctoral student to do anything but write one's dissertation, I blame Jacob Milgrom. Milgrom's extensive writings on the topics of Leviticus, sacrifice, and Jewish ritual purity threatened to derail any progress I made toward completing my degree. In the course of reading everything of his that I could get my hands on, I suddenly realized that much of what he and others had discovered in priestly literature provided me with a new lens through which to read the Gospel accounts of the life of Jesus. I knew then that I would write this book.

Fortunately, my responsible self returned, and I refocused enough to finish my dissertation. Unfortunately for this book, I was convinced that my dissertation required me to write another book before I could turn my attention to the topic of ritual purity. Consequently, what you hold in your hands is a book that I would have liked to have written ten years ago but am nevertheless happy to finally get off my mind and onto paper.

Given the long time between conceiving the idea for this book and actually getting around to writing it, many of my debts to others are long forgotten, erased not, I hope, by ingratitude but by a faulty memory. Nonetheless, I am thankful to mentors, colleagues, and students at Duke University, the College of Emmanuel and St. Chad, Saint Louis University, and McMaster University for many stimulating conversations about various aspects of this book. Thanks especially to Paula Fredriksen and Cecilia Wassen for input at a critical juncture in the writing of this project. Defective as my memory may be, I cannot fail to remember my family: my partner, Jennifer, and my two children, Solomon and Maggie. They bring me such richness and joy by lovingly refusing to let me work as much as I erroneously think I would like to work.

Finally, I am immeasurably grateful to my parents, Peter and Agnes Thiessen. I simply cannot remember a day in my childhood when my parents did not work diligently to instill in me the belief that one could find life in the texts that are the focus of this book. For this reason, I dedicate this book to them.

A Clarification

This book is *not* about the historical Jesus. That is to say, I am *not* here seeking to sift through the historical evidence in order to discover what Jesus really said and what Jesus really did. I am *not* trying to get behind the Gospels to uncover the real Jesus—either to prove that the Gospels accurately portray him or to demonstrate that they have re-created him for purposes of their own. My objective is *not* to weigh the literary evidence in order to discover data of historical value in order to write an account of the historical Jesus.

For such a treatment, one must begin with John P. Meier's 3,500-page *A Marginal Jew*.[1] Nonetheless, I harbor two reservations about any such project. First, the only way back to the historical Jesus is through literary sources: the four Gospels of what we call the New Testament, the works of Josephus, and the Gospels that did not make it into the New Testament. The question of historicity can be asked (and at best, partially answered) only after one has determined more accurately what the Gospel writers actually say about Jesus. Yet our efforts to interpret these texts are themselves contested. Read two or three commentaries on Mark or Matthew, and you will frequently find two or three competing interpretations of a passage. If we can't agree on the literary evidence we do have, I think it unlikely that we could ever come to a consensus about something we can never have: unmediated access to the historical Jesus.

---

1. On the question of the historical Jesus's views on ritual impurity, see Kazen, *Jesus and Purity Halakhah*; Kazen, *Scripture, Interpretation, or Authority*; Wassen, "Jesus' Table Fellowship"; Wassen, "Use of the Dead Sea Scrolls"; Wassen, "Jewishness of Jesus and Ritual Purity"; and Wassen, "Jesus' Work as a Healer."

Second, and more fundamentally, I find the methodology of most historical Jesus research to be too blunt to do what historical Jesus scholars require of it. The criteria of authenticity, as scholars call them, can do very little in separating the authentic from the inauthentic. In what follows, I will not argue for the authenticity of this or that saying or deed. Instead, I will show the ways in which the Gospel writers depict Jesus. Such depictions, of course, relate in some way to history—that is, they must fall somewhere along a spectrum from being entirely historically accurate to being entirely historically inaccurate. That these believers in Jesus repeatedly remember him in a certain way must shed some light on the historical realities that occasioned the composing of such stories.[2] What does it say about the historical Jesus that some of the earliest stories about him repeatedly place him in contact with people who have abnormal conditions that make them ritually impure?

When it comes to the question of Jesus and the Jewish law, particularly aspects of it such as ritual purity, commentators through the centuries have almost universally misconstrued the Gospel writers' portrayals.[3] Frequently, such misconstruals arise out of Christian presuppositions regarding the Jewish law—especially those assumptions that are indebted to certain understandings of the apostle Paul's thinking about the Jewish law.[4] Given later Christian rejection of and contempt for the Jewish ritual purity system, the logic seems to go, surely Jesus himself must have abandoned this external system in favor of interior spiritual realities. But, as I will show in the following chapters, the Jesus that the Synoptic Gospel writers depict is a Jesus genuinely concerned with matters of law observance. Concerning the historical value of the literary evidence we have, Paula Fredriksen puts it well: "Perhaps . . . Jesus did think that God's Torah (that is, Leviticus and Deuteronomy) was an outdated set of taboos, but we have no evidence that he did, and, in the behavior of the later church, we actually have counterevidence. . . . On the evidence of Paul's letters, the Gospels, and Acts, these apostles chose to live in Jerusalem, worship in the Temple, and keep the festivals, the Sabbath, and the food laws. Could they really have understood nothing?"[5]

---

2. Here see Allison, *Constructing Jesus*; Rodríguez, *Structuring Early Christian Memory*; Keith and Le Donne, *Jesus, Criteria, and the Demise of Authenticity*; and Bernier, *Quest for the Historical Jesus*.

3. For example, Lambrecht, "Jesus and the Law"; Crossan, *The Historical Jesus*; Borg, *Conflict, Holiness, and Politics*; N. T. Wright, *Jesus and the Victory of God*; and Dunn, "Jesus and Purity."

4. Even here, I think most scholarship understands Paul wrongly. See my own account of this in *Paul and the Gentile Problem*.

5. Fredriksen, "What You See," 89.

Introduction

In a 2018 sermon, American megachurch pastor Andy Stanley stirred up controversy when he suggested that leaders in the early Jesus movement sought "to unhitch the Christian faith from their Jewish scriptures." He then asserted to his congregation that "we must as well."[1] Responses to Stanley's remarks went viral as numerous Christians accused him of imitating the ancient arch-heretic Marcion, who sought to disconnect Christianity from the Old Testament.[2] And in an academic context, Notger Slenczka, a systematic theologian at the University of Berlin, has recently argued that the Old Testament should not have canonical authority; rather, it should function more like the Apocrypha does for Protestants.[3] Again, theologians have responded with charges that Slenczka is guilty of both heresy and anti-Jewish thinking.

But most Christians find their Old Testament to be troublesome. For instance, I have heard from numerous Christians that, despite their best and most pious intentions to read through the Bible (whether in a year or a lifetime), they have found their efforts stymied once they hit Leviticus and Numbers. These Christians usually are committed to the belief that the Bible in its entirety is the inspired word of God and that by reading it they are drawing closer to God. Yet the realities of the text seem to undermine and unsettle this theological conviction. For instance, how many pastors or priests willingly *choose* to preach from texts like Leviticus or Numbers? Many Christian

---

1. For the full sermon, see Stanley, "Aftermath, Part 3."
2. Contrary to my usual practice, I have chosen to use the Christian term *Old Testament* at the outset of this chapter because of the way it functions precisely as the *Old* Testament for the people under discussion.
3. The debate that has ensued has occurred almost exclusively in German and so is not well-known to English speakers outside of academic circles. See, for instance, Slenczka, "Die Kirche," 83–119.

leaders and thinkers seek to fight this reluctance toward the Old Testament, but even these efforts hint at their own discomfort. I noticed this hesitance the first time I was tasked with preaching from the *Revised Common Lectionary*, a series of scripture readings that usually contains an Old Testament text, a psalm, a New Testament text, and a Gospel text. The Old Testament text for that Sunday (the second Sunday of Lent in Year B) was from Genesis 17. Genesis 17 is *the* chapter on circumcision in the Bible, yet the editors of the *Revised Common Lectionary* had cut out all the portions of the chapter that actually talk about circumcision. Those people who came to church thinking that they would hear a sermon on Genesis 17 actually heard a very carefully edited, essentially Christianized (or de-Judaized) version of Genesis 17.[4]

Since the Holocaust, many Christians have been made aware of the always-present danger of anti-Judaism in Christian thinking. In at least some Christian circles, accusations of anti-Judaism hold considerable power and can function as an effective way to dismiss the claims or arguments of another person. And ever since the pioneering work of Geza Vermes in his 1973 book titled *Jesus the Jew*,[5] it has been common for people to emphasize that Jesus was, in fact, a Jew. These developments should be very welcome to all, yet the same people who speak most about Jesus's Jewishness often go on to argue that Jesus was not very Jewish in certain ways. My belief is that such people, whether preachers, writers, or scholars, are guilty of the same error committed by the editors of the *Revised Common Lectionary* in their carefully curated version of Genesis 17.

For instance, N. T. Wright, a prolific Christian scholar who wields immense influence inside and outside of academic circles, speaks of "a very Jewish Jesus who was nevertheless opposed to some high-profile features of first-century Judaism."[6] Such arguments, as James Crossley notes, boil down to the claim that Jesus was "Jewish . . . but not that Jewish."[7] One of my central aims in writing this book is to show that the Gospel writers portray a Jesus who really was *that* Jewish. I will do this by focusing on one area where scholars almost always conclude that Jesus really wasn't that Jewish after all: his interactions with those who were ritually impure. Matthew, Mark, and Luke repeatedly depict Jesus as the one who rescues people from the forces of impurity that

---

4. This treatment of Gen. 17 fits a larger trend of omitting from the lectionary Old Testament passages that deal with practices that Christians do not generally observe. For instance, the three-year lectionary cycle contains only two readings from all of Leviticus (both from Lev. 19), neither of which pertains to issues of sacrifice or ritual impurity. More broadly, see Strawn, *Old Testament Is Dying*.

5. Vermes, *Jesus the Jew*. See now Moller, *Vermes Quest*.

6. N. T. Wright, *Jesus and the Victory of God*, 93.

7. Crossley, "Multicultural Christ," 8–16. See also Arnal, *Symbolic Jesus*.

exist within the world.[8] In all three of these Gospels, Jesus encounters people who are ritually impure due to *untreatable* conditions: "leprosy" (*lepra*),[9] an abnormal genital discharge, and death.

Having just referred to ritual impurity, I know that I am in danger of turning many readers off, but bear with me a bit longer! My conviction is that we cannot fully appreciate how the Gospel writers communicate Jesus's significance apart from an accurate understanding of the ways in which first-century Jews constructed their world. I am persuaded that we often misunderstand the Gospel writers' depictions of Jesus because we naturally and unthinkingly transfer him and the people of the literary world of the Gospels into our own conceptual world. When coming across something foreign or different, it is natural to translate (often unconsciously) whatever is foreign into something understandable. But modern readers of the Gospels will not rightly understand Jesus apart from a more thorough comprehension of ancient Jewish (and non-Jewish) ritual purity concerns, precisely because these purity concerns map out the reality of the world as the Gospel writers conceived it.

Many modern readers of the New Testament find the Jewish ritual purity system to be alien at best and irrational at worst. Surely, such thinking goes, it is an embarrassment to modern religious adherents that their sacred texts refer to natural bodily processes as impure. How can any enlightened person consider someone who experiences natural bodily processes, such as sex, childbirth, or menstruation, to be impure? For Christian readers, the embarrassment or discomfort created by these passages is often ameliorated only by the supposed fact that Jesus and Paul rejected ritual purity concerns because such laws were focused on trivial, external issues, when God cares about interior dispositions and attitudes. Consider the words of the early twentieth-century German theologian Adolf von Harnack: "[Jews] thought of God as of a despot guarding the ceremonial observances in His household; [Jesus] breathed in the presence of God. [The Jews] saw Him only in His law, which they had converted into a labyrinth of dark defiles, blind alleys and secret passages; [Jesus] saw and felt Him everywhere."[10] Harnack's words describe Judaism as dead legalism focused on external ceremonies and then contrast this negative portrayal of Jewish religiosity to Jesus's free spirituality.

8. See the related argument of Bolt, *Jesus' Defeat of Death*.

9. Throughout this book, I will avoid the term *leprosy*, preferring instead *lepra*, the transliteration of the Greek word that Septuagint translators used to render the Hebrew word *ṣāraʿat*. It is an unfortunate reality that almost all modern Bibles translate this word as "leprosy," something it was almost assuredly not. See chap. 3 for a detailed discussion.

10. Harnack, *What Is Christianity?*, 50–51.

One can see in Harnack's claims the belief that Judaism is a religion, while Christianity is a relationship with God.

The claim that Jesus opposes the ritual purity system is all too common within theology, biblical interpretation, sermons, and the everyday thinking and language of many Christians. It is a claim that transcends internal Christian divisions between liberals and conservatives, between Catholics, Orthodox, and Protestants. For instance, John Dominic Crossan argues that Jesus saw himself as the "functional opponent, alternative, and substitute" to the Jewish temple in Jerusalem.[11] For Crossan, this opposition to the ritual purity system and the Jerusalem temple was connected to economic, class, and gender inequities. In other words, at least one central aspect of Jewish life—ritual purity and the temple cult—perpetuated an unjust social system that Jesus sought to overcome. In this light, Jesus stands for equality while Judaism stands for inequality.[12]

Likewise, Marcus Borg has argued that Jesus envisaged "a community shaped not by the ethos and politics of purity, but by the ethos and politics of compassion."[13] And Richard Beck makes a similar contrast: "Sacrifice—the purity impulse—marks off a zone of holiness, admitting the 'clean' and expelling the 'unclean.' Mercy, by contrast, crosses those purity boundaries. Mercy blurs the distinction, bringing clean and unclean into contact. Thus the tension. One impulse—holiness and purity—erects boundaries, while the other impulse—mercy and hospitality—crosses and ignores those boundaries."[14] One can see a dramatic presentation of this purported contrast between the Jewish elite and Jesus in Stuart L. Love's chart:

	Elite	Jesus
Core Value	God's holiness	God's mercy
Mission	Maintain political control	Inaugurate Israel's theocracy
Structural Implications	Strong boundaries Exclusive strategy	Weak boundaries Inclusive strategy
Scriptural Support	Law, except Genesis	Genesis and prophets

Adapted from Love, "Jesus Heals the Hemorrhaging Woman," 93.

Such arguments are indebted to a larger theological agenda that equates Jesus and Christianity with compassionate love on the one hand, and Judaism

11. Crossan, *Historical Jesus*, 355.

12. One can see the popularity of this reading in the attempts of some scholars who apply social-scientific criticism to the New Testament. For instance, Neyrey, "Idea of Purity in Mark's Gospel"; Rhoads, "Social Criticism"; and Malina, *New Testament World*, 161–97.

13. Borg, *Meeting Jesus Again*, 49. Cf. Borg, *Jesus in Contemporary Scholarship*, and Borg, *Conflict, Holiness, and Politics*.

14. Beck, *Unclean*, 2–3.

with sterile, heartless law observance on the other. As such, they are religious apologetics masquerading as historical research. "This is not history," Paula Fredriksen argues, "nor is it realistic description. It is caricature generated by abstractions, whereby a set of politically and ethically pleasant attributes define both Jesus (egalitarian, caring, other-directed, and so on) and, negatively, the majority of his Jewish contemporaries."[15]

What I advocate in this book is that readers, whatever their modern religious, theological, or ideological convictions, work sympathetically to understand ancient Jewish thinking about ritual purity on its own terms. Whatever we might think about systems of ritual purity, such systems were integral to the thinking of all ancient people, Jesus and the Gospel writers included. In this book, then, I focus on how an early reader who was knowledgeable of the Jewish purity laws (and ancient Mediterranean purity laws more generally)[16] might have interpreted the Synoptic Gospels' portrayals of Jesus.

Outline of *Jesus and the Forces of Death*

In chapter 1, I outline how ancient Jews mapped their world in relation to two different binaries: holy/profane and pure/impure. I discuss what these four categories mean and distinguish between different types of impurity. I also outline the role of Israel's priests in relation to these four categories.

In chapter 2, I begin by examining the ways that the Gospel writers situate Jesus's early life and public mission. I will begin with the initiatory role that John and his immersion of Jesus play in Jesus's mission, moving to a detailed examination of Luke's account of Jesus's family's law observance, in particular their adherence to ritual purity rites after Jesus's birth (Luke 2:21–23). Each Gospel writer connects the inauguration of Jesus's mission to John the Immerser's work of water purifications. These materials demonstrate that the Gospel writers emphasize immersion practices that would have been familiar to most Jews in Jesus's day. Luke's Gospel furthers this emphasis by showing how committed Jesus's family was to temple and Torah piety. Within the Gospel narratives, then, nothing prior to the inception of Jesus's work suggests that he would later go on to reject the ritual purity thinking that was common to his fellow Jews.

15. Fredriksen, "What You See Is What You Get," 96.

16. Although my primary focus is on the Jewish ritual purity system, in chaps. 3–5 I will also discuss non-Jewish purity thinking because modern readers are generally unaware of how ubiquitous such thinking was in the ancient Mediterranean world. See Frevel and Nihan, *Purity and the Forming of Religious Traditions*; Parker, *Miasma*; and Lennon, *Pollution and Religion*.

Chapters 3, 4, and 5 examine stories of Jesus's interactions with those suffering from the three general sources of impurity: *lepra*, genital discharges, and corpses. Each chapter will demonstrate Jesus's efforts to destroy the source of these ritual impurities. Together these chapters show that, according to the Gospel writers, when Jesus meets someone having a ritual impurity, he removes the source of that impurity from that person's body. In other words, Jesus does not abolish the ritual purity system;[17] rather, he abolishes the force that creates the ritual impurity in the person he meets. Jesus is, as Mark puts it, the holy one of God (Mark 1:24; cf. Luke 4:34; John 6:69), embodying a contagious power of holiness that overwhelms the forces of impurity.[18] Since, like most modern interpreters of the Gospels, I believe that the Gospel of Mark was written first, I place primary emphasis on Mark's account of Jesus's life. But I will also supplement the evidence of Mark with accounts from Matthew and Luke to show that in no way was Mark's treatment of Jesus an outlier in terms of early accounts of Jesus's mission. If any of the Gospels is unique, it is the Gospel of John, which does not generally deal with matters of ritual purity. Nonetheless, I will discuss pertinent aspects of John's Gospel briefly in chapter 4.

On the question of the synoptic problem (that is, the literary relationship between Matthew, Mark, and Luke), I believe that Mark's Gospel was written first and that both Matthew and Luke knew and used Mark. Further, I have become convinced that Luke knew and used Matthew's Gospel. This places me among a growing number of scholars who believe that Luke knew Matthew (the Farrer hypothesis), even as the majority of scholars still posit that Luke did not know Matthew but that both Luke and Matthew independently made use of the Gospel of Mark and another Gospel referred to as Q (the two-source hypothesis). For the latter scholars, I acknowledge that this book will contain an unsatisfying gap in that it does not examine the place of ritual impurity in Q's portrayal of Jesus.[19] Alas, I refuse to write about something that I do not believe existed.

In chapter 3, I will examine stories of Jesus's encounters with those suffering from *lepra*. I will devote particular attention to Mark 1:40–45 since it is the first and fullest story of Jesus's interactions with someone suffering from

---

17. See here Fredriksen, "Did Jesus Oppose the Purity Laws?"

18. Tom Holmén ("Jesus' Inverse Strategy," 25) argues that Jesus's purity is contagious, but this is inaccurate since purity is not a *force* but a *state* of being (and really a negative state, denoting the *absence* of impurity, not the actual presence of something). Instead, it is Jesus's *holiness* that functions as a force that can overpower impurity. Blood dedicated to God, for instance, is (implicitly) holy in priestly thought since it removes impurities (Lev. 17:11).

19. On the Farrer hypothesis, see Goodacre, *Case against Q*, and Poirier and Peterson, *Markan Priority without Q*.

the condition. One of the chief intentions of Mark's telling of this story, I will argue, is to convey to his readers that Jesus is opposed to the existence of ritual impurity. Jesus *wants* to heal those suffering from a condition that results in ritual impurity. To be clear, opposition to ritual impurity is not opposition to the ritual purity system itself. Fundamental to Mark's (and Matthew's and Luke's) portrayal of Jesus is the belief that Jesus desires to rid people of the conditions that create ritual impurity. This very desire indicates Jesus's belief that ritual impurity exists and that he needs to deal with it.

In chapter 4, I will discuss Jesus's healing of a woman who has suffered from a twelve-year genital discharge (Mark 5:25–34; Matt. 9:20–22; Luke 8:42b–48). Where doctors failed, Jesus succeeds. The story shows that the woman's confidence that Jesus is able to destroy the source of ritual impurity is accurately rooted in the nature of Jesus. Even though Jesus does not intend or choose to heal the woman, his body cannot help but emit a power that destroys her impurity. The story implies that Jesus's body can function like an unthinking force of contagion that inevitably destroys impurity.

In chapter 5, I will treat Jesus's interactions with corpses. I will show how the Gospel writers emphasize Jesus's power over death. In fact, we will see that the trend over time was for these early Christ followers to depict Jesus's raising of the dead at greater distance from both the time of death and the body of the dead person.

For the Gospel writers, the removal of the sources of ritual impurity was fundamental to Jesus's work. In chapter 6, I will turn to a different form of impurity—pneumatic or demonic impurity. The Gospel writers portray Jesus's expulsions of demons from people, frequently referring to these demons as impure spirits (Greek: *pneumata*).

These purifying aspects of Jesus's mission illuminate yet another aspect of Jesus's understanding and observance of the Jewish law: the Sabbath. Thus, in chapter 7, I will provide a coherent explanation for Jesus's purported disregard for holy time. Do the Gospel writers think Jesus disregards sacred time, even as they consistently demonstrate his commitment to the realm of the holy and his opposition to the impure? The answer, I contend, is that they depict Jesus using sacred time to extend the dominion of the holy God, who is the source of life, over the forces of impurity and death. In other words, they do not believe his Sabbath healings profane the Sabbath; instead, they portray his Sabbath actions as bringing about the wholeness of life that God intended the Sabbath to engender.

Finally, I will briefly summarize the preceding chapters and connect them to the Gospel portrayals of Jesus's own death and resurrection. Here, I think, is where we encounter both a literary and a theological payoff to highlighting the Gospel writers' portrayal of Jesus's interaction with ritual impurities. This particular understanding of Jesus's destruction of the sources of ritual impurity helps connect Jesus's mission to his death and resurrection. Jesus's skirmishes with these various ritual impurities—all forces of death, as I shall argue—foreshadow his crucifixion, in which death takes over Jesus's body. At the very point where death seems to have overwhelmed Jesus, Israel's God raises him from the dead, setting him eternally triumphant over even death itself.

What I intend to provide in the following pages, then, is a foundation for Christians seeking to retain their theological conviction in the importance of the Old Testament, including texts that deal with laws related to ritual impurity. The Jesus of the Gospels only makes sense in light of, in the context of, and in agreement with priestly concerns about purity and impurity documented in Leviticus and other Old Testament texts. I also hope to provide all readers with a better sense of the way in which the Gospel writers depict Jesus in relation to the Jewish law: not in opposition to it but in concert with it. I hope this depiction of a law-observant Jesus is not only of antiquarian interest but also a stimulant for Jewish-Christian dialogue, redirecting these conversations from erroneous and malignant understandings of the Jewish law and Jesus's purported rejection of it to the Gospel writers' conviction that in Jesus, the God of Israel was addressing the fundamental problem of human nature: human mortality.

CHAPTER 1

Mapping Jesus's World

L et us try to imaginatively step into the world of ancient Jewish purity thinking. First, God has structured the world in a variety of ways, but perhaps most fundamental for Israel's existence is its structure around two binaries: the holy and the profane, and the pure and the impure. The central text for this map came when God consecrated Israel's priests—setting them apart from other Israelites. At that time, God informed the priests of their essential role in Israelite society: "You are to distinguish between the holy and the profane, and between the impure and the pure" (Lev. 10:10). While the majority of the writings within what Christians now call the Old Testament and what Jews call the Bible or Tanakh are not explicitly concerned with these four categories, by the time of Jesus, many extant writings were in some way indebted to this mapping of the world, as shown by their use of this language.

These categories should not be equated one with the other, as many readers of these texts have assumed.[1] The word *holy* is not synonymous with the word *pure*. Neither is the word *profane* synonymous with the word *impure*. The category of the holy pertains to that which is for special use—in this sense, related to Israel's cult and therefore to Israel's God (Lev. 11:44; 20:7, 26; 22:32). For example, the Sabbath is holy (Exod. 31:14), as is the temple (Ps. 11:4). On the other hand, the category of the profane, a word that comes from the Latin *profanus* ("outside the temple"), refers to that which is secular or for common use. Here the English use of the word *profane* to refer to bad

---

1. For examples of this common misunderstanding in New Testament scholarship, see Neyrey, "Symbolic Universe of Luke-Acts"; Borg, *Conflict, Holiness, and Politics*, 8; D. Garland, *Reading Matthew*, 107; and Grappe, "Jesus et l'impureté."

language might unfortunately lead to confusion. There is nothing dirty or impure or sinful about something being profane.

This first binary provides one map of the entire world—*all* things are either holy or profane. And most things within the world belong within the category of the profane. For example, six days of the week are profane, as are noncultic Israelite buildings. An object or a person cannot be both holy and profane at the same time. In itself, there is nothing wrong with or sinful about being profane. As we will see, though, it is dangerous and possibly sinful when something holy, such as the temple or the Sabbath, is profaned or when something profane encroaches upon something holy.

The second map of the world is constructed by the categories of the pure and the impure. Once again, all things in the world fit into one of these two categories: something is either impure or pure. And again, no thing or person can be both pure and impure at the same time. A profane object, such as someone's house, can be either pure or impure. The same applies to holy objects—they can be either pure or impure. Israelite priests, who are consecrated (= holy), can be either pure or impure. To reiterate, the category of the holy is not synonymous with the category of the pure; neither is the category of the profane synonymous with the category of the impure. These are four *distinct* categories. And an Israelite person will always be characterized by two of these adjectives, existing in one of four possible states:

Holy and pure	Holy and impure
Profane and pure	Profane and impure

In priestly thought, the tent in the wilderness or the temple in Jerusalem is holy space inasmuch as God, who is holy and the source of all holiness, dwells there. The tent or temple is, in essence, a cordoned-off area that has a series of boundaries around it: the outer courtyard provides a protective barrier around the tent or temple, and the walls of the temple provide an additional barrier, permitting only priests to enter into the holy place. Even within the temple itself, an internal curtain protects the most holy place, into which only the high priest may enter and only once a year, on the Day of Atonement (Lev. 16).

What necessitates these barriers and what requires that God's presence, his *kavod* or glory,[2] be protected by a tent or temple is the existence of impurity

---

2. On God's *kavod* as the priestly language for God's earthly presence, see Sommer, *Bodies of God*, 73–74.

in the world. In the realm of the profane, impurities can exist. There they can affect people without having immediate consequences. But Israel's priests, at the instruction of their God, set up barriers to keep these impurities from entering where they must not—the Jerusalem temple, where Israel's God dwells among humans. The various boundaries to the temple and the prohibitions regarding which people could not enter into sacred space were established in order to preserve God's holy presence on earth, a presence threatened by impurities, to which Israel's God was opposed. Were people to enter into sacred space with their impurities, they would be cut off from the people of Israel (Lev. 22:3). These boundaries, then, were meant not only to safeguard God's presence but also to protect God's people from the consequences of wrongly approaching God.

Because of this dual protective function, I would qualify Paula Fredriksen's claim that compassion and purity have as much to do with each other as a fish and a bicycle.[3] Fredriksen rightly aims to dismantle Christian scholarship that seeks to contrast Jesus's compassion with the requirements of the ritual purity system. I would suggest, though, that compassion animates the Jewish purity system; it was a protective and benevolent system intended to preserve God's presence among his people, a presence that could be of considerable danger to humans if they approached God wrongly.

For examples of how hazardous God's presence could be (unrelated to ritual impurity per se), one need only consider two priests, Nadab and Abihu, who approached this God with strange fire and died as a result (Lev. 10). Or recall Uzzah, who wrongfully touched the ark of the covenant and died (2 Sam. 6). Access to sacred space was heavily restricted, not out of a lack of compassion but out of the belief that this holy God not only was merciful and loving but also was a powerful force that could be dangerous. The fact that Nadab and Abihu were priests and sons of Aaron matters not at all, nor does it matter that Uzzah piously meant to keep the ark of the covenant from falling to the ground. How much more would the unwitting or witting introduction of impurity into the realm of the holy endanger people? This depiction of God makes sense of the Israelites' request that Moses speak to them on God's behalf so that they would not have to endure the fear-inducing experience of encountering God directly (Exod. 20:18–21). Leviticus 15:31 nicely encapsulates the priestly concern over people coming too close to the tabernacle or temple while in a state of impurity: "Therefore, you shall separate the people of Israel from their impurity, so that they do not die by their impurity by defiling my tent which is in their midst" (cf. Num. 19:13, 20).

3. Fredriksen, "Compassion Is to Purity."

Contemporary Christians might compare this thinking to the way C. S. Lewis portrays Aslan in *The Lion, the Witch and the Wardrobe*. Upon finding out that Aslan is a lion, not a man, Susan asks, "Is he quite safe? I shall feel rather nervous about meeting a lion." To which Mrs. Beaver responds, "If there's anyone who can appear before Aslan without their knees knocking, they're either braver than most or else just silly." A young Lucy reiterates Susan's question: "Then he isn't safe?" Mr. Beaver then answers, "Safe? . . . Don't you hear what Mrs. Beaver tells you? Who said anything about safe? Course he isn't safe. But he's good. He's the King, I tell you."[4] Israel's priests did not believe that their God was some domesticated deity. Contrary to numerous modern caricatures, this depiction of God is not something unique to the Christian Old Testament—the God of the New Testament isn't meek and mild either. Luke, for instance, relates the fatal consequences that Ananias and Sapphira experienced for lying to the early leaders of the Jesus movement: without warning, God killed them (Acts 5). Simply put, approaching the God of Israel in the wrong way is dangerous. It is no wonder then that the Gospel writers depict Jesus exercising a fierceness in relation to the Jerusalem temple and to what he perceives to be an impious use of the sacred space associated with God's earthly presence (Mark 11:15–17; cf. Matt. 21:12–17; Luke 19:45–48; John 2:13–17).

Although humane, these ritual requirements meant that humans would need to keep their distance from God as long as they found themselves in a state of impurity. If impurities were to accumulate in God's dwelling, God would be forced to abandon it. When Israelites allowed impurities to build up in the tent or temple, they suffered the consequences. The boundaries around the tent or temple functioned to protect both the inside (God's presence) and the outside (any Israelite in a state of impurity) from the results of impure forces. Such thinking was commonplace in the ancient Mediterranean world. As Fredriksen puts it, ancient "gods tended to be emotionally invested in the precincts of their habitation, and they usually had distinct ideas about the etiquette they wanted observed when humans approached them there."[5]

The Multiple Forces of Impurity

Within this map, which divides the world into realms of holy and profane and pure and impure, it is necessary to focus on one particular category more closely—the category of the impure. Numerous scholars have argued that there

4. Lewis, *The Lion, the Witch and the Wardrobe*, 80.
5. Fredriksen, "Compassion Is to Purity," 56. See also Milgrom, "Israel's Sanctuary."

are two types of impurity in Leviticus: ritual and moral.[6] Unfortunately, here too people frequently confuse these two forms of impurity, leading to numerous interpretive or mapping errors. Jonathan Klawans provides a helpful comparison of these two forms of impurity that can be charted in the following way:

Ritual	Moral
unavoidable	avoidable
from a natural substance	from an action
communicable	noncommunicable
bathed away	atonement/punishment
not an abomination	an abomination
not sinful	sinful

This comparison highlights key differences between moral impurity, which is sinful, and ritual impurity, which is not inherently sinful. Conflating moral impurity with ritual impurity—something that New Testament scholars, theologians, clergy, and laypeople have frequently been guilty of doing—impinges upon our understanding of the Gospel narratives. As I noted above, there are times when these two categories, ritual and moral impurity, bleed into each other. When a person does not remove a ritual impurity using the prescribed method at the prescribed time, it can lead to moral impurity—sin. Consequently, I think it helpful to map these two categories in a way that reflects that these impurities form a spectrum and are not always mutually exclusive (see fig. 1 below).

Although the Gospel writers portray Jesus's interactions with and forgiveness of the morally impure (e.g., Mark 2:5), this book will focus almost exclusively on what Klawans calls ritual impurity. It does so precisely because interpretations of the Gospels frequently focus on Jesus's dealings with

6. Klawans, *Impurity and Sin*, and Hayes, *Gentile Impurities and Jewish Identities*, 19–24. Klawans elsewhere acknowledges that "the adjectives 'ritual' and 'moral' are problematic: The terms do not appear in the texts, and neither one is a category as such in biblical or postbiblical Jewish literature" (*Impurity and Sin*, 22). Christophe Nihan prefers to call ritual impurity "physical impurity" because a physical substance causes this sort of impurity ("Forms and Functions of Purity," 311–67). Nonetheless, while not all impurities arise out of physical substances, all impurities do result in physical consequences: they may pollute bodies, land, or sacred space. David P. Wright favors the terminology of permitted and prohibited impurities ("Unclean and Clean [OT]"). And Yitzhak Feder prefers to speak of three types of impurity: uncleanness (from regular genital discharges), infection (from abnormal discharges, *lepra*, and corpses), and stains of transgression (from actions such as murder and sexual misconduct; "Contagion and Cognition"). Additionally, Thomas Kazen rightly notes that to speak of moral and ritual purity as two distinct things is problematic inasmuch as it suggests that "purity ceases to be a ritual category when applied to moral matters" (*Emotions in Biblical Law*, 27). While I appreciate these various concerns, no alternative terminology improves upon this standard nomenclature.

Figure 1

Ritial——————— ——————**Moral**

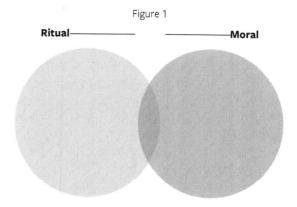

moral impurities (sins) but not (or not correctly) on his dealings with ritual impurities.[7]

In addition to these two forms of impurity, Leviticus contains one additional type of impurity—what I would call genealogical impurity—which I treat briefly in this book's appendix. Another form of impurity—one that the priestly writings do not envisage but that the Gospel writers do—is demonic (or pneumatic) impurity. Jewish scriptures refer only once to an impure spirit,[8] when the prophet Zechariah foretells the day that God will purify the land of Israel: "And on that day, says Yʜᴡʜ Sabaoth, I will cut off the names of the idols from the land, so that they will not be remembered again; and the prophets and the impure *ruaḥ/pneuma* I will remove from the land" (Zech. 13:2). Whether Zechariah, himself of priestly descent (1:1; cf. Ezra 5:1), refers here to some sort of demonic presence is uncertain, but some later Jews (see chap. 6) did use this and other similar phrases to refer to demons.[9]

Making Sense of Ritual Impurity

To prepare the way for the Jesus of the Gospels, we must consider some components of Jewish ritual purity. We are fortunate, therefore, to have the work of anthropologist Mary Douglas, who has greatly stimulated the study

7. There is no shortage of secondary literature on the topic of forgiveness of sins. See, for instance, Hägerland, *Jesus and the Forgiveness of Sins*.

8. I will always render *spirit* as *ruaḥ* (or *ruḥot* when referring to the plural) when discussing Hebrew texts, and *pneuma* (or *pneumata* when referring to the plural) when discussing Greek texts because the word *spirit* or *spiritual* often wrongly suggests something nonmaterial to modern readers. See the helpful discussion of P. Robertson, "De-spiritualizing *Pneuma*."

9. See Lange, "Considerations concerning the 'Spirit of Impurity,'" and the discussion in chap. 6.

of ritual purity. Both in her own writings on Leviticus and Numbers and in appropriations and criticisms of her work, ritual purity has become a focus in scholarship on Jewish scriptures and early Judaism and, to a lesser degree, on the New Testament.[10] We also have the extensive writings of Jacob Milgrom, whose research on Leviticus and Numbers, culminating in his magisterial three-volume commentary on Leviticus, spans decades.[11]

As we saw above, the three major *sources* of ritual impurity according to the priestly literature of Jewish scriptures are genital discharges of blood or semen, *lepra*, and corpses (cf. Lev. 12–15; Num. 19). In the following chapters, I shall examine more fully the symptoms of and legislation pertaining to these three physical sources of ritual impurity. Here I restrict myself to a few overarching observations.

When the profane comes into contact with something ritually impure, the profane becomes ritually impure. The legislation of Leviticus 12–15 and Numbers 19 deals with some of these ritual impurities. Such combinations of the profane and the impure were natural and generally inevitable. For instance, childbirth, menstruation, and sexual intercourse result in ritual impurity. These are natural human functions. The majority of Israelites would have at one time or another experienced such ritual impurities. Priestly legislation does not prohibit Israelites from contracting such impurities, nor does it punish them for doing so. Priestly law assumes that people will endure such impurities and provides them with the ritual means to remove those impurities. Only in the event that people do not properly dispose of their impurities does the issue become one of wrongdoing. When a person who has a ritual impurity comes into sacred space, he or she sins. This person should have used the divinely appointed ritual means to remove the impurity before coming into contact with the sphere of holiness. Thus, Leviticus 7:20 stipulates that a person who eats the meat of a sacrifice while in a state of impurity should be cut off from Israel (cf. Lev. 22:3, 9). It is at points such as these that the ritual impurity of the profane person transforms into some form of moral impurity. By not remedying their ritual impurity before contacting the holy, such people display irreverence toward Israel's holy God.

Once holy space reaches its impurity threshold, God must abandon the polluted sacred space. The consequence of polluting holy space is that, if

10. See Douglas, *Purity and Danger*; Douglas, *In the Wilderness*; Douglas, *Leviticus as Literature*; and Douglas, *Jacob's Tears*. For a series of essays interacting with her arguments, see Sawyer, *Reading Leviticus*, as well as the important qualifications of Lemos, "Universal and the Particular," and Lemos, "Where There Is Dirt."

11. Milgrom, *Leviticus 1–16*; Milgrom, *Leviticus 17–22*; and Milgrom, *Leviticus 23–27*. For readers looking for a condensed treatment of Leviticus, see Milgrom, *Leviticus: A Book of Ritual and Ethics*, which distills many of the insights of his three-volume work.

left unaddressed, the impurity will cause the holy God who dwells in the temple to forsake it. And when the holy God abandons the temple, this holy space becomes profane because its own holiness derives from God. Impurity and holiness are, in the words of Milgrom, "semantic opposites, and as the quintessence and source of [holiness] resides with God, it is imperative for Israel to control the occurrence of impurity lest it impinge on the realm of the holy God. The forces pitted against each other in the cosmic struggle are no longer the benevolent and demonic deities that populate the mythologies of Israel's neighbors but the forces of life and death set loose by humans themselves through their obedience to or defiance of God's commandments."[12]

On the basis of ancient portrayals of those suffering from *lepra*, Milgrom argues that what these three sources of ritual impurity share in common is that they represent death: the corpse, obviously, is a dead body; the *lepros*—that is, the one suffering from *lepra*—looks corpse-like; and those who experience a genital discharge suffer the loss of life force contained in genital blood or semen. From this observation, he concludes that in Jewish thinking ritual impurities represent the forces of death.[13] To be sure, extrapolating from *priestly* texts to make broader claims about *Jewish* thinking is problematic. Even if this was the priestly understanding of impurity, we simply cannot conclude that all ancient Jews shared this understanding. It is also dangerous to suppose that an entire symbolic and theological system motivated and gave shape to the priestly ritual purity system.[14] Notwithstanding these criticisms, Milgrom is right to note that a number of ancient Jewish texts connect two sources of impurity explicitly with death: the corpse, obviously, but also *lepra* (see Num. 12:12; 2 Kings 5:7; and probably Job 18:13). It is not, then, unreasonable to conclude that the loss of genital fluids likely also represented the loss of life force and thus simulated death.

Nonetheless, some scholars have argued that this association of impurity with death is not entirely convincing. How can something like sexual intercourse or birth, events connected to genital emissions, represent death?[15] And

12. Milgrom, "Dynamics of Purity," 32. In chap. 6, I shall address Milgrom's claim that these forces are devoid of demonic meaning.

13. See Milgrom, "Rationale for Biblical Impurity." Milgrom is followed by many interpreters, including Frank H. Gorman Jr. in *Ideology of Ritual*.

14. See the criticisms of Watts, *Ritual and Rhetoric in Leviticus*.

15. For instance, Frymer-Kensky, "Pollution, Purification and Purgation," and Maccoby, *Ritual and Morality*. That ancient Jews could connect birth to death can be seen in a hymn from Qumran, which states, "I was in distress like a woman giving birth the first time when her labor-pains came over her and a pang racks the opening of her womb to begin the birth in the crucible of the pregnant woman. For children come through the waves of death and the woman expectant with a boy is racked by her pangs, for through the waves of death she gives

if the emission of genital blood and semen signifies the loss of life force, which thereby explains its impurity, then shouldn't any loss of blood, not only genital blood, be defiling?[16] Consequently, they argue that ritual impurity stands for mortality in general—the fact that humans are born and die. In this sense, they are distinct from the realm of the holy—from God, who is immortal, without beginning or end, birth or death. A saying preserved in a fifth-century CE Jewish commentary on Genesis nicely captures this distinction between God and humanity, connecting birth to death: "It was taught: Whatever has offspring dies, decays, is created, but cannot create; but what has no offspring neither dies nor decays, creates but is not created. R. 'Azariah said in the name of Rabbi: This was said in reference to the One above."[17] If this saying does go back to Rabbi 'Azariah of the first century CE, it shows that some Jews at the time perceived childbirth (and implicitly sexual intercourse) to be connected to death. This gap between humans (as well as the rest of creation) and Israel's God is what necessitates the tabernacle and temple cult apparatus.[18] What is holy must be the antithesis of death and mortality: life.

Consequently, ancient Jews envisaged the protocols pertaining to access to the temple cult as necessary requirements for proximity to God, who had decided to camp among his mortal people. Only by following these regulations could Israel maintain God's presence in its midst. As Benjamin Sommer observes, "A central theme of priestly tradition—perhaps, the central theme of priestly tradition—is the desire of the transcendent God to become immanent on the earth this God had created."[19] Sommer's insights repay further reproduction: "The goal of the events at Sinai as P [= a strand of priestly writing] describes them is divine immanence, and the laws are but the

---

birth to a male" (*1QHodayot^a* XI, 7–10). Ancient Near Eastern cultures, such as the Assyrians and Babylonians, also associated birth with death, as I show in chap. 4. (Ultimately, in an age when pregnant women experienced high mortality rates, it would be unsurprising for most people to associate childbirth and death!)

With regard to sexual intercourse, in the thirteenth century, Nachmanides states, "The reason for the defilement of seminal emissions, even though it is part of the process of procreation, is like the reason for the defilement of death. . . . The individual does not know if his seed will be wasted, or if a child will result" (as cited in Milgrom, *Leviticus 1–16*, 934).

16. Maccoby, *Ritual and Morality*, 49.

17. *Genesis Rabbah* 12.7.

18. I would stress, in agreement with Lemos, that such rituals likely did not arise out of theological reflection; rather, the rituals gave rise to theological reflection that connected corpses, *lepra*, and genital emissions with death or mortality. She rightly cautions that "the type of analysis that seeks ever to schematize almost always sees ritual as secondary to belief and the body as secondary to the mind" ("Where There Is Dirt," 294). Or, as Walter Burkert puts it, "Ideas do not produce ritual: rather, ritual itself produces and shapes ideas, or even experience and emotions" (*Homo Necans*, 28).

19. Sommer, *Bodies of God*, 74.

means to that end. It follows that the many modern scholars who speak of P as essentially legalistic or as glorifying the law misrepresent this document. P's main concern is not law but the divine presence that observance of the law makes possible."[20] All the regulations about ritual purity and offerings, then, actually purport to maintain what modern religious people might call Israel's "relationship with God." In other words, the ritual purity system was, within the world that Israel's priests inhabited, foremost about life with God and was therefore a matter of life and death.

The Priests' Protective Role

God had tasked Israel's priests with policing these boundaries. First, the priests distinguished between the holy or sacred and the profane or common. Similarly, they were to distinguish between the clean or pure and the unclean or impure. As Milgrom puts it, "The making of distinctions is the essence of the priestly function."[21] They were divinely tasked with the central job of creating and maintaining boundaries to keep the forces of impurity contained so that they imperiled neither God's presence nor Israel's coexistence with God.

Yet Jewish scriptures contain accusations that Israel's priestly caste had at times been derelict in its duties, confusing holy and profane, pure and impure. Consequently, one of the later prophets, himself a priest, condemns the priesthood for failing to enforce these separations: "[Israel's] priests have violated my law. They have profaned my holy things, between holy and profane they have not distinguished, nor between impure and pure. And from my Sabbaths they have hidden their eyes. I am profaned in their midst" (Ezek. 22:26; cf. 44:23). Israel's actions profaned holy space (the holy things of the Jerusalem temple), holy time (the Sabbath), and the source of holiness (Israel's God). With similar words, Zephaniah says that Jerusalem's "priests profane what is holy, they do violence to the law" (Zeph. 3:4). The prophet Malachi also accuses the priests of having failed in their responsibility to teach the nation to distinguish between the categories of holy and profane and impure and pure: "But you have turned aside from the way; you have caused many to stumble in the law; you have destroyed the covenant of Levi" (Mal. 2:8). Again, the prophet Hosea protests priestly teaching: "My people are destroyed due to lack of knowledge. Since you have rejected knowledge, O priest, I will reject you as priest before me" (Hosea 4:6). Ezekiel portrays this breakdown of

---

20. Sommer, *Revelation and Authority*, 57.
21. Milgrom, *Leviticus: A Book of Ritual and Ethics*, 95. See also Olyan, *Rites and Rank*, 15–27.

boundaries when he accuses Israel of permitting foreigners to keep watch over YHWH's sanctuary (Ezek. 44:8). And, according to Numbers, God had demanded that the Levites guard the boundary between the holy and the profane. The Levites alone were to minister before the tent of meeting; anyone else who drew near to the tabernacle was to receive the death penalty (Num. 1:51; 3:10, 38; 18:7).[22] According to these prophets, then, on a number of occasions Israel's priests neglected their God-given duty to instruct Israel in the law: "The law perishes from the priest" (Ezek. 7:26). This dereliction of priestly duty profanes God himself, according to Ezekiel 22:26.

Modern readers should not understand such accusations against the priests to be a rejection of the purity system or the priestly authority over the realm of the sacred. Rather, these polemics indicate that many Jews were convinced of the importance of the purity system and believed it paramount that the priests guide Israel in distinguishing correctly between the holy and the profane and the pure and the impure. For the prophets, the proposed solution to failure within the ritual purity system was not the abandonment of the system but a more accurate delineation and maintenance of boundaries.

According to Israel's priests, God had provided Israel with a series of simple ritual actions that were designed to remove impurities and thus to allow limited access to the temple. God had given them the means to counter some of the forces of impurity. In effect, God had armed Israel with ritual practices that were efficacious in removing those impurities; these practices were basically a combination of time and water (and, in special instances, blood or ashes). But these ritual detergents were limited in their ability to remove impurity. They essentially removed the lingering effects of whatever condition made the person impure, but they did not, could not, and never were intended to remove the physical conditions that caused impurity. They did not, for instance, heal abnormal genital discharges, cure *lepra*, or turn corpses back into living beings. Proper maintenance, not transformation, of the current conditions of the world was their sole, divinely ordained goal.

The Apocalyptic Transformation of the Jewish World

Did Israel's priests long for a time when such rituals would be unnecessary? The prophet Ezekiel, himself a priest, envisages better, bigger, and stronger barriers and not some cosmic transformation in which impurities cease to exist entirely (Ezek. 40–48). One might point to Ezekiel 37 and the valley of

---

22. See here Milgrom, *Studies in Levitical Terminology*.

dry bones, in which God's *ruah* transforms impure corpse remains into living, and therefore pure (or purifiable), humans again. Yet even this remarkable transformation does not appear to portend some new reality where impurity *ceases* to exist.

Further, while the priestly writer does not dwell on the topic of the demonic, many later Jews certainly did and connected demons to the realm of the impure. So too some hoped for anti-impurity forces to enter into the world. In fact, we see an explosion of apocalyptic expectations that foresaw a new world where the current state of things would undergo radical transformation.[23] At times, such apocalyptic fervor was connected to a hope in a messianic figure who would deliver Israel (and the whole world) from its present state.[24]

It is within this world of apocalyptic hope that one must situate the Gospel writers and their portrayals of Jesus.[25] The Gospel writers depict Jesus as being divinely equipped to deal with the actual sources of impurity. Once the underlying conditions that create ritual impurity are removed, people are free to follow the simple steps that will remove the lingering ritual impurity. We see this explicitly, as I will discuss in chapter 3, in Jesus's treatment of the man with *lepra* (Mark 1:44). The Jesus of the Gospels is the holy one of God, a man who embodies a contagious power or force that is opposed to and ultimately destroys the powers that create impurity and death.

23. See here J. Collins, "Apocalyptic Eschatology."
24. On messianic thinking in early Judaism, see Novenson, *Grammar of Messianism*.
25. Some trace this apocalyptic thinking back to the historical Jesus. See Schweitzer, *Quest of the Historical Jesus*, and J. Weiss, *Jesus' Proclamation*.

CHAPTER 2

Jesus in a World of Ritual Impurity

Modern biographers stress the family backgrounds of their subjects, believing that one's earliest years often exert a powerful influence throughout one's life. Ancient biographies (*bioi*) also frequently, but not always, dwelled on the childhood of their subjects.[1] When we turn to the Gospels, how do the Gospel writers depict Jesus's familial upbringing and the inauguration of his mission?

Jesus and John the Immerser

Although Mark's Gospel lacks an infancy narrative, it introduces its readers to Jesus in a way that frames him within the context of the water immersions of John: "John the Immerser [*baptizōn*] appeared in the wilderness, proclaiming an immersion [*baptisma*] of repentance for the forgiveness of sins. And all the region of Judea and all the inhabitants of Jerusalem went out to him and were immersed [*ebaptizonto*] by him in the Jordan River, confessing their sins. . . . At that time, Jesus came from Nazareth of Galilee and was immersed [*ebaptisthē*] by John in the Jordan River" (Mark 1:4–5, 9). Both Matthew and Luke follow Mark on this point (Matt. 3:13–17; Luke 3:21–23), locating Jesus's

---

1. See for instance, Xenophon's *Cyropaedia* and Plutarch's *Life of Cato the Younger*, as well as Pelling, "Childhood and Personality," and Burridge, *What Are the Gospels?*

immersion prior to the beginning of his mission.[2] John's immersive practices may remind modern readers of the later Christian rite of baptism (the common moniker "John the Baptist" no doubt contributes to this understanding), but Jews in Jesus's day would have connected John to contemporary Jewish ritual bathing practices. For instance, Josephus links John's immersions to moral impurity but stresses that it related to the purification of the body as well.[3] Josephus's connection between moral and bodily purity finds a correspondence in the *Community Rule* from Qumran. In that work, the author asserts that no ritual purification is efficacious as long as one walks in a way that contradicts the law: "[The sinner] will not become pure by the deeds of atonement, nor will he be purified by the purifying waters, or made holy by seas or rivers, nor will he be purified by all the waters of washing. Impure, impure will he be all the days he rejects the decrees of God" (III, 4–6).[4]

While we know very little about the specifics of John's immersive rituals, the location of such actions provides us with a number of significant details. First, John's use of the Jordan River may have evoked Elisha's command to Naaman to immerse (*ebaptisato*) himself seven times in the Jordan in order to be purified of his *lepra* (2 Kings 5:14 Septuagint [hereafter LXX]). Second, it is possible that people would have associated John's actions with some form of eschatological entrance into the land of promise, since Joshua led Israel through the Jordan in order to possess the land (Josh. 3:15; LXX uses the verb *baptō* in reference to the priests entering into the water of the Jordan). Josephus's account of a man named Theudas who drew many Jews to the Jordan in order to mimic Joshua's crossing of it indicates that the story likely resonated with many first-century CE Jews and could have motivated John as well.[5] Third, and of relevance for our discussion of ritual purification, the use of running water, or what later rabbis referred to as "living water" (*mayim*

---

2. The Gospel of John, too, connects Jesus to John but lacks any mention of Jesus's immersion. This silence may indicate discomfort among early Christ followers regarding the relationship between Jesus and John. The Gospel of Matthew makes this discomfort apparent through John's words to Jesus: "I need to be immersed by you, and yet you come to me [for immersion]?" (3:14). Relatedly, the *Gospel of the Nazarenes* depicts Jesus's family encouraging him to go to John for immersion, but Jesus responds, "In what way have I sinned, that I would need to be immersed by him?" (fragment 2, in Jerome, *Against Pelagius* 3.2). Here the criterion of embarrassment works to suggest that John's immersion of Jesus is historically certain.

3. Josephus, *Jewish Antiquities* 18.117.

4. The belief that water purifications were ineffective if not accompanied by appropriate morality was commonplace in the Greco-Roman world. For instance, an oracle of the Delphian priestess at Pytho states, "The holy places of the gods are open to the righteous, nor have they any need of lustration; no defilement touches virtue. But thou who art evil at heart, depart; for never by sprinkling thy body shalt thou cleanse thy soul" (*Greek Anthology* 14.74).

5. Josephus, *Jewish Antiquities* 20.97–98; cf. Acts 5:36.

hayyim),[6] suggests that John was concerned with using the strongest form of water purificant available to humans. The previously mentioned passage from the *Community Rule*, for instance, exclaims that even the waters of the ocean and river are unable to sanctify the person who rejects God's decrees, implicitly stressing the stubbornness of such moral stains and the difficulty of removing them when using a detergent as powerful as living water. That John uses living water, then, suggests that he too believes that living water is a potent ritual detergent.

John's immersions fit well with the water purifications that occurred at Qumran and in first-century CE Judaism more broadly. Such parallels have led some scholars to conclude that John himself might have been an Essene. As Josephus's description demonstrates, and as Joan Taylor concludes, "To Jews in general John's call for immersion would have been understandable as a call to become ritually clean."[7] That John would be knowledgeable of and concerned about ritual purification should not surprise. After all, he was of priestly descent, at least according to Luke (1:5). As a priest, John would have received careful instruction in purification practices and principles. Thus, when the Gospel writers portrayed Jesus undergoing this immersion, readers would naturally situate Jesus within the context of Jewish ritual purifications and would assume that he was sympathetic to the priestly vocation of distinguishing pure from impure and keeping the holy realm distinct from the profane. Moreover, John's words encourage readers to form this conclusion. In all three Synoptic Gospels, he makes clear that while he uses water to purify, the one who is about to come (Jesus) will immerse people in a detergent of immeasurable power: the holy *pneuma* and, in Matthew and Luke, fire (Mark 1:8; Matt. 3:11; Luke 3:16).[8] John, as a priestly figure, may be committed to purification, but he is limited by the ritual detergent available to him—even living water can achieve only so much. Consequently, he expresses the expectation that one will come soon who will wash with a newly available pneumatic detergent to perform a full purification.

Jesus's Family according to Matthew and Luke

Whereas Mark begins his Gospel with John's immersion of Jesus, Matthew and Luke begin with two distinct infancy narratives, introducing readers to

---

6. Mishnah, *Mikwa'ot* 1.4–8; cf. Lev. 14:5–6, 50–52; 15:13; Num. 19:17; Deut. 21:4.

7. Taylor, *The Immerser*, 63. For a convincing argument that John at some point belonged to the Qumran community, see Marcus, *John the Baptist*, 28–33.

8. While Origen (*Homilies on Ezekiel* 5.1.2) takes the reference to fire as a fire of judgment, it is more likely that John connects fire to the *pneuma* because both have the ability to purify. Cf. Num. 31:23.

Jesus's family. Matthew, for example, opens his Gospel with a lengthy genealogy, deliberately situating Jesus within the story of Israel and identifying him as one of the key climaxes of that history: according to Matthew, fourteen generations separate Abraham from David, David from the Babylonian exile, and the Babylonian exile from the birth of Jesus.

Luke, on the other hand, begins with Jesus's relatives, Zechariah and Elizabeth. According to Luke, Elizabeth is Mary's relative (Luke 1:36), and his depiction of Mary's visit with Elizabeth suggests that the relation is quite close. He begins his Gospel with the story of Zechariah and Elizabeth, together with the miraculous birth of John, in order to place Jesus within a specific context for his readers. Luke claims that Zechariah was a priest of the line of Abijah and that Elizabeth was also of priestly descent, being "one of the daughters of Aaron" (1:5). Unsurprisingly, he portrays Jesus's priestly relatives as devout Jews: both Zechariah and Elizabeth were "just before God, living blamelessly in all the commandments and ordinances of the Lord" (1:6). The fact that Luke emphasizes Elizabeth's priestly pedigree signifies how punctilious Zechariah and his family were in keeping the Jewish law. According to Leviticus 21:14, the high priest must marry a woman of his own people (Hebrew: *am*; Greek: *genos*).[9] Building upon this requirement, some Jews believed that *all* priests should marry only women of priestly descent. For instance, Josephus avers,

> Not only did our ancestors in the first instance set over [the temple] men of the highest character, devoted to the service of God, but they took precautions to ensure that the priests' lineage should be kept unadulterated and pure. A member of the priestly order must, to beget a family, marry a woman of his own race [*genos*], without regard to her wealth or other distinctions; but he must investigate her pedigree, obtaining the genealogy from the archives and producing a number of witnesses. . . . And whoever violates any of the above rules is forbidden to minister at the altars or to take any other part in divine worship.[10]

Josephus's claims indicate the care that some Jews thought ought to be taken in arranging marriages for priestly men, confirming with records the genealogical pedigree of any potential wife.[11] Later, the rabbis too suggest that priests regularly married women of priestly descent.[12] Philo, though, shows that not all Jews interpreted Leviticus 21 in this way, distinguishing between

---

9. See Milgrom, *Leviticus 17–22*, 1819–20.
10. Josephus, *Against Apion* 1.30–32, 36.
11. See Büchler, "Family Purity," and Tervanotko, "Members of the Levite Family."
12. E.g., Jerusalem Talmud, *Ta'anit* 4.5.

the high priest, who must marry a woman of priestly descent, and ordinary priests, who were permitted to marry lay Israelite women.[13] Luke, therefore, appears to follow the more stringent legal position found in Josephus, who was, after all, of priestly descent himself, in suggesting that Zechariah acted righteously in marrying a woman of priestly descent even though he was not the high priest.[14]

The piety of Zechariah and Elizabeth emerges also in Luke's depiction of Zechariah's being chosen "according to the custom of the priesthood" to enter into the sanctuary of the Lord in order to offer incense there (Luke 1:9). Luke's description agrees with later rabbinic literature, which details how priests were chosen by lot in order to offer incense in sacred space.[15] That an angel of the Lord appeared to him in the temple shows the divine favor that rested upon this pious priest and his family. This angelic visitation in the temple precincts also underlines Luke's belief that the temple complex is the locus of the divine presence (cf. Acts 22:17–21). Like Abraham and Sarah, Zechariah and Elizabeth would have a son in their old age, a son who would practice supererogatory forms of Jewish piety from birth (1:15), abstaining from wine and strong drink like a priest who enters God's sanctuary or a Nazirite who takes a vow of holiness (Lev. 10:9; cf. Num. 6:1–4; Judg. 13:7).[16] Just as priestly literature prohibits the consumption of intoxicating liquids for those who come into proximity with the holy (cf. Eph. 5:18), so too does Luke. John must abstain from alcohol because he will be filled with the holy *pneuma* from conception. Finally, at John's birth, Luke again emphasizes the law observance of Zechariah and Elizabeth by noting that John was circumcised on the eighth day after his birth (1:59; cf. Gen. 17:12–14; Lev. 12:3).

When Luke finally turns to Jesus's own parents, the same emphasis upon Torah piety persists. Luke mentions that Jesus, too, underwent circumcision on the eighth day after his birth (Luke 2:21).[17] He also claims that Mary and Joseph went up to Jerusalem at the time of purification, "according to the law of Moses" (2:22), in order to present Jesus to the Lord "just as it is written in the law of the Lord" (2:23) as well as to offer a sacrifice "as it is stated in the law of the Lord" (2:24). Luke describes their actions in presenting Jesus in the temple and offering sacrifices as doing what was "customary under the

13. Philo, *On the Special Laws* 1.110–11.

14. See Josephus, *The Life* 1. In contrast to the second-century CE *Protevangelium of James*, Luke does not suggest that Zechariah was the high priest.

15. E.g., Mishnah, *Tamid* 5.2–6.3.

16. As Bovon notes, the words of Luke 1:15 "are closer to Lev. 10:9 than to Num. 6:3; thus they are more reminiscent of the regulations for priests (and their children!) preparing for service than they are of the life of a Nazirite" (*Commentary on the Gospel of Luke*, 36).

17. On eighth-day circumcision in Luke-Acts, see Thiessen, *Contesting Conversion*, 114–19.

law" (2:27) and notes that in their trip to Jerusalem they had completed everything that was "required by the law of the Lord" (2:39). Luke's refrain that
their actions comport with the law underlines how devout Mary and Joseph
were regarding law observance. Furthermore, Luke repeatedly demonstrates
his belief that the law of Moses (2:22) is the law of Israel's God (2:23, 24,
39). We shall return to this story shortly, since it presents us with a potential
problem surrounding at least one Gospel writer's portrayal of Jesus's family
and ritual purity.

The piety of Jesus's family continues throughout his youth. Luke portrays
Jesus's parents' annual ascent to Jerusalem for the Passover festival, stating
that when Jesus was twelve, they went up to Jerusalem as was "the custom
of the feast" (2:42).[18] Again, we see Jesus's parents involving him in Jewish
law observance. Luke's infancy narrative, then, emphatically places Jesus
within the context of a Jewish family committed to observing the law. Both
his parents and his extended family participate in central Jewish customs from
circumcision to the temple cult.[19] Nothing within Luke's infancy narrative,
then, prepares readers for a Jesus who breaks with customary forms of Jewish
piety in the first century CE.

In fact, Luke's portrayal of the adolescent Jesus implies that Jesus himself
remains devoted to these forms of piety, since when he goes to Jerusalem at
the age of twelve, he stays in the temple precincts to listen to the teachers
and to ask them questions. When his parents finally find and chastise him
for frightening them, his response stresses his temple devotion: "Did you not
know that it is necessary for me to be in my father's house?" (2:49). Luke's
depiction of Jesus suggests that while Jesus may be precocious, he is precocious precisely regarding his superlative piety: Jesus needs to be in the temple,
a building that he describes as his father's house (en tois tou patros mou),[20]
where he learns from teachers and questions them, amazing all who hear him
speak (2:47). Jesus's knowledge is remarkable in that even though he has not

18. The NRSV's translation ("they went up as usual for the festival") is surely incorrect,
although it agrees with Luke's claim in 2:41 that they went up annually. In fact, the Gospels
suggest that the adult Jesus continued this annual pilgrimage for the Passover (Mark 14:12;
Matt. 26:12; Luke 22:8–9; cf. John 13).

19. See also Klinghardt, Gesetz und Volk Gottes, 267–69.

20. I take the Greek phrase en tois tou patros mou to mean "my father's house," even
though it could be rendered "my father's business." See, e.g., Origen, Homilies on Luke 18.5
and 20.3; Cyril of Jerusalem, On Luke, sermon 5; and Epiphanius, Heresies 66.42.12. See Gen.
41:51 LXX, which translates the Hebrew "all the house of my father" (kol-bet avi) as pantōn
tōn tou patros mou. Luke uses a similar expression elsewhere: at Tyre, Paul and his traveling
companions boarded a ship, and the locals who came to say farewell returned "to their homes"
(eis ta idia, Acts 21:6).

reached the age of thirteen (an important age in later rabbinic thought in terms of halakhic responsibility),[21] it impresses the teachers in the temple. While we may not know the specifics about Jesus's own piety or theology, one thing we do know at this point in Luke's narrative: Jesus believes that the temple is the earthly dwelling of Israel's God. The Gospel of Matthew presents Jesus as assuming this fact late in life, claiming that those who swear by the Jerusalem temple swear by the one who dwells in the temple (Matt. 23:21). In fact, all the Gospel writers portray Jesus as continuing to believe that the Jerusalem temple is the earthly abode of Israel's God. So seriously does Jesus take this belief that he angrily chastises people at the temple for what he perceives to be their deep irreverence for holy space (Mark 11:17; Matt. 21:13; Luke 19:46; John 2:16), which, following Isaiah 56:7, Jesus believes to be the dwelling of God.[22] For the Jesus of the Gospels, then, the Jerusalem temple is God's house and therefore needs to be treated with what Paula Fredriksen calls the proper etiquette.[23]

Jesus's Birth and Purification

One story about Jesus's early life might present problems for my argument in this book.[24] If it is true that the Synoptic Gospel writers are intent on portraying Jesus in a way that shows his commitment to the ritual purity system, then how can we account for Luke's supposedly error-filled portrayal of the newborn Jesus and his presentation in the temple? The potentially troublesome text states, "And when the days of their [*autōn*] purification were completed according to the law of Moses, they brought [Jesus] to Jerusalem to present him to the Lord (as it is written in the law of the Lord, 'Every male who opens the womb shall be called holy to the Lord') and to offer a sacrifice according to what is said in the law of the Lord, 'a pair of turtledoves or two young pigeons'" (Luke 2:22–24). Raymond Brown summarizes the supposed errors Luke is guilty of in these verses in the following way: "Imprecisely Luke seems to think that both parents needed to be purified ('their purification' in 2:22), that the child needed to be brought to Jerusalem to be presented to the Lord (2:22–23), and that the offering of two young pigeons was related

21. Mishnah, *Avot* 5.21; Mishnah, *Niddah* 5.6.

22. John's Jesus likewise calls the Jerusalem temple "my father's house," a claim that John connects to Ps. 69:9, which associates Jesus's actions here with his zeal for the Jerusalem temple (John 2:16–17).

23. Fredriksen, "Compassion Is to Purity," 56.

24. The following section is a revised and slightly expanded version of Thiessen, "Luke 2:22, Leviticus 12." Used by permission.

to the presentation (2:24 in sequence to 2:22b)."[25] According to the scholarly consensus, then, Luke's belief that both Mary and Joseph (and/or Jesus, a possibility that Brown does not mention)[26] need to undergo purification conflicts with the law, which requires only the purification of the new mother: "And the Lord said to Moses: Tell the sons of Israel, 'Any woman who conceives and gives birth to a male will be impure for seven days. Just like in the days of the separation of her menstruation she will be impure. And on the eighth day the flesh of his foreskin will be circumcised. And thirty-three days she will remain in her impure blood. She will neither touch anything holy nor enter into the sanctuary until the days of her [autēs] purification end'" (Lev. 12:2–4 LXX).

Well before the rise of historical-critical biblical scholarship, readers of Luke's Gospel noticed this discrepancy between Luke 2:22 and Leviticus 12:2–4. While the majority of manuscript witnesses to Luke 2:22 contain the plural pronoun autōn (tou katharismou autōn, "their purification"), a number of non-Greek witnesses attest to the third-person feminine singular pronoun autēs ("her"). Other manuscripts have the third-person masculine singular pronoun autou ("his"), and still other manuscripts contain no genitive pronoun qualifying the word katharismou (simply "purification").[27] The absence of a personal pronoun removes any problem in the text, suggesting that a scribe attempted to avoid the question of who underwent this rite of purification.[28] Similarly, since manuscripts containing the feminine singular pronoun autēs agree with Leviticus 12:4 LXX (autēs),[29] a scribe likely harmonized the Gospel of Luke with the text of Leviticus. The remaining variants, autou and autōn

25. Brown, "Presentation of Jesus," 3. Brown is not alone in concluding that Luke demonstrates his lack of knowledge of Jewish customs. See Mann, "Rabbinic Studies in the Synoptic Gospels"; Klostermann, Das Lukasevangelium, 41; Marshall, Gospel of Luke, 116; Fitzmyer, Gospel according to Luke I–IX, 424; Nolland, Luke 1:1–9:20, 117; Räisänen, Die Mutter Jesu, 127; C. F. Evans, Saint Luke, 212; Schneider, Das Evangelium nach Lukas, 71; Stein, Luke, 113; and Bovon, Luke 1:1–9:50, 99.

26. For example, Fitzmyer (Gospel according to Luke I–IX, 424) and Nolland (Luke 1:1–9:20, 117) conclude that "their" (autōn) refers to Joseph and Mary, while Origen (Homilies on Luke 14.3–6) believes autōn refers to Mary and Jesus.

27. For the manuscript evidence, see Hatch, "Text of Luke 2:22."

28. It is also possible that a scribe who knew the Hebrew of Lev. 12:4 took the unpointed Hebrew phrase ימי טהרה not as "the days of her purification" but as "the days of purification," since one could interpret טהרה as a feminine noun and not as the masculine noun טהר with the third-person feminine singular possessive suffix ה. If so, the scribe harmonized Luke 2:22 with his reading of Lev. 12:4. Compare the earlier occurrence of טהרה in Lev. 12:4, which the Masoretes pointed as a feminine noun (i.e., the final he lacks a mappiq) but the LXX translator renders as akathartō autēs.

29. While there are a number of variants to this verse in manuscripts of LXX Leviticus, all manuscripts contain the feminine singular pronoun autēs. See Wevers, Leviticus, 138–39. The Hebrew reads עד־מלאת ימי טהרה.

("his" and "their"), create difficulties for two reasons, one textual and one theological. First, neither of these readings matches the priestly legislation on childbirth impurity, which only mentions the mother's impurity. Second, readers could take either variant to suggest that *Jesus* suffered ritual impurity, an interpretation that likely would have troubled early Christian scribes, who struggled with aspects of the Gospels' depictions of Jesus's humanity.[30] Although both readings are equally difficult theologically, the early, diverse, and weighty external support for *autōn* suggests that it is an earlier reading than *autou*. This conclusion suggests that the other variants (*autēs* and no personal possessive pronoun) are attempts both to remove a perceived discrepancy between Leviticus 12:4 and Luke 2:22 and to modify a theologically difficult text.

Both the ancient efforts to correct Luke and the modern claims that Luke misunderstood the Jewish ritual purity system create an issue for one of the central assertions of this book. If I would like to argue convincingly that the Gospel writers were each committed to portraying Jesus (and in Luke's case, his broader family) as being devoted to the Jewish law and especially committed to the subset of Jewish laws pertaining to ritual purity, Luke 2:22–24 presents a potential problem. If scholars are correct to conclude that Luke makes a number of mistakes in discussing the Jewish law and ritual purity here, how likely is it that he was actually interested in portraying Jesus and his family as observing such laws? The purpose of the remainder of this chapter, then, is to question the near consensus that Luke has misunderstood Jewish purity laws dealing with childbirth. First, I will show that readers of the priestly legislation pertaining to purification after childbirth could conclude that either the newborn or someone else might become impure from a new mother; second, I will demonstrate that some Second Temple Jews did believe that infants were born in a state of ritual impurity, or at least were susceptible to becoming ritually impure through their ritually impure mothers.

Leviticus 12:1–8 and Childbirth Impurity

According to the legislation of Leviticus 12, a woman giving birth to a male child is impure, "like a menstruant," for seven days (Lev. 12:2). This

---

30. See Plummer, *Critical and Exegetical Commentary*, 63. Even the possibility that Mary might be deemed impure was problematic for early Christian interpreters. For instance, despite Luke 2:22, Origen says of Lev. 12, "For the Lawgiver added this word [i.e., "conceived"] to distinguish her who 'conceived and gave birth' without seed from other women so as not to designate as 'unclean' every woman who had given birth but her who 'had given birth by receiving seed'" (*Homilies on Leviticus* 8.2.2; trans. Barkley, 154). On the scribal tendency of making New Testament texts fit more neatly with burgeoning orthodox Christian theology, see Ehrman, *Orthodox Corruption of Scripture*.

phrase stresses, as Jacob Milgrom puts it, "that the quality of the impurity and not just its length is equivalent to that of the menstruant (see [Lev.] 15:19–24)."[31] After this seven-day period, the child undergoes circumcision, and the mother's impurity continues, albeit in a downgraded state (12:4), for an additional thirty-three days. In contrast, if the mother gives birth to a female child, she bears a menstrual-like impurity that lasts for fourteen days, and her downgraded impurity continues for a further sixty-six days. At the completion of this period, the mother must bring a lamb (or a turtledove or pigeon, if she is too poor to afford a lamb) for a burnt offering and a pigeon or turtledove for a purification offering (Lev. 12:6–8). During the period of impurity, the new mother is permitted neither to touch holy things nor to enter Israel's sanctuary.[32] Of Leviticus 12, Milgrom observes, "The active agent in this chapter is solely the new mother. It is she who must scrupulously keep count of the days of her purification period and, at its termination, bring its requisite offerings." Considering the singular attention that the priestly legislation pays to the mother, Milgrom asks the following: "What of the Israelite child? Is he (or she) rendered impure by contact with the mother? The text is silent. Nor is there even a hint of an answer in Scripture. Does its silence mean that the newborn is exempt from the laws of *niddâ*, or must we assume that the child's impurity is taken for granted, that the child is isolated with the mother during the seven (or fourteen) days, and that at the termination of this period it undergoes immersion with her? There is no clear answer."[33]

Leviticus does not explicitly address the question of the purity or impurity of the newborn child. Yet the reader cannot take this silence as proof that the newborn child suffers no impurity. After all, Leviticus is not an exhaustive description of all the purity laws enjoined upon Israel; rather, the

31. Milgrom, *Leviticus 1–16*, 744. For a helpful depiction of these stages of impurity, see Whitekettle, "Leviticus 12," 401.

32. As I noted in chap. 1, scholars debate why Leviticus excludes new mothers from sacred space. Wenham (*Book of Leviticus*, 188) and Milgrom (*Leviticus 1–16*, 767) argue that the blood loss of childbirth aligns the experience with death, while Frymer-Kensky ("Pollution, Purification, and Purgation") and Maccoby (*Ritual and Morality*, 49–50) argue that childbirth is the experience of new life, which must be kept out of holy space. Either interpretation suggests that the mortality of humanity is the issue and that such mortality cannot approach God. Yet there are numerous texts that associate the womb or the birth process with death. In chap. 3 I discuss these texts more fully, but I note here that the *Thanksgiving Hymns* from Qumran, for instance, claim that children are born amid "the breakers of death" (1QHodayot^a XI, 7–10), while rabbinic literature calls the womb an open grave (Mishnah, *Ohalot* 7.4) and depicts the new mother as being on the very verge of death (Babylonian Talmud, *Shabbat* 129a).

33. Milgrom, *Leviticus 1–16*, 743, 746. In contrast, in his brief discussion of Luke 2:22, Milgrom confidently concludes, "Leviticus leaves no room for doubt that only one person needs to be purified: the new mother" (*Leviticus 1–16*, 762). See the similar remarks of B. Levine, *Leviticus = Va-yikra*, 72.

priestly writer lays out a system of purity that is at times elliptical, requiring understanding of the whole in order to apply it appropriately to individual cases. The legislation regarding childbirth is remarkably succinct, especially when compared to the detailed descriptions of impurity associated with other genital discharges (Lev. 15) and *lepra* (Lev. 13–14). This brevity leads to the omission of important information, for at the end of her initial seven- or fourteen-day period of impurity, Leviticus does not mention the way in which a woman removes this heightened degree of impurity. Nonetheless, Milgrom argues that an immersion requirement is "omitted for the simple reason that it is taken for granted except in cases in which it is not self-understood."[34] If in Leviticus 12 the priestly writer leaves unstated so central a rite to purification as immersion, it is equally conceivable that he omits other aspects of the purity legislation pertaining to childbirth.

Cross-cultural parallels strengthen the possibility that Leviticus leaves unstated the assumption of the child's ritual impurity. In the ancient Mediterranean world, the new mother and her newborn child both suffered ritual impurity. Just as Leviticus prescribes a lengthier period of impurity for the birth of a female than it does for a male, Hittite purity laws state that the male newborn and his mother remain impure for three months, while the female newborn and her mother remain impure for four months.[35] Similarly, a second-century BCE sacred law from a sanctuary devoted to Isis, Sarapis, and Anoubis prohibits entry for eight days to anyone who has been at the birth of a child (*lechous*).[36] Presumably, this would include the newborn child.

---

34. Milgrom, *Leviticus 1–16*, 756. As Milgrom notes, some early rabbis assumed that immersion occurred at the end of this initial period of impurity and debated whether it was also required after the second stage of impurity (cf. Mishnah, *Niddah* 10.7).

35. For further examples, see Milgrom, *Leviticus 1–16*, 763–65, and, more broadly, D. Wright, *Disposal of Impurity*. Additionally, the birth equipment and the midwife become impure. See Beckman, *Hittite Birth Rituals*, 251.

36. Te Riele, "Une Nouvelle Loi Sacrée en Arcadie." Te Riele (329) notes that the Greek word *lechous* can be read either as referring to childbirth (*léchous*) or as referring to the woman who has just given birth (*lechoûs*), but he prefers the former reading. In late fourth-century BCE Cyrene, we have "cathartic laws" that discuss pollution in the case of birth (Supplementum epigraphicum graecum ix.72.a.4). While mocking such people as superstitious, Theophrastus gives evidence of people who view the new mother as ritually impure: "[The superstitious person] refuses to step on a gravestone, view a corpse or visit a woman who has given birth, and says it's the best policy for him not to incur pollution" (*Characters* 16.9). Diogenes Laertius claims that Pythagoras taught that "purification is by cleansing, baptism and lustration, and by keeping clean from all deaths and births and all pollution" (*Lives of Eminent Philosophers* 8.33). And Censorinus, in the mid-third century CE, suggested that "for the first forty days of pregnancy, and for forty days after birth, women were expected to avoid sacred spaces (although they could enter temples after the first forty days of pregnancy to pray for a safe delivery)" (*The Birthday Book* 11.7). For conceptions of birth impurity in Greece, see Parker, *Miasma*, 48–52, and Wächter, *Reinheitsvorschriften im griechischen Kult*, 25–36. Plutarch's

Reading Leviticus, one could conclude that the newborn child was impure. First, that the purification period of the new mother differs on the basis of the gender of the newborn child suggests that the woman's impurity relates directly to the child. If the newborn does not experience ritual impurity, why would *its* gender have any bearing on the length of the *mother's* purification process?[37] Second, why does the circumcision of the male newborn take place on the eighth day after birth? Is it possible that the priestly writer believed that the male child suffered the same degree of impurity as the mother during the first seven days after birth and that circumcision needed to be delayed in order for this heightened level of impurity to pass? Finally, Leviticus 12 twice likens the initial phase of impurity (the seven-day period after a male's birth or the fourteen-day period after a female's birth) to the impurity of a menstruant (12:2–5; cf. 15:19–24).[38] Accordingly, if we are to understand childbirth impurity, we must do so in light of the lengthier discussion of menstrual impurity. Of particular relevance is Leviticus 15, which asserts that a male who lies with a woman during her menstruation contracts an impurity lasting seven days

---

own statements about childbirth show that at least some people connected it to impurity out of disgust, something that aligns with the work of Kazen, *Emotions in Biblical Law*, 71–94. Plutarch states, "For there is nothing so imperfect, so helpless, so naked, so shapeless, so foul, as man observed at birth, to whom alone, one might almost say, Nature has given not even a clean passage to the light; but, defiled with blood and covered with filth and resembling more one just slain than one just born, he is an object for none to touch or lift up or kiss or embrace except for someone who loves with a natural affection" (*On Affection of Offspring* 496B; cf. *Moralia* 758A).

37. For attempts to explain this correlation scientifically, see Macht, "Scientific Appreciation of Leviticus 12:1–5," and Magonet, "But If It Is a Girl." Philo provides an ancient scientific explanation, arguing that the male embryo takes forty days to form, while the female embryo takes eighty days (*Questions and Answers on Genesis* 1.25). Philo is indebted here to wider Greco-Roman thinking on the differing developmental periods of male and female embryos, as a comparison with the Hippocratic work *On the Nature of the Child* demonstrates:

A fetus has already been formed and reached the stage described in 42 days at the longest in the female, and in 30 days at the longest in the male, for the articulation of these parts generally takes place in these times, or a little more or less. Also the cleaning (sc. of the lochia) after birth in women usually occurs over 42 days after the birth of a female child: this is the longest and most complete cleaning, but danger would also be escaped if the cleaning lasted just 25 days. After the birth of a male child, the cleaning takes place over 30 days: again this is the longest and most complete cleaning, and danger would also be escaped if the cleaning lasted 20 days. (18.1)

Of particular relevance in this lengthy quotation is the claim that lochia, or postnatal bleeding, lasts for a longer duration after the birth of a female baby than it does after a male baby's birth. I have argued that a similar medical belief about embryological development lies behind the legislation of Lev. 12 (Thiessen, "Legislation of Leviticus 12").

38. Elliger argues that Lev. 12 was originally part of the legislation dealing with bodily emissions found in Lev. 15 (*Leviticus*, 157). While this suggestion has no textual support, it does recognize the interconnections between the two chapters.

(15:24).[39] As Jonathan Magonet argues, "The act of intercourse creates a single entity, 'one flesh,' and both are equally affected by the status of uncleanness of the other."[40] The resulting seven-day period of impurity contrasts with other forms of impurity contracted from the menstruant, which last only until evening (15:19–23). Since, unlike these other forms of contact, sexual intercourse with a menstruant brings about direct contact with menstrual blood, the woman transmits the full strength of her impurity to the man (15:24). Just as the menstruant endures impurity for a seven-day period, so the man who has intercourse with her undergoes a seven-day period of impurity.

If childbirth impurity is analogous to menstrual impurity, then presumably one contracts childbirth impurity in the same manner.[41] Direct contact with the blood of childbirth, therefore, logically ought to result in an impurity similar to direct contact with menstrual blood. Consequently, although Leviticus does not state so explicitly, one could conclude that a person who touches the blood of the new mother endures the same impurity as that which the mother herself experiences—a seven- or fourteen-day period of impurity followed by a lessened state of impurity lasting thirty-three or sixty-six days. As Magonet notes, "If any entity can be considered to be a 'single flesh' made up of two persons, it is a mother bearing a child."[42] One potential implication, then, is that the newborn child, having been in direct contact with both the mother's reproductive system and the new mother's blood at its birth, becomes impure in the same way as the mother and, like her, is thus in need of the same purification rites. In light of both the ancient Near Eastern context and the logic undergirding the legislation of the book of Leviticus, the reader cannot take the silence surrounding the purity of a newborn in Leviticus 12 as evidence that the newborn existed outside the purity system.

Childbirth Impurity in the Second Temple Period

The evidence of Leviticus does not demonstrate unequivocally that the newborn child requires purification, nor does it help to determine the purification

---

39. In contrast (or perhaps in addition), according to Lev. 20:18, a man who has sexual intercourse with a woman who has any type of genital discharge (the menstruant, the new mother, or the *zavah*) is subject to the *karet* penalty (cf. Ezek. 18:6; 22:10). It may be that Lev. 20:18 assumes intentionality not inadvertence, although this has to be inferred from the text. Cf. Jerusalem Talmud, *Horayot* 2.5; Milgrom, *Leviticus 1–16*, 940–41; and Milgrom, *Leviticus 17–22*, 1754–56.

40. Magonet, "But If It Is a Girl," 151.

41. See also the Qumran *Temple Scroll*, which equates menstrual and childbirth impurity (11Q19 XLVIII, 15–17).

42. Magonet, "But If It Is a Girl," 151.

beliefs and ritual practices of Luke and his contemporaries. It is, therefore, necessary to determine whether evidence exists that demonstrates that later Jewish readers believed that newborns suffered impurity. The second-century BCE book of *Jubilees* provides the earliest indication that some Jews did conclude that newborns suffered the same ritual impurity endured by their mothers. In his discussion of the creation of Adam and Eve, the author states,

> In the first week Adam and his wife—the rib—were created, and in the second week [God] showed her to him. Therefore, a commandment was given to keep (women) in their defilement seven days for a male (child) and for a female two (units) of seven days. After 40 days had come to an end for Adam in the land where he had been created, we [i.e., the angels] brought him into the Garden of Eden to work and to keep it. His wife was brought (there) on the eightieth day. After this she entered the Garden of Eden. For this reason a commandment was written in the heavenly tablets for the one who gives birth to a child: if she gives birth to a male, she is to remain in her impurity for seven days like the first seven days; then for 33 days she is to remain in the blood of purification. She is not to touch any sacred thing nor to enter the sanctuary until she completes these days for a male. As for a female she is to remain in her impurity for two weeks of days like the first two weeks and 66 days in the blood of purification. Their total is 80 days. After she had completed these 80 days, we brought her into the Garden of Eden because it is the holiest in the entire earth, and every tree which is planted in it is holy. For this reason the law of these days has been ordained for the one who gives birth to a male or a female. She is not to touch any sacred thing nor to enter the sanctuary until the time when those days for a male or a female are completed. (3.8–13)[43]

At first glance, *Jubilees* says nothing about the impurity of the newborn child. Yet the narrative explanation that the author gives for these differing periods implies that the child undergoes a time of impurity. For the analogy between Adam and Eve and the new mother to work, the reader must assume that both have endured a period of impurity prior to their entry into the garden. The author states that Adam was kept in "the land where he had been created" for forty days and that Eve was kept out of the garden until the end of an eighty-day period. He also claims that the garden of Eden was the holiest place on earth and that the trees in it were holy (3.12). In fact, in *Jubilees* Eden functions as the temple: "[Noah] knew that the Garden of Eden is the holy of holies and is the residence of the Lord" (8.19).[44] The author

---

43. Translations of *Jubilees* in this chapter are from VanderKam, *Book of Jubilees*.
44. On the garden of Eden as the temple, see G. Anderson, "Celibacy or Consummation in the Garden?," 129–31; Hayward, "Figure of Adam," 6–7; and Ego, "Heilige Zeit," 214.

would narrate the exclusion of Adam and Eve from this sanctum after their creation only if he believed that, as "newborns," they suffered ritual impurity. Once time, in accordance with Leviticus 12, removed their newborn impurity, God permitted them entrance into the holy place (that is, the garden) and allowed them to touch the holy things (that is, every holy tree within it). Such a connection between childbirth and the formation of Adam and Eve from the ground suggests that the author likens the earth to the womb, an equation found in other Jewish texts (e.g., Ps. 139:13–15; Job 1:21; Eccles. 5:15; Sir. 40:1).[45] As a result of this narration of the creation of Adam and Eve and their subsequent period of purification outside the garden of Eden, we can conclude that the author believed that newborns suffer the same ritual impurity associated with childbirth that their mothers endure.[46]

Similarly, 4Q265, a fragmentary text from Qumran, juxtaposes a series of laws with the creation of Adam and Eve. Joseph Baumgarten's reconstructed text demonstrates that this work also links God's placement of Adam and Eve in the garden of Eden to the childbirth legislation of Leviticus 12. Like the author of *Jubilees*, the author of 4Q265 believed that the garden and its trees were holy: "[For] the Garden of Eden is holy and all its young shoots are holy" (fragment 7, line 14). Consequently, Adam must wait forty days before entering Eden, while Eve must wait eighty days (lines 11–13). Again, like the author of *Jubilees*, this author connects the purity legislation of Leviticus 12, along with the differing periods of purification after the birth of a male and a female, to this account of the creation of Adam and Eve. As Baumgarten states, "The entrance of Adam and Eve into the garden, after their respective periods of purification, can with little difficulty be viewed as paradigmatic for the acceptance of newly born infants of both sexes into the sacred sphere."[47]

Both *Jubilees* and 4Q265 connect the creation of Adam and Eve and their delayed entry into Eden to the laws of the new mother in Leviticus 12. Although neither work explicitly states that all subsequent newborn Israelites endure childbirth impurity, this inference seems to be the logical conclusion to this juxtaposition of Levitical legislation and primeval narrative.

To be clear, this evidence does not demonstrate that all Jews in the Second Temple period understood Leviticus 12 to signify that newborns endured childbirth impurity. Another text from Qumran, 4Q266, provides the clearest evidence that some Jews did not believe this, since it does not permit

45. On this point, I am indebted to Meyer, *Adam's Dust*, 48.

46. So too J. Baumgarten, "Purification after Childbirth," and H. Harrington, *The Purity Texts*, 62, 100. In addition, see J. Baumgarten's critical edition with commentary, "265. 4QMiscellaneous Rules."

47. J. Baumgarten, "Purification after Childbirth," 5.

the new mother to nurse her child and requires the use of a wet nurse (6 II, 10–11). The underlying assumption of this legal ruling is that if the mother nurses the newborn child, she will convey impurity to her child. The author of 4Q266 agrees, then, with *Jubilees* and 4Q265 in their belief that newborn children are susceptible to impurity, but he disagrees with them regarding when (at the time of birth or during the initial period of impurity) such transference of impurity occurs. Relatedly, the *Infancy Gospel of James 5*, a late second-century CE Christian work, claims that Mary's mother, Anna, gave birth to her but did not breastfeed her until Anna underwent purification. The author of this work shares with the author of 4Q266 the belief that a newborn child is susceptible to childbirth impurity and attempts to protect Jesus's mother from this ritual impurity. As Martha Himmelfarb concludes, "[This] reading of the text of Leviticus is so persuasive that it is hard not to agree that P must have shared the view that the new mother conveyed impurity to those who touched her during the first stage of her impurity. Surely it would not have escaped P's notice that the newborn baby could not avoid such contact."[48]

The Presentation of the Newborn Jesus in the Jerusalem Temple

Despite the concern *Jubilees* and 4Q265 demonstrate over the possibility of the impurity of the newborn, Leviticus 12 does not address the child's status. Himmelfarb provides a compelling reason as to why this is the case: "Leviticus 12 betrays no anxiety about this contact. Perhaps P ignores the question because it does not think it important. The consequences of impurity as specified in Leviticus 12 are hardly relevant to a newborn, who is most unlikely to have the opportunity to enter the sanctuary or touch holy things and who is certainly incapable of eating sacrificial meat and other kinds of consecrated food."[49] Since *Jubilees* and 4Q265 narrate the entrance of Adam

---

48. Himmelfarb, "Impurity and Sin," 26.

49. Himmelfarb, "Impurity and Sin," 26. Himmelfarb's remarks are similar to the conclusions of Wilfried Paschen, who argues that the new mother transmits impurity throughout the entire period of her purification (*Rein und Unrein*, 60). The *Canons of Hippolytus* (see esp. canon 18) demonstrate that in the fourth century CE some Christians still believed that childbirth brought about impurity, requiring the separation of both new mothers and midwives from sacred space. Of midwives, the *Canons* state, "The midwives are not to partake of the mysteries, until they have been purified. Their purification shall be thus: if the child which they have delivered is male, twenty days; if it is female, forty days. They are not [to] neglect the confinements, but they are to pray to God for her who is confined. If she goes to the house of God before being purified, she is to pray with the catechumens who have not yet been received and have not been (judged) worthy to be accepted." Such a requirement assumes that anyone coming into contact with the genital discharges associated with childbirth becomes ritually impure, even though the

and Eve into the garden of Eden—that is, into holy space—the authors of these works *must* make clear that Adam and Eve have completed the period of purification that Leviticus 12 requires. This observation illuminates what Luke is trying to do in Luke 2:22. Like *Jubilees* and 4Q265, but in contrast to Leviticus, Luke explicitly portrays the entrance of the newborn Jesus into holy space when his parents present him to the Lord at the Jerusalem temple. While the priestly writer of Leviticus did not need to address the purity status of the newborn, Luke is compelled to do so in order to portray a ritually pure Jesus in the temple precincts. As I emphasized at the beginning of this chapter, Luke's infancy narrative stresses the law observance of Jesus's family (cf. 1:6, 9; 2:22–24, 27, 41–42); if he is not careful in his depiction of Jesus's presentation at the temple, he might inadvertently depict the infant Jesus polluting God's temple.

In fact, Luke elsewhere works to demonstrate that the Jesus movement was not guilty of profaning or defiling the sacred space of the temple. After the apostle Paul enters the Jerusalem temple in Acts, he faces accusations that he has desecrated the temple by bringing a gentile, Trophimus the Ephesian, into the temple precincts and presumably beyond the court of the gentiles (Acts 21:28; 24:6). Luke makes clear, though, that these charges are false: Paul and his Jewish—not gentile—companions entered the temple only after undergoing purification (21:26), something that Paul stresses in his own defense before Felix (24:18). Acts → But is this irons

This connection between Jesus's presentation in the temple and the need for the preceding purification rites also explains another of the perceived errors Brown detects in Luke's understanding of the law. As noted above, Brown argues that Luke wrongly conflates the childbirth offerings with temple presentation. But this combination of the legislation of Leviticus 12 with the presentation in the temple makes good legal sense. Since Luke portrays Jesus's parents presenting him to the Lord, Luke must ensure that his readers realize that all the requisite childbirth purification rites occurred prior to this presentation. In other words, Luke does not mistakenly conflate two separate rites; rather, the one rite, the presentation in the temple, necessitates the second (but chronologically prior) rite, purification from ritual impurity.[50]

---

time period that a midwife endures this impurity is half the time of the new mother. For this and other examples, see Bradshaw, *Canons of Hippolytus*.

50. Because it does not relate to ritual purity, I leave untreated the question of why Luke depicts Jesus's presentation in the temple in supposed fulfillment of Exod. 13, when this was not a common practice among early Jews. Although we cannot be certain as to Luke's reasoning, we should exercise caution in claiming that Luke here misunderstood the Jewish law when in so many other places he shows considerable knowledge of the Jewish law and contemporary practices.

Conclusion

I have taken considerable time to look at the discrepancy between Luke 2:22 and Leviticus 12 because of the way New Testament scholars have made use of it. On the basis of Luke's supposed errors in Luke 2, Joseph Fitzmyer states, "What has to be recognized is that Luke, not being a Palestinian Jewish Christian, is not accurately informed about this custom of the purification of a woman after childbirth."[51] Similarly, Brown avers, "The result is a strange combination of a general knowledge of Judaism with an inaccurate knowledge of details—an indication that the author scarcely grew up in Judaism or in Palestine. The need to explain the customs to the audience supposes that for the most part they also were non-Palestinian Gentiles. . . . Much of this could be explained if Luke was a Gentile proselyte to Judaism before he became a Christian: one who had a 'book-knowledge' of Judaism through the LXX."[52] Brown's conclusion is of particular interest. If Luke shows us anything in his writings, it is that he is a knowledgeable and skillful interpreter of the Greek translations of Jewish scriptures. In other words, his Gospel repeatedly demonstrates that Luke has an intimate "book knowledge," as Brown puts it, of Judaism. How likely is it that such a careful and knowledgeable reader of Jewish scriptures would have unwittingly contradicted Jewish scriptures with regard to childbirth impurity? I would argue, in contrast to Brown, that were Luke to have only book knowledge of Judaism, his portrayal of the purification in Jerusalem would conform more closely to the written legislation of Leviticus 12.

What *Jubilees* and 4Q265 suggest is that although Luke's reference to Mary's time of purification does not match the wording of Leviticus 12, it does reflect a legal position that was espoused by some Jews in the Second Temple period. It is not Luke, therefore, who betrays his ignorance of actual Jewish customs and the Jewish ritual purity system in the first century CE; it is modern scholars. It is, of course, rather ironic that modern (and predominantly Christian) scholars accuse an ancient author of having only *book knowledge* of Judaism as it was practiced in Jesus's day, for it is we modern readers who have only a book knowledge of ancient Judaism. We face the considerable challenge of trying to inhabit the foreign world of early Judaism. Thanks to the relatively recent discoveries of the scrolls at Qumran and the survival of other early Jewish literature, we are able to piece together fragments of that world, but our knowledge will only ever be imperfect at best.

51. Fitzmyer, *Gospel according to Luke I–IX*, 424.
52. Brown, *Birth of the Messiah*, 448–49.

Nonetheless, even with this fragmentary evidence, we can conclude that Luke knew contemporary Jewish legal positions regarding childbirth and, as noted above, sided with those Jewish writers who thought it impossible that a child could somehow remain ritually pure having just entered into the world at the precise point in time and location that a newborn mother becomes ritually impure.

Luke 2:22 contradicts neither the legislation of Leviticus 12 nor the childbirth practices of Jesus's Jewish contemporaries. In fact, Luke's views on childbirth impurity coincide with some of the stricter legal rulings on childbirth impurity in Second Temple Judaism. Luke may subscribe to an essentialist, as opposed to a nominalist, understanding of the Jewish law.[53] An essentialist understanding of ritual impurity is that ritual purity has an ontological reality: corpses, *lepra*, and genital discharges contain or emit a real substance or power into the world.[54] In the case of childbirth, the genital discharge involved in the birthing process truly is impure. If so, anyone who comes into contact with the discharge must, by the very laws of nature, become ritually impure. The book of *Jubilees* subscribes to this legal essentialism, as do numerous works from Qumran (likely 4Q265 among them). Luke too is best understood as subscribing to this understanding of the law. In other words, instead of conveying his ignorance of the Jewish law, Luke's description of Jesus's birth and subsequent purification demonstrates Luke's familiarity with the Jewish law as some Jews in the Second Temple period understood it. In fact, it appears to fit within what modern scholars would likely classify as a stricter interpretation of the Jewish law. Such an assertion might find additional confirmation in the fact that, as I noted earlier in the chapter, Luke held to a stricter understanding of which women priests ought to marry (women of priestly descent). And both of these legal positions also coincide with Luke's stricter legal understanding regarding circumcision: it *must* occur on the eighth day after birth if it is to have covenantal validity, leaving no room for gentiles to become Jews.[55]

53. On legal essentialism and legal nominalism (or formalism), see Amihay, *Theory and Practice in Essene Law*, 19–30. For earlier iterations of this dichotomy, albeit using different and problematic terminology, see Schwartz, "Priestly View of Descent at Qumran," and Hayes, *What's Divine about Divine Law*.

54. A nominalist understanding of ritual impurity is that there is no real, ontological essence to impurity—it is a legal or cultural fiction. One can see such a nominalist understanding of ancient Mediterranean purity and holiness codes in the writings of Sextus Empiricus, a late first-century CE doctor and philosopher, who avers, "For things which are in some cults accounted holy are in others accounted unholy. But this would not have been so if the holy and the unholy existed by nature" (*Outlines of Pyrrhonism* 3.220).

55. See Thiessen, *Contesting Conversion*, chap. 5.

In this chapter I have focused almost exclusively on the infancy narrative of the Gospel of Luke. I have done so for a number of reasons, even though Luke is the latest of the three Synoptic Gospels. First, Luke's Gospel provides readers with the clearest portrayal of the Torah and temple piety of Jesus's family. To my mind, the later we date Luke's Gospel (and Acts), the more interesting this fact becomes. Whether Luke wrote in the 80s or 90s, as most scholars presume, or in the second century CE, as a number of scholars have recently argued,[56] his account of Jesus, while following many of the major contours of Mark and Matthew, adds significant details that stress the law observance of Jesus's family. Such editorial work demonstrates how imperative Jewish law observance was for Luke. Well after the destruction of the Jerusalem temple, and well after the Jesus movement had become predominantly gentile in its ethnic makeup, Luke *still* stressed common aspects of Jewish piety.

Second, it is almost a scholarly consensus that the author of the Third Gospel was a gentile follower of Christ.[57] If so, Luke's Gospel contrasts with the Gospels of Matthew and Mark, who were both Jewish followers of Christ.[58] The preceding discussion, though, might call this consensus into question, for it demonstrates that Luke was deeply knowledgeable about the way some of his Jewish contemporaries interpreted the Jewish law.

Third, and finally, Luke's treatment of childbirth impurity raises a number of methodological issues not only for this chapter but also for the entirety of this book. To my knowledge, no interpreter has ever concluded on the basis of a legal argument (halakhah) that does not at first glance agree with Leviticus 12 that the author of, say, *Jubilees* or 4Q266 must be a non-Jew. The same observation applies more broadly to other writers like Josephus or Philo. A different legal position in a Second Temple Jewish writer is always treated as evidence of legal development or diversity, never as a sign of ignorance of the Jewish law or Jewish practices, never as a sign of non-Jewish identity, and never as a sign that someone has abandoned or rejected the Jewish law. But if this is the case, what gives New Testament scholars the license to treat Luke (or any other New Testament writer, for that matter) as markedly different from these other writings, apart from the fact that a couple of centuries after he wrote, Christians incorporated his writings into something that came to

---

56. E.g., Tyson, *Marcion and Luke-Acts*, and Pervo, *Dating Acts*.

57. E.g., Plummer, *Gospel according to St. Luke*, xx; Caird, *Gospel of St. Luke*, 105; Kümmel, *Introduction to the New Testament*, 149; Schmithals, *Das Evangelium nach Lukas*, 9; Fitzmyer, *Gospel according to Luke I–IX*, 41–42; C. A. Evans, *Luke*, 2; Bock, *Luke 1:1–9:50*, 6; Bovon, *Gospel of Luke 1:1–9:50*, 8; and Carroll, *Luke*, 2.

58. See, for instance, Runesson, *Divine Wrath and Salvation*; Kampen, *Matthew within Sectarian Judaism*; and VanMaaren, "Gospel of Mark within Judaism."

be called the New Testament, a collection of texts that became foundational to something (Christianity) that defined itself in opposition to Judaism?

To put it differently, one of the central assumptions of this book is that the Gospel writers actually provide evidence of the legal diversity of early Jews and should not be used, as many scholars have used them, to posit a first-century CE break between Christianity and Judaism. This legal diversity in the first century CE raises anew the possibility that Luke was himself a Jew, an argument most often associated with the work of Jacob Jervell, a scholar whom Isaac Oliver has aptly described as a "singular and dissident voice" that was "too prophetic for that time." In *Torah Praxis after 70 CE*, Oliver himself repeatedly and convincingly points to Luke's concern for Torah observance as evidence for Luke's Jewishness.[59] While Luke's ethnicity is not the topic of this book, Oliver's argument that Luke and Matthew provide evidence of legal diversity among early Jews is. The following chapters will examine Jesus's mission and his encounters with the ritually impure in light of the methodological assumption that legal differences do not signify indifference to or rejection of the Jewish law.

59. Oliver, *Torah Praxis*, 21. See Jervell, *Luke and the People of God*, and Jervell, *Unknown Paul*. Others who conclude that Luke was Jewish include Munck, *Acts of the Apostles*, 264–67; Ellis, *Gospel of Luke*, 51–53; Salmon, "Insider or Outsider?"; Sterling, *Historiography and Self-Definition*, 328; and Strelan, *Luke the Priest*.

CHAPTER 3

Jesus and the Walking Dead

The first ritually impure person Jesus encounters in Mark's Gospel is a man who has what Mark calls *lepra*. This story, I will argue, stresses Jesus's desire to remove the sources of ritual impurity from those who endure it. Matthew and Luke not only retain this story but also add further stories about Jesus and those with *lepra*. Such additions demonstrate that Matthew and Luke continue to find significance in narratives of Jesus healing those with *lepra*. First, though, the Greek word *lepra* requires careful unpacking because of the ways that modern scholars and readers have often mistranslated and therefore misunderstood it. This misunderstanding has concealed the Gospel writers' interests in depicting Jesus's relation to ritual impurity and therefore contributes to contemporary readings of the Gospels in which Jesus opposes the ritual purity system.

What Is *Lepra*?

The Synoptic Gospels portray Jesus encountering people who have *lepra*, a Greek word frequently translated into English as *leprosy* (e.g., Mark 1:40–42; Matt. 8:2–3; 10:8; 11:5; Luke 5:12–13; 7:22; 17:12). The term *leprosy* conjures up all kinds of dreadful images in the modern imagination. For example, I recall being taught as a child that leprosy is a disease that causes people to lose all feeling within their bodies. Due to this lack of sensation, lepers frequently lose limbs, unwittingly doing damage to their bodies because they cannot sense the harm that they are inflicting upon themselves. I was also

43

taught that leprosy is a highly contagious disease, one requiring those who suffer from it to be quarantined in order to protect others from contracting the disease. No wonder, then, that the Gospel writers would want to portray Jesus showing compassion to a man suffering from such a degenerative and contagious disease! In identifying *lepra* with leprosy, modern readers of the Gospels encounter nothing unfamiliar in these stories; rather, they find them to be moving examples of compassionate care of those who suffer from debilitating medical illnesses. Such an interpretation has not only inspired the work of Mother Teresa and the Missionaries of Charity among modern-day lepers in India but has also, through analogy, led to thoughtful care for those experiencing both the physical suffering and the stigma that are often associated with HIV/AIDS.[1]

While these efforts to care for people who suffer in modern times are truly admirable, this sort of historical reconstruction unwittingly rips Jesus out of the world of the first century CE and relocates him within our own conceptual world. It is true that leprosy, or Hansen's disease as it is called in modern medicine, is a chronic bacterial infection that can result in the loss of feeling to body parts. Nonetheless, leprosy does not typically result in the loss of limbs. Instead, it can shrink tissue, thus giving the appearance of shorter fingers or toes. Further, contrary to popular thinking, leprosy is not highly contagious—while the bacteria that causes leprosy (*Mycobacterium leprae* [and *Mycobacterium lepromatosis*, which was discovered in 2008]) is disseminated through coughing and sneezing, contraction of the disease ordinarily occurs through prolonged contact with those who are infected. Even then, apparently 95 percent of people are naturally immune to the disease.[2] Thus, while leprosy is a serious medical condition, common portrayals of it tilt toward the fantastical.

More fundamentally, the Greek term *lepra*—*tsara'at* in Hebrew—does not refer to the disease that we call leprosy today. While almost all English Bibles render this word as *leprosy*, this translation runs contrary to both archaeological and literary evidence, which suggest that leprosy did not exist in the Mediterranean world until well after the composition of Leviticus.

For instance, despite medical records dating back to the beginning of the Old Kingdom (almost 3000 BCE), early Egyptian literature does not contain a single reference to leprosy. And despite extensive archaeological work, the earliest evidence of leprosy in Egypt comes from four corpses that date to

---

1. See, for instance, W. H. P. Anderson, "Christian Missions and Lepers," and Manus and Bateye, "Plight of HIV and AIDS Persons."

2. For a helpful summary, see Mark, "Alexander the Great," 287–91. My discussion of the archaeological and literary evidence for leprosy in antiquity is indebted to this article.

approximately 200 BCE.[3] Similarly, our earliest evidence for leprosy in Judea comes from first-century CE Jerusalem.[4] Although there is literary evidence of leprosy in sixth-century BCE India,[5] it appears to have been unknown in the Mediterranean world until the third century BCE.

Greco-Roman medical literature wrestles with the recent appearance of this disease in the West. In the early second century CE, a physician named Rufus of Ephesus maintains that "the ancients knew nothing of *elephantiasis* [that is, leprosy], and we must wonder that people capable of contemplating everything in the tiniest detail missed such a serious and common disease." Rufus claims that it was the third-century BCE Alexandrian Straton "who gave us the basic knowledge of this disease."[6] A similar sentiment is found slightly earlier in Plutarch, who states,

> Philo, the physician, claimed that the disease called *elephantiasis* had been known for only a short time, because none of the ancient physicians had written a treatise on it, though they discussed many others that were minute and minor and, to most people, obscure. . . . Those present [when Philo made this claim] were amazed at the idea that new diseases came into existence and took shape at that date; but they thought it would be no less amazing if such remarkable symptoms had gone unnoticed for so long. The majority, however, preferred the second hypothesis, because it placed the blame on humanity, for they regarded nature as being unable to innovate in such matters.[7]

Although Plutarch claims that Philo and his contemporaries were divided over whether leprosy was a new disease or had previously gone unnoticed, they failed to consider one other possibility: that the disease was introduced

3. Contrary to Grmek, *Diseases in the Ancient Greek World*, 152–76. The one supposed exception is the Ebers Papyrus, an Egyptian medical work that dates to the sixteenth century BCE, which its translator, Bendix Ebbell, claims mentions leprosy by the name of "Chon's swelling" (*Papyrus Ebers*, 126). This identification is incorrect, since the symptoms that the work describes relate to a disease called "gas gangrene," as argued by Andersen, "Medieval Diagnosis of Leprosy," 11. On the earliest evidence of leprosy in Egypt, see Dzierzykray-Rogalski, "Paleopathology of the Ptolemaic Inhabitants." In fact, Grafton Elliot Smith and Warren Royal Dawson were able to find only one Egyptian corpse that had Hansen's disease, and it was from sixth-century CE Nubia. Building on their work, Vilhelm Møller-Christensen examined twelve hundred Egyptian remains and found only one additional case of leprosy, which came from the same Christian cemetery in which Smith and Dawson identified their own case. Further, he also examined almost six hundred individuals excavated from Lachish, an ancient Canaanite settlement, and found no evidence of leprosy. See Smith and Dawson, *Egyptian Mummies*, 160, and Møller-Christensen, "Evidence of Leprosy," 304.

4. See Matheson et al., "Molecular Exploration."

5. See Bhishagratna, *Sushruta Samhita*, 2:36–37.

6. According to Oribasius, *Collectio medica* 4.63–64; trans. Mark, "Alexander the Great."

7. Plutarch, *Moralia* 731A–B.

into the Mediterranean world at a particular point in time through migration. If Plutarch's testimony can be trusted, it locates the first Mediterranean instances and knowledge of leprosy both chronologically and geographically in third-century BCE Egypt—something that finds support in the leprous Egyptian corpses dating to 200 BCE. In the first century BCE, the Roman philosopher Lucretius still thinks that the disease, which he refers to as *elephas morbus*, is restricted to the area near the Nile River.[8] It then appears to have moved to Europe, where, according to Plutarch's testimony above, it first became known both to Philo, a first-century BCE Greek physician working in Rome, and to Aretaeus of Cappadocia, who wrote the earliest detailed description of leprosy in Western medicine.[9] The testimonies of Lucretius, Rufus, and Plutarch find confirmation in the first-century CE writings of Pliny the Elder, who believes that the disease was unknown in Italy prior to the days of Pompey the Great—that is, the mid-first century BCE—and that it was of Egyptian origin.[10] Nonetheless, leprosy does not appear to be particularly prevalent in first-century CE Italy, since Celsus claims that, "almost unknown in Italy, the disease, which the Greeks call *elephantiasis*, occurs frequently in certain regions."[11]

All of this evidence leads paleopathologists to conclude that leprosy originated in India, where we have sixth-century BCE evidence of its existence, and spread to Egypt in the third century BCE and then into the Levant and Europe by the first century BCE. Samuel Mark, in contrast to scholars who have argued that the armies of Alexander the Great brought the disease back from India, notes that leprosy is much more likely to afflict the weak, making armies, which generally consist of young, healthy men, an unlikely transmitter of the disease. Instead, he argues that the burgeoning slave trade that brought numerous Indians, particularly women and children, to Egypt in the third century BCE provided the likely migration path for the disease.[12]

Regardless, the internal evidence of Leviticus, and Jewish scriptures more broadly, confirms that the Hebrew word *tsaraʿat* did not refer to leprosy. Leviticus points to the existence of white flesh, and white hair within that flesh, as potential evidence of *lepra* (Lev. 13:3–4, 10, 13, 16–17, 19–21, 24–26, 38–39). It is precisely the whiteness of the skin that leads the priest to diagnose the presence of *lepra* and to declare the person impure. White, flaky skin,

8. Lucretius, *Nature of Things* 6.1114–15.
9. See Hude, *Corpus Medicorum Graecorum II*, 85–90.
10. Pliny the Elder, *Natural History* 26.5.7–8; cf. 20.52.144.
11. Celsus, *On Medicine* 3.25.1.
12. Mark, "Alexander the Great."

then, seems to be one of the key symptoms of *lepra*. But it is the distinctive whiteness, among other things, that the leprologist Robert Cochrane claims precludes the possibility of identifying the *lepra* described in Leviticus 13–14 with the disease of leprosy: "There are two details in the Levitical record which cannot apply to leprosy—its 'whiteness' and the affection of the scalp. In the first place, leprosy lesions are *never* white. In the second place, leprosy of the scalp very rarely occurs and does not occur apart from advanced lepromatous leprosy."[13] *Lepra*'s whiteness is the most pertinent detail for our discussion. Like Cochrane, Greco-Roman medical writers describe leprosy in ways that simply do not fit Leviticus 13–14. For instance, Celsus depicts leprosy in the following way: "The surface of the body presents a multiplicity of spots and of swellings, which, at first red, are gradually changed to be black in colour."[14] Pliny portrays leprosy in similar terms: "The plague usually begins on the face, a kind of freckle on the tip of the nose, yet presently the skin dries up over all the body, covered with spots of various colours, and uneven, in places thick, in others thin, in others hard as with rough itch scab, finally however going black."[15]

Additionally, three other ancient Israelite texts compare *lepra* to snow and thus might corroborate the whiteness of *lepra* (Exod. 4:6; Num. 12:10; 2 Kings 5:27). English translations may be guilty of overinterpreting these texts, which compare *lepra* to snow but say nothing explicit about the *color* of this disease. E. V. Hulse, for instance, argues that the comparison to snow is related to the flake-like condition of the skin, which peels or falls off the body like snowflakes.[16] As evidence for this claim, he notes that *lepra* is related to the words *lepis* ("a scale") and *lepō* ("to peel"). While Hulse rightly stresses that one symptom of this disease is flaky skin, he fails to do justice to the frequent appeals to the whiteness of flesh in Leviticus 13. White, flaky skin seems to be one of the key symptoms of *lepra*.[17] If leprosy—Hansen's disease—is never white, then a leper in the modern sense would never have been declared impure by the legislation of Leviticus 13–14. Still, even clearer evidence that Leviticus does not refer to leprosy exists: the laws pertaining to *lepra* describe the rituals that Israel must observe if either clothing (Lev. 13:47–59) or a house (14:34–35) becomes infected with *lepra*. Clearly a medical condition is not in view here, since houses and clothing do not contract leprosy.

13. Cochrane, *Biblical Leprosy*, 13.
14. Celsus, *On Medicine* 3.25.1.
15. Pliny the Elder, *Natural History* 26.5.2–6.
16. Hulse, "Nature of Biblical 'Leprosy,'" 93.
17. Cf. Mishnah, *Nega'im* 1.1.

To what condition(s) does the *lepra* of Leviticus 13–14 (and other texts) refer? In his three-volume commentary on Leviticus, Jacob Milgrom relates that upon reading the description of *tsaraʿat* in Leviticus 13–14, a contemporary dermatologist concluded that the symptoms described there actually do not correspond to any known skin conditions. Milgrom ultimately concludes from this that trying to identify which modern medical condition Leviticus depicts is wrongheaded; what Leviticus 13–14 describes "is ritual, not pathology."[18]

To summarize, all of our evidence, both archaeological and literary, indicates that leprosy did not exist in the Mediterranean world prior to the third or second century BCE and thus would have been unknown to the priestly community responsible for the production of the book of Leviticus. On this most scholars agree. But what about in Jesus's day? After all, as I noted above, leprosy *did* exist in Judea and in the Mediterranean world more broadly in the first century CE. When the Gospel writers refer to *lepra*, did *they* mean to refer to leprosy? The answer, in short, is no.[19]

After leprosy arrived in the Middle East and Europe, Greek writers did not refer to it as *lepra*, which the Greek translators of Jewish scriptures *always* used to translate the skin condition described in Leviticus 13–14 and which the Gospel writers used. Instead, when referring to leprosy, Greek and Latin writers usually used the words *elephas* or *elephantiasis*, never *lepra*. On the other hand, they used the word *lepra* for a variety of relatively minor skin disorders. For instance, the Hippocratic Corpus, written between 430 and 330 BCE and attributed to Hippocrates, the so-called father of Western medicine, uses *lepra* to refer to conditions similar to psoriasis or fungal infections.[20] Subsequent medical writers, such as Pliny the Elder, frequently mention *lepra* in the same context as scurvy (*psora*) and distinguish it from *elephantiasis*.[21] Galen, writing in the second century CE, uses the term in similar ways for sores and scabs.[22] Even later writers, such as Oribasios of Alexandria in the fourth century CE and Paulos of Aegina in the seventh century CE, continue to differentiate *lepra* (scale disease) from *elephantiasis* (leprosy). If the Gospel writers intended to refer to leprosy when they mentioned Jesus's

---

18. Milgrom, *Leviticus 1–16*, 817.

19. In contrast to R. T. France, who claims that "it is generally agreed that λέπρα [*lepra*] in the Bible is used for a wider range of diseases than 'true leprosy' (Hansen's disease), though including it" (*Gospel of Mark*, 117).

20. E.g., *Humors* 17, which mentions skin diseases that are aggravated by the possibility of rain, or *Affections* 35, which claims that *lepra* and other conditions are not diseases but minor disfigurements.

21. Pliny the Elder, *Natural History* 28.33.128; 35.51.180.

22. Galen, *Method in Medicine* 5.12.368K.

healings of *lepra*, then they were unique in the Greek-speaking world—so unique, in fact, that no one would have known that it was actually leprosy to which they referred, since the first writer to use *lepra* to refer to leprosy was the doctor John of Damascus in the late eighth or early ninth century CE. Only as a result of John's mistaken conflation of leprosy with *lepra* did it become common among later writers to interpret the *lepra* of the Gospels as leprosy.[23] To this day, this misidentification persists in biblical translations, commentaries, and sermons.

Lepra-Like Conditions in the Ancient Near East

But properly identifying *lepra* raises its own set of questions. If *lepra* was not the medical disease leprosy, why did the priestly community that composed Leviticus care so much about it? One possible explanation comes from other ancient Near Eastern cultures. For instance, Vilhelm Møller-Christensen notes that there are numerous references to a disease called *sbh* in Egyptian papyri dating from the twenty-first to the twenty-third dynasties (roughly 1100 BCE to 700 BCE). That *sbh* was likely equivalent to *lepra* can be seen in the fact that later Coptic translators of both Jewish scriptures and the New Testament consistently used the Coptic equivalent of the hieroglyphic *sbh* to translate *lepra*.

Sam Meier notes another parallel in ancient Mesopotamian concerns over house fungus. The twelfth tablet of the omen tablets known as *Šumma ālu ina mēlê šakin* discusses a fungus it calls *katarru*, which gives differing portents of the future depending upon its color and location in a house. Not all of these portents, though, are evil. For instance, black fungus foretells future success. In fact, we have one surviving letter written to an Assyrian king that discusses the *katarru* fungus and its treatment: "There exists an apotropaic prayer and also a ritual for the special *kamunu*-lichen which has appeared in the inner court yard of the temple of Nabû, and the *katarru*-lichen on the wall of the central storehouses. Adad-šumi-uṣur will perform it tomorrow morning. He should perform it several times."[24] This letter shows that the concern over house fungus was real—so important, in fact, that it merited disturbing the king over its presence in a temple. It also demonstrates that the Assyrians had an established ritual in place to protect a person from any evil that might result from the fungus—both a prayer to ward off evil and a

---

23. See Andersen, "Medieval Diagnosis of Leprosy."

24. S. Meier, "House Fungus." Translation of Letter #110 is from Oppenheim, *Letters from Mesopotamia*, 167.

ritual for the fungus's removal. Meier reconstructs the basic aspects of this latter ritual in the following way:

1. The fungus is observed.
2. A special scraping instrument is acquired.
3. An exorcist scrapes the fungus off the wall with the instrument.
4. An exorcist disposes of the fungus by burning.

But differences exist between priestly depictions of *lepra* and Assyrian depictions of house fungus. Most significantly, the former usually views *lepra* as a naturally occurring phenomenon devoid of meaning, while the latter finds portentous significance in its presence. When *lepra* is unnatural, though, Leviticus attributes its presence in a house not to demonic activity but to God's doing. Such a statement suggests that *lepra* in clothing or on a human body might also be due to Israel's God (Lev. 14:34; cf. 2 Sam. 3:29). After all, when the king of Israel hears that the king of Aram wants him to heal Naaman's *lepra*, he asks whether he is God to have such power over it. The assumption appears to be that God is the source of, and therefore the only remedy for, *lepra*. Further, whereas these ancient Near Eastern texts often bring up the presence of the demonic, Jewish scriptures discuss *lepra* only in relation to ritual impurity.[25]

Other ancient Near Eastern literature also discusses a *lepra*-like skin condition occurring in humans. James Kinnier Wilson, for instance, points to a Babylonian omen text that states, "If the skin of a man exhibits 'white *pūsu*-areas,' or is 'dotted with *nuqdu*-dots,' such a man has been rejected by his god and is to be rejected by mankind." While Kinnier Wilson identifies this disease as leprosy, it clearly is not, since, as discussed above, the white areas are not indicative of leprosy. Instead, this condition sounds similar to the skin conditions of Leviticus 13–14. Associated medical terms from the second millennium BCE, such as *saharšubbù*, *išrubu*, and *garābu*, indicated conditions that caused the person who suffered from them "to roam outside the city walls like the wild ass."[26] Those Assyrians and Babylonians who suffered from conditions akin to the *lepra* of Leviticus 13–14, then, may have had to endure social isolation. Herodotus mentions a similar concern in Persia: Any person "who has *leprēn* or the *leukēn* may not come into a

---

25. But see below where later Jewish authors connect *lepra* and the demonic.
26. Vorderasiatische Abteilung Tontafel 7525, Vorderasiatisches Museum, Berlin. Kinnier Wilson, "Organic Disease in Ancient Mesopotamia," 206. Translation of the Babylonian omen text also comes from Kinnier Wilson.

town or consort with other Persians. They say that he is so afflicted because he has sinned in some way against the sun."[27] In fact, even in the early third century CE, the Roman writer Aelian attests that "all the peoples of Asia" abhor *lepra*.[28] In sum, concern over *lepra* existed in ancient Israelite society as well as in other ancient Near Eastern cultures, but those concerns were not entirely equivalent.

As seen above, even though they do not identify it with leprosy, numerous Greco-Roman writers discuss *lepra* and the ways one can treat it. Greek and Roman physicians, therefore, identify the term with a variety of minor medical skin conditions—more akin to psoriasis, eczema, or scurvy than to Hansen's disease. In contrast, *lepra* and other ritual impurities signified the forces of death in at least some Jewish thinking. As Milgrom puts it, "The main clue for understanding the place of [*lepra*] in the impurity system is that it is an aspect of death: its bearer is treated like a corpse."[29] The story of Miriam, the sister of Moses and Aaron, demonstrates this connection (Num. 12). In response to the complaints of Miriam and Aaron, God comes down to them in a pillar of cloud and rebukes them. When the cloud ascends, Miriam has *lepra*. Her brother Aaron acts as the mediator between Miriam and Moses, stating, "Do not let her be as in death, as a miscarried baby whose flesh is half consumed when it comes out of its mother's womb" (12:12). This gruesome depiction of a stillborn child's flesh connects the appearance of *lepra* to corpse-like skin. The peeling off of the skin that *lepra* caused reminded priestly thinkers of the deterioration of a corpse, thus functioning as a sign of death—Miriam looked like the walking dead.

We see this same association between *lepra* and death in Deuteronomic literature when the king of Aram asks the king of Israel to cure Naaman of his *lepra*. The king's response, "Am I a god, [that I am able] to kill and to make alive?" (2 Kings 5:7), implies that healing Naaman of his *lepra* is equivalent to giving life to the dead. Such power resides only with God. The first-century Jewish historian Josephus likewise equates those suffering from *lepra* with the dead: "And [Moses] expelled those with *lepra* from the city, permitting them to dwell with no one, since they differ in no way from a corpse."[30] Finally, later rabbis also repeatedly emphasize this connection: "[*Lepra*] is the equivalent of death, as it is written, 'Let her not be as one dead.'"[31]

27. Herodotus, *Histories* 1.138; translation slightly modified from the Loeb Classical Library.
28. Aelian, *Nature of Animals* 10.16.
29. Milgrom, *Leviticus: A Book of Ritual and Ethics*, 128.
30. Josephus, *Jewish Antiquities* 3.264.
31. E.g., Babylonian Talmud, *Sanhedrin* 47a; cf. Babylonian Talmud, *Nedarim* 64b; *Exodus Rabbah* 1.34.

Perhaps connected to this association, in its discussion of the way the priest identifies whether someone has *lepra*, the Qumran work known as the *Damascus Document* states that the priest must examine the "living" skin and the "dead" skin of the afflicted person.[32] The work elsewhere talks about the priest examining "the dead and living hairs" of the person who might have *lepra*.[33] This interpretive expansion of Leviticus 13–14 suggests that the community associated with the *Damascus Document* would have likewise identified *lepra* with death. The connection between *lepra* and death helps explain why Israel's priests believed this condition caused ritual impurity, which in turn helps modern readers better understand the Gospel writers' portrayals of Jesus's interaction with those with *lepra*.

Lepra in Second Temple Judaism

How did Jews in Jesus's day understand these laws? And how did they observe the laws pertaining to *lepra*? Were those suffering from *lepra* treated according to the legislation of Leviticus 13–14? Did Second Temple Jews agree with one another on the interpretation and application of this legislation? Thanks to the discoveries at Qumran, we have a good deal of literary evidence about what at least one group of Jews thought with regard to *lepra* in the century or so before Jesus. According to the *Temple Scroll*, for instance, every Jewish city must contain a quarantined area designated for those who have *lepra* so that they do not enter into a city and thus spread impurity through contact with others.[34] Only once the *lepros* has undergone purification can he or she enter again into the cities of Israel.[35] This legislation depends upon Leviticus 13:45–46 and Numbers 5:1–3, both of which require that Israel send those with *lepra* out of the camp.

The Qumran community criticized their opponents for their lax treatment of those who had *lepra*. One letter accuses their opponents of wrongly permitting those with *lepra* to return prematurely to their regular life, which apparently included allowing them to enter into buildings that contained sacred food after they had undergone ritual bathing.[36] To the minds of the people at Qumran, this custom disregarded the requirement that when *lepra* leaves people, not only must they have their hair shaved off and undergo ritual

---

32. 4Q269 7 4–7; 4Q272 1 I, 1–5.
33. 4Q266 6 I, 10.
34. 11Q19 XLVIII, 14–15.
35. 11Q20 XII, 10.
36. 4Q396 III, 4–11. Here see Feder, "Polemic regarding Skin Disease." For *lepra* at Qumran and in the Gospels, see Berthelot, "La place des infirmes."

bathing, but they must also wait an additional seven days before entering their tents (Lev. 14:8). The rituals of Leviticus 13–14 suggest that even after the underlying condition causing the impurity disappears, the ritual impurity still lingers. The apparent logic at work here is that, like the corpse (as we shall see in chap. 5), the *lepros*'s impurity is so potent that it affects everything within the same building. Even if the *lepros* does not touch the sacred food, the food becomes impure just by being in the same room. Consequently, priests who permit this premature introduction of the former *lepros* back into society (i.e., after the condition disappears but before the seven-day lingering ritual impurity dissipates) endanger not only sacred food but also themselves, because they willfully sin. Such willful sinning makes them guilty of "despising" and "blaspheming" God. For the Qumran community, then, *lepra* was of such grave importance that any *perceived* laxity in treating it would provoke the community's censure. Note, though, that the *Temple Scroll* demonstrates diversity in the ways that early Jews interpreted and observed the laws of *lepra*. Some thought the *lepros* needed to be quarantined for seven additional days after the underlying condition disappeared; others believed that such a person could reenter the community during this seven-day period. Neither believed themselves to be guilty of rejecting the law.

This exclusion of the *lepros* from city life was not unique to the Qumran community. Josephus, for instance, claims that Moses prohibited those with *lepra* from entering into cities or from living with others. Instead, they were to live as if they were dead—that is, as though they were corpses that were highly contagious to others.[37] He makes a similar assertion in his defense of Jews against the Egyptian priest Manetho, who maintained that the Egyptians had expelled Moses from Egypt because he suffered *lepra*. According to Josephus, this accusation was blatantly false since Moses himself legislated that those who had *lepra* could dwell neither in a city nor in a village with other people but had to conduct lives of solitude.[38]

The earliest rabbinic literature, though composed after the Gospels, contains a similar trajectory of thought. According to the Mishnah, those with *lepra* defile everything within an enclosure and even everything that sits beneath a tree with them.[39] This ruling agrees with the Qumran community's understanding of the defiling power of *lepra* and of the need to be quarantined. Considerably later, the Aramaic paraphrase of 2 Kings 15:5 states that after God struck King Azariah with *lepra*, he dwelled outside Jerusalem until

37. Josephus, *Jewish Antiquities* 3.264.
38. Josephus, *Against Apion* 1.281.
39. Mishnah, *Nega'im* 13.7–12.

his death. This interpretive expansion might reflect contemporary Jewish practices, since 2 Kings merely states that Azariah lived in a separate house (presumably from the royal palace). Nonetheless, the Mishnah permits those with *lepra* to return to their homes after their initial purification as long as they avoid sexual intercourse.[40] Such a legal position, as noted above, was precisely what the Qumran community protested. At the same time, not all rabbinic references to *lepra* imply that the *lepros* needed to be separated from the community. Another rabbinic text, for instance, permits the *lepros* to enter into the house of study with those who do not suffer such an impurity, even as it distances the *lepros* from others by a tall partition.[41]

All the evidence, then, suggests that while many Jews in the first century CE would have thought that the *lepros* needed to exercise vigilance in maintaining distance from people so as not to transmit his or her impurity to other Jews, they disagreed on the length of time one must maintain this distance. Although contracting a second-degree impurity from a *lepros* was not sinful, the danger lay in the possibility that a person might unwittingly bring an impurity that was unknowingly contracted from a *lepros* in a crowded setting into contact with sacred food or sacred space.

A *Lepros* in the Hands of an Angry Jesus

I needed to clear extensive ground so that modern readers of the Gospels can understand rightly the significance of Jesus's encounters with those who have *lepra*. While Greco-Roman writers perceived *lepra* to be a disease, they did not identify it with leprosy. Instead, it was a minor medical condition. On the other hand, Jews thought of *lepra* primarily as a condition that caused ritual impurity, not exclusively or even chiefly as a medical condition. Turning to the Gospels, if *lepra* was little different from eczema or scurvy medically speaking, why did the Gospel writers care to present Jesus performing a miracle that was roughly equivalent to using dandruff shampoo or an antifungal ointment twice a week? What does the fact that Jesus overcomes something as seemingly mundane as skin blemishes say about his mission and identity? Surely there were more pressing medical conditions in the first century upon which Mark, Matthew, and Luke could have focused! The answer must be that they did not want to demonstrate Jesus's opposition to Jewish ritual concerns about *lepra*, as is so often the argument of New Testament scholars; rather, these early followers of Jesus wanted to depict him in a way that showed his

40. Mishnah, *Nega'im* 14.2.
41. Mishnah, *Nega'im* 13.12.

opposition to the very existence of *lepra* itself. The difference between these two interpretations is substantial. The former denies the reality and power of ritual impurity; the latter acknowledges its reality but believes that Jesus's power transcends the power that creates the ritual impurity.

In Mark's Gospel one of the very first deeds of power that Jesus performs relates to a *lepros*—a man who suffers from *lepra*:

> And a *lepros* came to him, begging him, and saying to him, "If you desire to, you can purify me." Angered, [Jesus] stretched out his hand and touched him, and said to him, "I desire. Be pure!" And immediately the *lepra* left him, and he was purified. And growling at him, [Jesus] immediately cast him away, and said to him, "See that you say nothing to anyone. But go, show yourself to the priest, and offer for your purification what Moses commanded, as a testimony to them." Instead, [the former *lepros*] went out and began to talk about it, and to spread the news, with the result that [Jesus] was no longer able to enter into a town openly, but stayed outside in deserted places. (Mark 1:40–45)

Mark's story raises a number of questions, but here I focus only on the question of *why* Jesus gets angry when he encounters this man and hears his request. There is a considerable text-critical issue related to this anger: only a few manuscripts of Mark read "angered" (*orgistheis*), while the vast majority read "having compassion" (*splanchnistheis*).[42] Most modern translations follow the latter manuscripts, but according to the principles of text criticism, interpreters should generally prefer the more difficult reading since it is more likely that a scribe would remove a difficulty in a passage than create one. Although the external evidence is undeniably slight, the harder reading is indeed preferable here. Support for this conclusion comes from the fact that Matthew and Luke, who both use and revise Mark's Gospel, mention neither Jesus's compassion nor his anger.[43] This silence suggests that the version of

42. The reading *orgistheis* ("angered") occurs only in D (Codex Bezae), three Old Latin manuscripts, and the Diatessaron, whereas almost all other manuscripts read *splanchnistheis* ("having compassion"). Bruce M. Metzger (*Textual Commentary on the Greek New Testament*, 76) thinks that the former reading is original, as does Bart Ehrman ("Text and Tradition"). The strongest argument for the originality of *splanchnistheis* ("having compassion") can be found in Johnson, "Anger Issues." Ultimately, as I will highlight below, even if one finds Johnson's argument convincing, the story still portrays Jesus dealing roughly with the man.

43. I find unconvincing Peter J. Williams's argument that since we cannot know with certainty the literary relationship of the Synoptic Gospels, we should not consider the evidence of Matthew and Luke in assessing the text of Mark ("An Examination of Ehrman's Case," 4). The case for Markan priority, and therefore for Matthew's and Luke's dependence upon Mark (regardless of the precise relationship between Luke and Matthew), is uncontroversial to the majority of scholars. What scholars need to explain, then, is why both Matthew and Luke modify Mark's account in the way that they do.

Mark that they used had "angered," not "having compassion," since it is more likely that they would both omit the difficult "angered" than that they would both omit a reference to Jesus's compassion (cf. Matt. 8:1–4; Luke 5:12–16).

In contrast, Nathan Johnson argues that early Christians would have been happy to point to evidence of Jesus's anger in their disputes with Marcion: "In countering Marcion Origen appears to be *searching* for an angry Jesus, one who hands an unrepentant servant over to torture."[44] This observation is true enough as far as it goes. But if Mark 1:41 originally read *orgistheis*, it would hardly help Origen, since the verse depicts Jesus getting angry at someone who comes to him for *deliverance*, not at some unrepentant sinner. Instead, evidence that Matthew and Luke would feel inclined to remove this reference to Jesus's anger can be found in the way in which they remove Mark's references to Jesus's anger in more textually secure passages. For instance, Mark claims that when Jesus encountered a man with a withered hand on the Sabbath, he looked around *with anger* at those who would accuse him of wrongdoing for healing on the Sabbath (Mark 3:5). In their rewritings of this account, both Matthew and Luke omit the phrase "with anger" even though Jesus is arguably justified in being angry at those who would judge him for healing on the Sabbath (Matt. 12:13; Luke 6:10). Similarly, when his disciples attempt to prevent children from approaching him, Jesus *becomes angry* with his disciples (Mark 10:14). Again, both Matthew and Luke omit Mark's seemingly justifiable reference to Jesus's anger (Matt. 19:14; Luke 18:16).

Conversely, both Matthew and Luke feel quite comfortable referring to Jesus's *compassion*. For instance, in Matthew, Jesus feels compassion for the crowds (Matt. 9:36; 15:32), and his compassion leads him to heal the sick on other occasions (14:14; 20:34). Two of these instances, Matthew 9:36 and 15:32, are dependent upon Mark's prior use of compassion terminology in Mark 6:34 and 8:2. Luke, too, is comfortable using compassion language of Jesus, although he does so only once in recounting Jesus's compassion on the widow who is on her way to bury her only son (Luke 7:13)—another example of Jesus's interactions with the ritually impure that I will examine more fully in chapter 5. It is difficult to conceive of a reason why both Matthew and Luke would choose to omit a reference to compassion if it occurred in Mark's account of the *lepros*.[45] This assertion stands whether the two-source

44. Johnson, "Anger Issues," 197.

45. Johnson points to the occurrence of *splanchnistheis* in Mark 9:22, where a father asks Jesus to remove a demon from his son, and to its subsequent absence in both Matt. 17 and Luke 9 ("Anger Issues," 185). While his observation is correct, his use of this fact is unconvincing. It does not indicate that Matthew and Luke intended to remove the reference to compassion; rather, Mark 9:21–22 portrays Jesus asking the father how long his son has had this particular

hypothesis or the Farrer hypothesis is correct. According to the two-source hypothesis, both Matthew and Luke would have *independently* chosen to omit Mark's reference to compassion. According to the Farrer hypothesis, Matthew would have omitted the reference to compassion, and Luke, who had access to both Mark and Matthew, would have had to prefer Matthew's version of this story to Mark's. Neither scenario seems likely. On the other hand, given that both Matthew and Luke omit references to Jesus's anger in contexts where it seems eminently justifiable for Jesus to show anger (that is, in contexts where people either resist his healing or try to keep children away from him), it makes considerable sense that Matthew and Luke would omit a reference to Jesus's anger when it seems entirely unwarranted.

Finally, an angry Jesus also fits with Mark's depiction of Jesus's indignation in 1:43: Jesus growls at or scolds (cf. Mark 14:5) the man and casts him away (Mark uses the Greek word *ekballō* here, the same word he commonly uses of Jesus's exorcisms of demons). Evidently, something about the encounter with this man has upset Jesus. But what is it? Scholars usually suggest one of four possible reasons for Jesus's anger: the man himself, the *lepra* that the man has, a demonic presence connected to the disease, or the entire ritual purity system, which was, according to some scholars, unduly harsh to this man in requiring his isolation.[46] Mark, unfortunately, does not say. Such ambiguity

---

condition and then has the man asking Jesus for compassion and help. Both Matthew and Luke omit this entire exchange, perhaps to shorten the passage by removing superfluous dialogue. In fact, Johnson claims that Luke "lacks *every* use of *splanchnizomai* from Mark" ("Anger Issues," 185). This claim sounds more impressive than it is. Apart from the contested appearance in 1:41, and apart from the previously explained absence in Luke's parallel to Mark 9:21–22, the verb appears only two times in Mark (6:34; 8:2). In those instances, Luke does not merely remove the verb *splanchnizomai*. Instead, Luke omits the entirety of Mark 6:34 and completely removes the story in which Mark 8:2 is found (Mark's doublet feeding story; 8:1–10). Additionally, Luke does contain a reference to Jesus's compassion (7:13). Similarly unhelpful is Johnson's suggestion that the reference to mercy (*éleēsen*) in Mark 5:19 and its absence from both Matthew and Luke supports his argument. Again, Matthew omits the entire dialogue between Jesus and the former demoniac. Luke, in contrast, merely abbreviates the words of Mark's Jesus. In sum, none of these passages are comparable to what Johnson suggests Matthew and Luke do in Mark 1:41.

46. William R. G. Loader, for instance, suggests Jesus is angry at the man's disrespect for the law, which he demonstrates in approaching Jesus in his impure condition ("Challenged at the Boundaries," 56). Stephen Voorwinde argues that Jesus might be mad at the man for his supposed sinfulness, which is the cause of his condition (*Jesus' Emotions in the Gospels*, 74). Though this claim is not rooted in Mark's account, evidence of such a connection between sin and *lepra* can be found elsewhere. Though it was written much later, *Numbers Rabbah* claims that *lepra* resulted from eleven sins (*Numbers Rabbah* 7.5) and that Israel began to suffer from it after their idolatrous worship of the calf in the wilderness (13.8). Cf. *Leviticus Rabbah* 18.1. For the claim that Jesus is angry at the *lepra*, see Gnilka, *Das Evangelium nach Markus*, 1:92–93. Those who suggest that Jesus is angry at a demonic presence include Sariola, *Markus und das Gesetz*, 66n86, and Marcus, *Mark 1–8*, 209. Finally, those who argue that Jesus is angered by

presumably helped give rise to the well-attested textual variant that describes Jesus as moved to compassion.

The fourth suggestion is the least plausible. If Jesus rejected the ritual purity system and the very reality of ritual impurity, then Mark should not have depicted Jesus *purifying* the impure man. Such behavior would undermine Jesus's purported message that such impurities do not actually exist. Rather, Jesus could have (and should have!) taught the man and the crowd that the system was exclusionary and encouraged them to consider the man pure. John Pilch claims that Jesus did precisely this: "Jesus declared the petitioner clean, that is, acceptable and welcome in the community. Jesus extended the boundaries of society and included in the holy community many who were otherwise excluded (lepers, tax collectors, prostitutes)."[47] In suggesting that Jesus extended boundaries to include those with *lepra*, Pilch implies that Jesus either overlooked the impurity connected to *lepra* or rejected the idea that *lepra* actually was impure. Such an interpretation of the story fits nicely with the thinking of many modern readers who cannot conceive of the possibility that ritual impurity exists. But in this sense, it is an outsider description of the social construction of ritual impurity. Most modern readers of the Gospels do not believe in the existence of ritual impurities, so we naturally interpret Jesus's actions in a way that coincides with our own worldview. Consequently, we read the story as depicting Jesus's struggle to convince the *lepros* and others to give up what we believe to be an imaginary binary of pure and impure. Not surprisingly, such an interpretation of the text places Jesus squarely within *our* world; despite living in first-century Galilee and Judea, Jesus knew (like us!) that ritual impurity was nothing more than a social construction that excludes others. His mission, then, was to proclaim and teach inclusion. The story itself, though, does not portray Jesus in this manner, since Jesus claims that he does desire to purify the man.

On the third suggestion: some early Jewish and Christian texts do connect *lepra* to the demonic. For instance, the *Damascus Document* refers to a *ruaḥ* in relation to this condition.[48] Additionally, the early Christian work known

---

the Jewish ritual purity system include France, *Gospel of Mark*, 118, and Myers, *Binding the Strong Man*, 152–54.

47. Pilch, *Healing in the New Testament*, 51. Similarly, John Dominic Crossan avers that Jesus "refuses to accept the disease's ritual uncleanliness and social ostracization" (*Jesus*, 82).

48. Cf. 4Q269 7 1–4; 4Q272 1 I, 1–5. So, for instance, J. Baumgarten, "4Q Zadokite Fragments," 162: "It is thus possible to take the attribution of scale disease to the [*ruaḥ*] in our text as involving the intrusion of evil or demonic influences." But see the cautionary remarks of Werrett, *Ritual Purity*, 31. More broadly, on the connection between the demonic and illness, see Wassen, "What Do Angels Have against the Blind?," and Machiela, "Luke 13:10–13."

as the *Acts of Pilate* retains a memory of Jesus's healing of *lepra*. In Jesus's trial before Pilate, various people whom Jesus healed come forward in his defense. One claims that with a word Jesus healed his *lepra* (6.2). Toward the end of the work, the author connects the condition to demonic activity, portraying Satan lamenting to personified Hades that all the people that he had made "crooked, blind, lame, or *leproi*" Jesus had, by a single word, healed (20.1). Finally, later rabbis refer to a demon who causes this condition.[49] Nonetheless, nothing in Mark's narrative makes this explicit. Thus, while it is historically plausible that Mark envisages a demonic presence connected to the *lepra*, the story does not focus on any demonic presence. In fact, even after he removes the *lepra*, Jesus continues his angry behavior—growling at the man and casting him away.

On the second suggestion: if Mark intends to portray Jesus as being angered by the presence of *lepra* in the man, then it demonstrates that Jesus loathes ritual impurity, much like Israel's God, who requires that no one approach his terrestrial residence—the sanctuary—while in such a condition. This interpretation would fit with Jesus's action in removing the *lepra* from the man and would also support research that connects concepts of impurity to the emotion of disgust.[50]

Nonetheless, I find the first suggestion to be the most convincing—Jesus is angry at the man. Again, Jesus's later actions of growling at and expelling the man (even though he no longer has *lepra*) from his presence appear to confirm this reading.

But *why* is Jesus angry at the man? After all, he comes to Jesus begging to be purified. And in his supplication, he shows a considerable degree of faith by verbally acknowledging that Jesus is powerful enough to purify him. Later rabbis would claim that it is as difficult to heal those suffering from *lepra* as it is to raise the dead. As noted above, Rabbi Yoḥanan claims, referring to the healing of Naaman's *lepra* in 2 Kings, that it "is the equivalent of death, as it is written, Let her not be as one dead."[51] Yet this man, as Mark portrays him, has no problem believing that Jesus *is* powerful enough to remove *lepra*. But Mark does not draw attention to the man's faith. In contrast, a father of a boy with an impure *pneuma* questions whether Jesus is able to do anything for his son later in Mark's narrative (Mark 9:22–23). Such doubts likewise anger Jesus. But here Mark narrates the story in order to structure the encounter around the question of whether Jesus *desires* to purify the man. This is the

49. Cf. Babylonian Talmud, *Ketubbot* 61b.

50. See here Kazen, *Emotions in Biblical Law*, 71–94; Kazen, "Role of Disgust"; and Feder, "Contagion and Cognition."

51. Babylonian Talmud, *Sanhedrin* 47a.

central question! The man's doubts pertain to whether Jesus *wants* to remove the *lepra*, not whether he is *able*. Does Jesus think this condition should be treated, and if so, is he willing to use his power to do so?

In other words, the story as Mark frames it focuses on Jesus's attitude toward ritual impurity. This is, after all, the first story in which a ritually impure person comes to Jesus. The very fact that the man is unsure whether Jesus desires to remove *lepra* demonstrates that Mark wishes to set the record straight on Jesus and ritual impurity. Presumably the man gives voice to a question or criticism that Mark believes was aimed at Jesus. The man's uncertainty angers Jesus because Mark thinks it is absurd that anyone would harbor doubts about Jesus's view of ritual impurity. For Mark's Jesus, ritual impurity is something real: it is a substance or miasma that *actually* exists in nature. Mark and Mark's Jesus, in other words, are legal essentialists. And *lepra* is of such momentous consequence that Jesus desires to purify those who suffer from it, becoming angry at the thought that anyone would believe otherwise. His response again focuses the reader's attention on Jesus's desire. Jesus says, "I desire! Be purified!" Such a heated encounter between the *lepros* and Jesus demonstrates the falsity of scholarly claims that Mark's Jesus was "indifferent" to or intended to "subvert" the laws pertaining to ritual impurity.[52]

But Jesus's concern for ritual purity does not end there. Instead of telling the man that he is pure and can now resume his regular life in the Jewish community, Jesus casts the man away, telling him to show himself to the priest and to bring the offering required for ritual purification (cf. Lev. 14:2–7). Mark's depiction of Jesus's interactions with the *lepros* perfectly fits the first stages of purification that Leviticus outlines: the person is first purified of the polluting condition (*lepra* itself, Lev. 14:2) but then must bring a sacrifice (and shave his or her hair) under the priest's direction (14:4–8), finally entering the community seven days after the underlying condition is removed. Here Jesus does not take upon himself the priestly prerogative of declaring someone pure or impure; rather, he sends him to the priest for such a pronouncement.[53] This action fits with Qumranic concerns, which do not permit the nonpriestly overseer to make such declarations. For example, the *Damascus Document* addresses how to identify *lepra*: "In the judgment of the law of skin disease in a person, the priest will come and stand in the camp, and the overseer will instruct him [i.e., the priest] in the details of the law. And

---

52. E.g., regarding subversion, see Crossan, *Historical Jesus*, 263; and regarding indifference, see Kazen, *Jesus and Purity Halakhah*, 8.

53. So too Loader, *Jesus' Attitude towards the Law*, 22.

even if he [i.e., the priest] is ignorant, he isolates [the diseased person], since the judgment belongs to them [i.e., the priests]."[54] This also coincides with rabbinic concerns, which stipulate that only a priest can declare whether the *lepros* has become pure: "Everyone is permitted to examine plagues, but the (declaration of) impurity and purity is in the mouth of the priest."[55] Like the Qumran community and the early rabbis, Jesus defers to the legislation of Leviticus 13–14, which states that only a priest may diagnose and make rulings about who is pure and who is impure (14:2–7). Since Jesus is not a priest, *he* cannot declare the man pure.[56] Jesus, then, fits within this larger stream of Jewish thinking about the declarative role that priests must play with regard to *lepra*.

In spite of this rather clear portrayal of Jesus's observance of Leviticus 13–14, interpreters frequently suggest that aspects of the story provide evidence of Jesus rejecting ritual purity laws. With regard to Jesus's command to go to the priest, Edwin Brodhead asserts, "Jesus sends the one declared clean specifically to the priest who had declared the [*lepros*] unclean. There the [*lepros*] is to bear witness to the power of Jesus and, by implication, to the impotence of the priest."[57] Numerous interpreters essentially agree with this conclusion, one that could perhaps be supported by Jesus's command to the man to show himself to the priest "for a testimony to them" (*eis martyrion autois*). Building on an adversarial reading of the preposition *eis* (that is, translating the phrase "as a testimony *against* them"), Simon Joseph observes that "Mark does *not* tell us that the man actually went to the priests or performed any sacrifices."[58] Yet such an observation says nothing about Mark's Jesus; after all, Jesus explicitly commands the man to offer precisely what Moses prescribes. Jesus intends for the man to fulfill the laws pertaining to *lepra* impurity because he thinks that they remain valid and significant. The man, in his (perhaps justifiable) exuberance, disobeys Jesus. But to conclude from this disobedience that neither Jesus nor Mark cares about the offerings required once one becomes purified from *lepra* is as preposterous as concluding that Jesus and Mark do not care about what one

---

54. *Damascus Document* XIII, 5–7.

55. Mishnah, *Nega'im* 3.1. The Mishnah never uses the noun *tsara'at* (= *lepra*), which is common in the Hebrew Bible, but instead uses the word *nega'im* ("plagues").

56. Cf. the similar acknowledgment in Heb. 7:13–14 about Jesus's nonpriestly status in relation to the earthly cult.

57. Brodhead, "Christology as Polemic and Apologetic," 25. For other negative readings of this phrase, see, for instance, Lohmeyer, *Das Evangelium des Markus*, 47. For more positive readings of this phrase, see Pesch, *Das Markusevangelium*, 1:146; Schweizer, *Good News according to Mark*, 58; and Gnilka, *Das Evangelium nach Markus*, 1:93.

58. Joseph, *Jesus and the Temple*, 118.

does with one's money since the rich man refuses to give his wealth away in order to follow Jesus (Mark 10:17–22). In fact, the man's disobedience could be Mark's way of implying that the misconception that Jesus disregarded ritual purity stems not from Jesus's actions or teachings but from the fact that this man did not do as Jesus commanded. Jesus intended for the man to obey the law of Moses and to show the priests that he too subscribed to the laws of ritual purity, but the man's disobedience led to later misunderstanding between Jesus and the priests. Ironically, whereas the *lepros* formerly could not enter into towns due to his condition, now Jesus finds himself unable to do so because of the man's disregard for the command to tell no one but to go to the priest (1:45).[59]

Others suggest that Mark's Jesus does not care about the laws of ritual purity because, according to Mark, Jesus stretched out his hand and touched the *lepros* (1:41).[60] Again, though, touching a person who has *lepra* is not sinful: one only needs to be careful neither to transmit that impurity into sacred space nor to handle sacred vessels or food. If Mark believes that Jesus became impure through contact with the *lepros*, this belief does not entail the conclusion that Jesus rejected the law. Mark intends to show that Jesus is doing something related to but different from the priestly service. Jesus's actions do not demonstrate, contrary to John Dominic Crossan, that he was the "functional opponent, alternative, and substitute" to the Jerusalem temple.[61] Nowhere in priestly literature or Second Temple Jewish texts do priests possess the ability to remove *lepra*. Their God-ordained job is to *diagnose*, not to *cure*.

Jesus's purification of the man is an astounding deed of power that Leviticus never envisages the priests performing. But this fact does not necessitate the conclusion that Mark intends any criticism of the priestly caste or rejection of the ritual purity system.[62] In Jewish scriptures we see two cases in which a person suffering *lepra* undergoes healing at the initiative of a prophet rather than a priest: Miriam through the prayer of Moses *not* Aaron (Num. 12)[63]

59. So too Marcus, *Mark 1–8*, 210.

60. E.g., Sariola, *Markus und das Gesetz*, 66–67.

61. Crossan, *Historical Jesus*, 355.

62. So too Preuss, *Biblical and Talmudic Medicine*, 18–19. Consequently, Robert L. Webb incorrectly claims that Jesus's actions are an "infringement of priestly prerogative" ("Jesus Heals a Leper," 200).

63. According to some texts, Moses was both a prophet and a priest. Implicitly, Exod. 24:6 and Lev. 8:30–9:24 portray Moses as a priest, and Ps. 99:6 explicitly states that Moses was a priest. In the first century CE, both Pseudo-Philo (*Liber antiquitatum biblicarum* 51.6) and Philo (e.g., *Who Is the Heir?* 182) claim that Moses was a priest, whereas Josephus claims that Moses was not a priest (e.g., *Jewish Antiquities* 3.188–91, 307).

and the Aramean Naaman through the actions of Elisha (2 Kings 5). There is a real difference, then, between priestly and prophetic roles in relation to *lepra*.[64] Jewish scriptures suggest that, though uncommon, certain people might be divinely empowered to remove this affliction from others. Like Moses and Elisha, the Jesus that Mark portrays is endowed with both great power and a strong desire to remove the sources of ritual impurity. In contrast to both Moses and Elisha, though, Jesus needs neither prayer nor the waters of the Jordan River to remove the man's *lepra*. Such differences raise questions about Jesus's identity.

Relatedly, later rabbis make the following claim: "In this world the priest examines for [*lepra*]; but in the World to Come, says the Holy One, blessed be He—'I will purify you.' Thus it is written, '*And I will sprinkle pure water upon you, and you will be pure*' [Ezek. 36:25]."[65] The rabbis acknowledge the limited power of the priests in the face of *lepra*, yet this is hardly a criticism of them. Rather, the observation points to the fact that at least some rabbis held out hope that one day God would address the wellspring of ritual impurity in ways that God had never empowered the temple cult or priestly personnel to do. Mark shares this same hope but believes that Israel's God is now, in Jesus, purifying those with *lepra*. The World to Come, the "kingdom of God" as Mark's Jesus puts it in Mark 1:14, has now invaded this world, and this eschatological purification process has begun.

In this story, then, Mark emphasizes that Jesus's actions both conform to the legislation of Leviticus and demonstrate his commitment to the temple cult and ritual purity system. By placing this miraculous cleansing early in his narrative and before the series of controversy stories in Mark 2:1–3:6, Mark aims to ensure that his readers will witness Jesus's reverence for the Jewish law. In fact, Jesus's commands to the man surely connect to and help answer the question with which the narrative begins: Does Jesus desire the removal of ritual impurity, or is he indifferent to the whole ritual impurity system? Consequently, the testimony that this purified man gives does not pertain to Jesus's *ability* to rid someone of ritual impurity. Rather, his testimony demonstrates that Jesus *desires* to rid people of what causes their ritual impurities. Through his interaction with Jesus, the former *lepros* has moved toward purity. Jesus destroys the impurity-creating condition, allowing the man to now observe the regulations of Leviticus 14 in removing the remaining ritual impurity. In showing the priests the tangible evidence that he no longer suffers

---

64. So too Baden and Moss, "Origin and Interpretation of *ṣāraʿat*," 646.
65. *Leviticus Rabbah* 15.9, emphasis original.

from *lepra*, the man would have enabled the priests to see and acknowledge that Jesus is involved in a powerful purification mission. As Joel Marcus notes, "The story is dominated by the motif of cleansing ('you are able to cleanse me,' 'be cleansed!,' 'he was cleansed,' 'offer for your cleansing')."[66] But it is also dominated by the motif of desire ("If you desire"; "*I* desire!"). Far from being indifferent to ritual impurity, then, an angry Jesus wages war in Mark's Gospel against the sources of ritual impurity.

One final passage from Mark merits discussion. Later in his Gospel, Mark portrays Jesus and his disciples sharing a meal in the house of Simon the *Lepros* (14:3; cf. Matt. 26:6). Mark makes no mention of whether the man still has *lepra* and, if so, whether Jesus addresses this condition. On the basis of this silence, Marcus argues that the man did indeed have *lepra* and that Jesus's presence in his house fits with his associating with tax collectors and sinners.[67] Nonetheless, I think it more likely that Mark refers to a man who was formerly a *lepros* and as a result became known as Simon the *Lepros*.[68]

Lepra in Matthew and Luke

Although Mark nowhere else mentions any interaction between Jesus and a *lepros*, Matthew and Luke do, adding to what they find in Mark. According to Matthew, when John the Immerser was in prison, he sent his disciples to Jesus to find out whether Jesus was "the one who is to come" (*ho erchomenos*, 11:3; cf. Luke 7:22).[69] This title appears to have had messianic connotations for early Christ followers, since all four canonical Gospels quote Psalm 118:26 (117:26 LXX) in depicting Jesus's triumphal entry into Jerusalem: "Hosanna to the Son of David, Blessed is the One Who Comes [*ho erchomenos*] in the name of the Lord" (Mark 11:9; Matt. 21:9; Luke 19:38; John 12:13). The Gospel of John adds one further reference to the One Who Comes, claiming that the crowds saw Jesus's miraculous provision of food (John 6:1–14) and exclaimed, "Surely, this is the prophet who comes into the world!" (6:14). And the Letter to the Hebrews also uses the

---

66. Marcus, *Mark 1–8*, 208. On the kingdom of God in Mark, see Marcus, *Mystery of the Kingdom of God*, and Marcus, "Entering into the Kingly Power of God."

67. Marcus, *Mark 8–16*, 933.

68. So too Lane, *Gospel of Mark*, 493, and Westerholm, *Jesus and Scribal Authority*, 69.

69. Matthew also moves Mark's story of the man with *lepra* so that it appears after the Sermon on the Mount, perhaps to show that Jesus has not come to abolish the (ritual) law (Matt. 5:17–20). Luke, on the other hand, keeps it near the beginning of Jesus's public work.

phrase messianically, citing Habakkuk 2:3 LXX: "In a little while, the One Who Comes [*erchomenos*] will come and will not delay." John's question, therefore, relates to Jesus's messianic identity.

In response, Jesus proves his messianic identity by pointing to, among other things, the fact that he purifies *leproi* (Matt. 11:5; Luke 7:22). According to this saying, such a description of his mission signals that Jesus really is the One Who Comes. The purifying of *lepra* was precisely what the messiah would do, a central messianic work. What is more, not only does Jesus treat those who suffer from *lepra*, but he also gives his disciples authority to do so (Matt. 10:8; cf. Luke 7:22). The power to remove *lepra* was, according to Matthew, a hallmark of the mission of Jesus and his followers and demonstrated that the long-awaited messiah had come.[70] Like Matthew 11:5 and Luke 7:22, the early Christian *Acts of Pilate* also implies that the healing of *lepra* was one of the works of Israel's messiah (6.2).

Assuming that Luke knew both Mark and Matthew, it becomes apparent that Luke retained every reference to *lepra* in Mark and Matthew, apart from the brief reference to Simon the *Lepros*. These stories, then, continue to be relevant to Luke's portrayal of Jesus. Further, Luke signals his abiding concern for *lepra* by adding his own material on the topic. Most significantly, Luke portrays ten men with *lepra* coming to Jesus to beg him to have mercy upon them (Luke 17:12–19). Unlike in the initial story of the single *lepros* whom Jesus touches, here Jesus merely speaks to them. But like that initial story, Jesus commands these ten men to go and show themselves to the priests. According to Luke, as they were on their way to the priests, they were purified of their underlying condition (17:14; cf. Lev. 14:2). Of the ten, only one man turns back and thanks Jesus. Luke emphasizes that this one thankful *lepros* is in fact a Samaritan, not a Jew. Jesus commends the man's confidence (*pistis*) that he has truly been purified of his condition. Even though he has not yet received priestly confirmation and undergone the seven-day rites needed to remove the remaining ritual impurity, he returns in gratitude and gives praise to God. It is implied that the others, all Jews it seems, were not yet thankful and did not praise God, because they had not yet heard the diagnosis of the Jerusalem priests and so did not yet believe. Like Mark's story about Jesus's healing of a *lepros* (and its retellings in Matthew and Luke), Luke's story here emphasizes Jesus's commitment to the legislation of Leviticus 13–14; these men are to go to the priest to receive the declaration that they are in fact pure, although Luke does not explicitly state that they are to offer sacrifices. Luke's portrayal here confirms that he is concerned to depict Jesus as displaying customary temple piety.

---

70. On the relationship between the messiah and healing in general, see Novakovic, *Messiah*.

Jewish Antecedents to Jesus's Treatment of *Lepra*

Wilhelm Bruners has argued that Luke composed the story of the ten men with *lepra* on the basis of Elisha's healing of Naaman (2 Kings 5:8–19).[71] His argument notes the connection between this story and Luke's only other addition to the *lepra* material found in Mark and Matthew, in which Jesus addresses the doubts of the people of Nazareth: "There were many *leproi* in Israel during the lifetime of Elisha the prophet, but none of them were purified, except Naaman the Syrian" (Luke 4:27). Both stories connect Jesus's dealings with *lepra* to the prophet Elisha. Jesus's references to the story of Elisha and Naaman suggest that Luke's Jesus places his own work, a mission that involves purifying *leproi*, within the context of Israel's history. But this story also highlights the problematic nature of many scholarly treatments of Jesus.

This tale of Elisha and Naaman is one of the few ancient narratives that discuss the healing of a *lepros*. According to 2 Kings, Naaman, a successful commander in the army of the king of Aram, suffers from *lepra*. One of Naaman's captured slaves, an Israelite girl, tells him that if he visits a prophet in Samaria, he will be cured of his *lepra*. When the king of Aram learns this, he sends a letter with Naaman to ask the Israelite king to have Naaman cured.[72] Nonetheless, when the king of Israel hears that the king of Aram desires to have Naaman's *lepra* treated, he concludes that Aram is merely looking for a pretext for war: "Am I a god? Can I put to death and make alive? For this man asks me to heal a man of his *lepra*!" (2 Kings 5:7). Not only does the king's reaction confirm that many ancient Jews associated *lepra* with death, but it also shows that the treatment of *lepra* was no simple matter of applying the correct ointment or salve. *Lepra* was a persistent and essentially untreatable condition, one that God alone could address.

The prophet Elisha, though, asserts that he can deal with Naaman's *lepra*, commanding Naaman to bathe seven times in the Jordan River in order that his flesh might be restored (2 Kings 5:10). Naaman's disappointed response indicates that he had expected a flashier healing procedure—a public appeal to God and a hand gesture over the affected area—not a straightforward command to rinse in some insignificant river. Nevertheless, he relents and bathes seven times in the Jordan, finding himself cured as a result.

---

71. Bruners, *Die Reinigung der zehn Aussätzigen*. On the importance of the Elijah/Elisha narrative for Luke, see C. A. Evans, "Luke's Use of the Elijah/Elisha Narratives"; Öhler, *Elia im Neuen Testament*, 77–89; and Kloppenborg and Verheyden, *Elijah-Elisha Narrative*.

72. This letter conforms to ancient medical practices, in which letters for medical aid were addressed to kings. See Zucconi, "Aramean Skin Care."

The story of Elisha and Naaman is remarkable for what it does not mention. At no point is there a reference to the Israelite priesthood, the temple, or any purification rites. Perhaps this is because Naaman is a non-Israelite, and the priestly ritual purity regulations therefore do not apply to him.[73] Regardless of the reason, no ancient or modern reader concludes from 2 Kings 5 that Elisha sets himself up in opposition to or as a replacement for the priests, the temple cult, or the ritual purity system.

The same point can be made in regard to Moses's sister, Miriam, who contracts *lepra* as a result of her complaints against Moses and his wife. Although Aaron is a priest, he can do nothing to remove the *lepra*; rather, he appeals to Moses to intervene on Miriam's behalf. Moses's prayer to God results in the *lepra*'s healing and her skin returning to its normal condition. Moses's successful intervention on Miriam's behalf surely does not undermine the priestly role of Aaron, who initially observes her ritual impurity. For that matter, the story does not portray Miriam making the requisite offerings after having been purified. But surely we should not conclude from this silence that Moses and his family were somehow lax in their observance of the law or that the priestly author/editor of Numbers intended to criticize the ritual purity system.

Why, then, when scholars turn to the Gospels and Jesus do they frequently conclude that similar healings of *lepra* somehow constitute a sharp criticism or rejection of Israel's priests or the Jerusalem temple or the ritual purity regulations? What is it about Jesus's treatment of *lepra* that leads readers to view it so differently from the healings of Moses or Elisha? In fact, while neither Elisha nor Moses commands the person healed of *lepra* to go to the priest for confirmation of purification or to offer the sacrifices required by the legislation of Leviticus 13–14, Jesus does so, both in Mark 1:44 (reiterated in Matthew 8:4 and Luke 5:14) and in Luke 17:14: "Go and show yourselves to the priests!" Consequently, Paula Fredriksen is right to conclude that Mark 1:44 "is an uncomplicated endorsement of a very elaborate sequence of ablutions and sacrifices (a bird, two male lambs, one perfect year-old ewe), detailed in Leviticus 14, by which the [*lepros*] moves from pollution to purity, from isolation back into life in the community."[74] These stories explicitly present a law-observant Jesus who

1. believes in the ontological reality of the ritual impurity associated with *lepra*,

73. Cf. Mishnah, *Nega'im* 3.1.
74. Fredriksen, *Sin*, 20–21. Similarly, M. Eugene Boring states, "Mark's view of the law is nuanced and dialectical. By placing the story here Mark makes a preemptive strike at accusations to come. Moses, priests, and sacrifice are here affirmed" (*Mark*, 72). Cf. Vermes, *Religion of Jesus*, 18.

2. desires to remove the sources of ritual impurity,

3. uses his power to remove these conditions, and

4. commands the newly healed *leproi* to go to the temple, where they should show themselves to the priests and make the appropriate offerings so that they can remove the remaining ritual impurity.

What more do modern scholars need to conclude that the Synoptic Gospel writers intended to portray how seriously Jesus took the impurity associated with *lepra*?

Conclusion

I have spent considerable time in this chapter clarifying what *lepra* is and is not. It is *not* leprosy. It *is* a minor skin condition that ancient Jews thought conveyed ritual impurity. The person who had *lepra* could not enter into the tabernacle or temple because impurity and holiness simply cannot mix. In Mark's depiction of Jesus's encounter with the man who had *lepra*, we see Jesus dealing with the source of this man's ritual impurity, the *lepra* itself. Translations that render *lepra* as "leprosy" and thus interpret the story as a miraculous healing of a horrific, highly contagious medical condition inevitably conceal from modern readers what would have stuck out plainly to ancient Jewish readers of Mark's Gospel, and even to gentile readers who were familiar with Jewish scriptures: the miraculous *purification* of one who was formerly ritually impure.

Like Moses and Elisha, then, the Jesus that the Gospel writers portray is one endowed with great power. He is a rarity—a person who has the ability to remove *lepra*. What this ability says about Jesus's identity remains open to debate at the point it occurs in the Gospel narratives. What is not open to debate, though, is the fact that Jesus, as these writers portray him, inhabited and was shaped by a world that was governed by the concerns of Jewish ritual purity. The Gospel writers depict Jesus acting in a way that fits perfectly with the laws of Leviticus 13–14. After cleansing people of their *lepra* (cf. Lev. 14:2), Jesus commands them to go to the temple to undergo the rituals necessary to remove the ritual impurity that continues to exist after the *lepra* leaves (Lev. 14:8, 9, 20).

CHAPTER 4

Jesus and the Dead Womb

After depicting Jesus's encounter with the man with *lepra* in Mark 1:40–45, Mark records a string of stories that relate to controversies surrounding Jesus's Sabbath practices and his claims to forgive people's moral impurities (Mark 2–3). (I will examine Jesus's Sabbath practices in chap. 7.) We must wait until Mark 5, a chapter containing an array of different impurities, for the next encounter between a ritually impure person and Jesus, and there we meet not one but two ritually impure people whose stories Mark has woven together. The narrative begins with a father and his sick daughter, then turns to a woman with an illness, and then returns to the young girl, whose sickness has ended in death. This Markan sandwich, as scholars refer to it, suggests that Mark connects the two stories in order to ensure that readers will interpret them in light of each other. The next two chapters of this book, therefore, examine Jesus's encounters with this girl and woman. In this chapter, though, I focus on the woman, whom Mark describes as having had a twelve-year flow of blood.

Numerous scholars have understood this story to relate to priestly laws about impurity. The woman is a *zavah*—a female "discharger" who endures a long-term genital flow. Consequently, they have turned to this passage to determine Jesus's attitude toward the Jewish law—particularly the ritual purity system. Marla Selvidge, for instance, maintains that "this story was written to free early Christian women from the social bonds of niddah, 'banishment,' during a woman's menstrual period." Elsewhere she extrapolates from this assertion to make a more expansive claim about Mark's attitude toward the entire Jewish purity system: "Mark 5:25–34 may stand preserved because it remembers an early Christian community's break with the Jewish purity system, which restricted and excluded women from cult and society."[1] Selvidge's comments have elicited numerous criticisms, and for good reason. First, her feminist concerns, as admirable as they may be, lead her to construct early Judaism in an unfavorable light.[2] Her legitimate concerns about patriarchy and sexism have become also an attack on Jews and Judaism. In her narrative, Christianity frees women from the sexist constraints of Judaism and the Jewish law, from the Jewish purity system that "restricted and excluded women from cult and society." Selvidge's exclusive focus on the ways in which Jewish regulations on purity pertained to women fails to acknowledge that men were also affected by purity rules. The Jewish law did not aim to exclude women from cult and society; rather, its purpose was to exclude ritual impurities, whether suffered by a man or by a woman, from the cult. No woman could be a priest in the Jerusalem temple, so women were indeed excluded from the inner realms of the sanctuary—but so too were all men who were not of priestly descent. Additionally, as I show below, most if not all ancient Mediterranean cultures held to similar purity codes related to sex, menstruation, and childbirth.[3] In other words, as foreign as such codes may seem to many modern readers, such restrictions were nearly ubiquitous in the ancient world.

Putting aside Selvidge's negative portrayal of Judaism, is it true that Mark intends for his readers to understand this story as the abolishment of Jewish laws dealing with genital discharges? This is one of the central questions of this chapter. In order to answer it, we must first look at the legislation regarding genital discharges in Jewish scriptures and then detail how such laws were understood in early Judaism, placing them within a broader context to show that these beliefs, far from being unique to Judaism, were common throughout the ancient Mediterranean world.

Leviticus and Genital Discharges

Leviticus contains detailed regulations pertaining to people, both men and women, who suffer from genital discharges. As I discussed in chapter 1, women

1. Quotations come from Selvidge, *Woman, Cult and Miracle Recital*, 30, and Selvidge, "Mark 5:25–34 and Leviticus 15:19–20," 619.

2. For this problematic trend in modern Christian theology, see Plaskow, "Feminist Anti-Judaism"; Kellenbach, *Anti-Judaism in Feminist Religious Writings*; and Kraemer and D'Angelo, *Women and Christian Origins*.

3. Only in a footnote does Selvidge concede that men too are excluded at times ("Mark 5:25–34 and Leviticus 15:19–20," 619n4).

who have recently given birth are subject to a lengthy two-stage impurity (Lev. 12). The woman who has given birth to a male child endures a heightened state of impurity for seven days and then a less intense form of impurity for another thirty-three days; the woman who has given birth to a female child endures a heightened state of impurity for fourteen days and then a lesser state of impurity for another sixty-six days.

But Leviticus 15 contains the greatest concentration of purity legislation relating to those with genital discharges. As Jacob Milgrom has argued, the chapter evidences the thoughtful work of an editor who has labored to structure this legislation in the following manner:

> Introduction—Leviticus 15:1–2a
>   Abnormal Male Discharges (the *zav*)—Leviticus 15:2b–15
>   Normal Male Discharges—Leviticus 15:16–17
>   Sexual Intercourse—Leviticus 15:18
>   Normal Female Discharges—Leviticus 15:19–24
>   Abnormal Female Discharges (the *zavah*)—Leviticus 15:25–30
> Motive and Summary—Leviticus 15:31–33[4]

This meticulously constructed text highlights a number of details regarding Jewish conceptions of impurities related to genital discharges. First, in the priestly writer's thinking, there is a distinction between normal and abnormal genital discharges. Nocturnal emissions, sex, and menstruation, for instance, are all normal, natural bodily processes. The distinction between normal and abnormal discharges, which the editor carefully signals through the structure of Leviticus 15, demonstrates the inaccuracy of Selvidge's claim that in Jewish thinking "a woman's normal biological rhythms were considered abnormal."[5] Jews did not consider menstruation to be unnatural; *impurity* language implies nothing about disease or abnormality. Josephus, in fact, makes it clear that Jews viewed the menstrual process as a bodily function "according to nature" (*kata physin*) and distinguished it from other genital discharges, which were presumably abnormal or atypical.[6]

---

4. Milgrom, *Leviticus 1–16*, 905.

5. Selvidge, *Woman, Cult and Miracle Recital*, 55. See the helpful comments of D'Angelo, "Gender and Power," 84. And, as Tarja Philip says, "Impurities are taken as part of human nature and life, and in themselves are not negative; they become negative only in relation to the holy" ("Gender Matters," 42).

6. Josephus, *Jewish Antiquities* 3.261.

Further, both men and women are subject to a one-day impurity after sexual intercourse (Lev. 15:18), but the resulting impurity does not imply that sexual intercourse is either unnatural or wrong. And the man with a seminal emission endures a one-day impurity (15:16), while the menstruating woman experiences a seven-day impurity (15:19). In none of these particular instances does Leviticus require these impure people to provide an offering at the end of their period of impurity. In fact, only after childbirth must a woman do so. Priestly literature views only a *zav*, a man with an irregular genital discharge, or a *zavah*, a woman who has a nonmenstrual vaginal flow of blood, as suffering something abnormal. Such cases are considered abnormal because the genital discharge they endure is open-ended—it does not necessarily last for a discrete amount of time. Unlike those suffering from normal genital discharges (excluding childbirth), the *zav* and the *zavah* must bring two birds for an offering once they become pure (15:15, 29–30).

The motivation and summary that the priestly writer provides for this set of regulations avers that these rules make known to the Israelites their impurities so that they do not enter into sacred space in an impure state. If they were to do so, as Leviticus 15:31 makes clear, their impurities would cause their deaths. Thus, God gave Moses and Aaron these detailed instructions in order to protect the Israelites, who would inevitably and naturally experience impurity from genital discharges, from inadvertently causing their own deaths by entering into holy space. In light of the protective nature of these priestly laws, one can see that compassion and concern for the preservation of human life is integral to such seemingly restrictive commandments. Again, when contemporary Christian theology distinguishes between Jesus's healing actions and the ritual purity system on the basis of compassion, it misunderstands and misdescribes the purpose of the ritual purity system. To use an example from modern health-care practices: we discourage people with weakened immunities from visiting hospitals because they might contract an illness while there. Only the most unsympathetic person would choose to interpret this suggestion as an oppressive restriction; rather, it is a defensive effort motivated by the desire to protect such people.

The Gospels do not depict Jesus seeking to treat a woman who is ritually impure because of menstruation or a man who is ritually impure as a result of nocturnal emissions. Such conditions require no special treatment because they are normal conditions for mortals and give rise to short-lived impurities that are easily removed. Instead, the Gospels portray Jesus's interaction with a person who endures one particular form of genital discharge: the woman who experiences a nonmenstrual genital discharge. Leviticus states that such a woman endures a ritual impurity for the entire time that her discharge continues. Once the discharge stops, she must wait an additional seven days before she can go and make her offering of two birds and reenter a state of ritual purity. During her impurity, everything she sits on or lies upon becomes ritually impure and can convey a one-day impurity to others (Lev. 15:26–27).

Relatedly, there is a textual issue that relates to whether contact with the woman herself conveys impurity to the one who touches her. While the Hebrew of Leviticus 15:27, both the Masoretic Text and the Samaritan Pentateuch, states that whoever touches *the things* upon which she sits becomes impure, the Septuagint translation and a number of medieval Hebrew manuscripts stipulate that anyone who touches *her* becomes impure. Milgrom argues that the Greek probably reflects the original reading and makes the most sense.[7] In support of this conclusion, Leviticus states that the *zav*, the male genital discharger, passes on impurity if he touches someone without having washed his hands (15:11). From this passage, one should likely infer that the *zavah* also transmits impurity by touch, unless she washes her hands. Even if Milgrom is wrong here, Mark and his readers would have used the Septuagint. Consequently, when they read Leviticus 15, or heard it read, it would suggest to them that contact with the *zavah* herself could convey impurity.[8]

Contrary to Selvidge, though, Leviticus 15 in no way suggests that the *zavah*, or anyone who has a genital discharge, needs to be quarantined. Throughout this passage, the author repeatedly assumes that the impure man or woman will continue to live within the house and have human contact. The only stipulation, as the conclusion makes apparent, is that the impure person must stay away from the tabernacle or temple apparatus.

Numbers 5

In contrast to Leviticus 15, Numbers 5 presents a different way for Israelites to deal with certain people suffering impurities. Here, within a larger discussion of the tabernacle camp in the wilderness, God says to Moses, "Command the sons of Israel that they send out from the camp every *lepros*, every *zav*, and everyone who is impure by a corpse—both the male and the female you shall send outside, you shall send them out of the camp so that they do not make impure their camps in the midst of which I dwell" (Num. 5:2–3). The proximity of God's presence, which dwells in the tabernacle located at the center of the wilderness camp, necessitates greater stringency regarding those who endure powerful ritual impurities. Although this legislation says nothing explicit about

7. Milgrom, *Leviticus 1–16*, 943.
8. So too Haber, "A Woman's Touch," 175, and Kazen, *Jesus and Purity Halakhah*, 143.

the *zavah*, the fact that God excludes the *zav* and then states that the Israelites
are to send out both impure men and impure women indicates that the passage
relates to women with abnormal genital discharges as well. Because the wilderness camp functions as a buffer between the tabernacle and the wilderness, it
requires a higher degree of purity. Not all who are ritually impure are excluded:
new mothers, people who have sex, men with nocturnal emissions, and women
who menstruate do *not* need to dwell outside the wilderness camp. Only those
suffering the most intense impurities—*lepra*, abnormal genital discharges, and
corpse impurities—need to leave the wilderness camp.[9] But even this limited
exclusion is rigorous, leading Shaye Cohen to conclude that "Numbers 5:1–4
is a utopian extension of Leviticus 15:31. The perimeter of the 'tabernacle,'
the central sanctuary, is coterminous with the perimeter of the 'camp.'"[10]

Numbers 5 therefore raises interpretive questions for later generations who
sought both to reconcile it to Leviticus 15 and to apply it to their own contexts.
How do these commandments function once Israel leaves the wilderness and
enters into the land that God promised Abraham? For later Jews, do such
injunctions still have relevance? Rabbinic tradition, for example, interprets
Numbers 5:2 as excluding the impure only from entering the sanctuary.[11] In
this reading, the legislation of Numbers 5:2, as stringent as it is, coincides
with the concerns of Leviticus 15; the intention of both texts is to exclude
the impure from the realm of the sacred.

Females and Genital Discharge Impurity in the Ancient Near East

Modern readers should not think that the Israelite purity system was distinctive; Israel agreed in large part with its neighbors when it came to the
impurity of genital discharges. In ancient Egypt, pregnant or menstruating
women (and thus, presumably, any woman with an irregular genital discharge)
and people who had recently had sex were excluded from entering cultic
settings. Herodotus, for instance, claims that Egyptians prohibited sexual
intercourse within temples and also required washing after sex before entering sacred space.[12] According to Hittite law, a woman needed to bathe after
sexual intercourse in order to become pure,[13] as did a man.[14] According to

9. Mishnah, *Kelim* 1.4.
10. Cohen, "Menstruants and the Sacred," 275. More broadly, see Frevel, "Purity Conceptions."
11. *Sifre Numbers* 1.
12. Herodotus, *Histories* 2.64.
13. *Keilschrifturkunden aus Boghazköi* 9.22.3.29–32.
14. "Mursili's Speech Loss," 1.19–20, in Laroche, *Catalogue des textes hittites*, 486.

Michaël Guichard and Lionel Marti, Paleo-Babylonian texts indicate that "women's menstruation (ki-sikil) was a serious source of impurity." They note that in eighteenth-century BCE Mari (modern-day Syria), women had to leave the palace during their menstruation because the building contained sacred chapels.[15] Again Herodotus confirms that such practices were long-lived in Babylonian (and Arabian) society.[16] While not an exclusion from a temple per se, one Middle Assyrian palace decree states, "When the time for making sacrifices draws near, a palace woman who is menstruating (lit.: unapproachable) shall not enter into the presence of the king."[17] Neo-Assyrian texts refer to a menstruant as a *harištu*, a "reclusive woman," and hint at the contagious impurity the menstruant endured. Like Leviticus, Assyrian culture also prohibited sex with a menstruating woman. Finally, while Zoroastrian texts remain notoriously tricky to date, we have some evidence that ancient Persians also excluded menstruating women from the realm of the sacred, since they could not approach sacred fire.[18]

This brief survey demonstrates how common it was for ancient Near Eastern cultures, like Israel, to ascribe impurity to various genital discharges. Likewise, these cultures believed that at least some genital discharges were associated with death or mortality, an assumption found in a Middle Assyrian clay tablet that describes a woman in childbirth in the following terms:

> The woman in childbirth has pangs at delivery,
> At delivery she has pangs, the babe is stuck fast,
> The babe is stuck fast. The bolt is secure—to bring life to an end,
> The door is made fast—against the suckling kid. . . .
> The mother is enveloped in the dust of death.
> Like a chariot, she is enveloped in the dust of battle,
> Like a plough she is enveloped in the dust of the woods,
> Like a warrior in the fray, she is cast down in her blood.
> Her eyes are diminished, she cannot see; her lips are covered,
> She cannot open (them) * the destiny of death and destinies * her eyes
> are dim.[19]

15. On Egyptian thinking, see Wilfong, "Menstrual Synchrony," and Frandsen, "The Menstrual 'Taboo.'" On Mesopotamian thinking, see Guichard and Marti, "Purity in Ancient Mesopotamia," 74. On childbirth impurity in Babylonian texts, see Stol, *Birth in Babylonia*.
16. Herodotus, *Histories* 1.198.
17. *Middle Assyrian Palace Decrees* 7, trans. Roth, *Law Collections from Mesopotamia*.
18. E.g., *Vendidad* 16.3.17 (39).
19. Lambert, "Middle Assyrian Medical Text," 32 (lines 33–42). The asterisks indicate sections where Lambert cannot make sense of the text.

Similarly, ancient Babylonian texts speak of the newborn as a ship moving from the quay of death or hardship to the quay of life.[20] Such texts demonstrate that many people associated the birth experience with the realm of death, an understandable association when one recalls the high rates of mortality for both mother and child at birth. What these regulations in cultures surrounding Israel suggest is that the exclusion of men and women with genital discharges from the realm of the sacred was a widespread feature of ancient purity systems that was due, at times, to the belief that such bodily functions were connected to the realm of death. In this regard, then, Jacob Milgrom's argument that the priestly writer associates birth, sex, and genital discharges with death finds confirmation in other ancient Near Eastern sources.

The Greco-Roman World

Although Selvidge does not treat these other cultures, she asserts that the Greco-Roman world did not exhibit these same purity concerns about menstrual and related discharges: "A woman's menstrual cycle was considered a time of cleansing [*katharsia*] to the Greeks. The Jews added a negative prefix and called it unclean."[21] But this claim is at best misleading. First, extensive evidence suggests that one needed to bathe after the same sorts of genital discharges that Leviticus mentions before one could enter into sacred spaces in Greek culture. Herodotus claims that, like the Egyptians, Greeks did not permit sexual intercourse in sacred space and required bathing before entering temples.[22] And there is evidence that a new mother (a natural biological state) was not permitted into sacred space.[23] Repeatedly, the Greek tragedian Euripides stresses that childbirth creates a ritual impurity that bars those who endure it from cultic sites.[24] According to Diogenes Laertius, Pythago-

---

20. Stol, *Birth in Babylonia*, who refers to *Babylonisch—assyrische Medizin in Texten und Untersuchungen* 248 1.62–63 and 3.58–59.

21. Selvidge, *Woman, Cult and Miracle Recital*, 55. As D'Angelo observes, Selvidge is far from alone: "It is frequently assumed among interpreters of the NT, both scholarly and popular, that purity is a Jewish concern of no real interest to either the Greeks or Romans" ("Gender and Power," 85). Cohen ("Menstruants and the Sacred," 287) points to the words of fourth-century CE emperor Julian regarding Christians: "All the rest we have in a manner in common with them—temples, sanctuaries, altars, purifications, and certain precepts. For as to these we differ from one another either not at all or in trivial matters" (*Against the Galileans* 306B). For a brief treatment of menstruation and childbirth in ancient Greece, see Nilsson, *Geschichte der Griechischen Religion*, 1:94–95.

22. Herodotus, *Histories* 2.64.

23. N. Robertson, "Concept of Purity," 196.

24. E.g., *Electra* 654; *Iphigenia at Tauris* 380–82; *Auge* fragment 266; *Cretans* fragments 16–19.

ras taught that "purification is by cleansing, baptism and lustration, and by keeping clean from all deaths and births and all pollution."[25] The philosopher Theophrastus demonstrates that this belief was relatively widespread, since he mocks "superstitious" people who refuse to visit a woman after she has given birth precisely because it is their policy to avoid "pollution."[26] Such a belief persisted in the Greco-Roman world, as evidence from the third century CE reveals. For instance, Censorinus states that women should avoid sacred space for the first forty days after giving birth,[27] and in the late fourth century CE, the city of Cyrene in Libya produced legislation pertaining to childbirth impurity.[28]

Second, while Selvidge is correct to claim that Greek medical literature refers to menstruation as a time of cleansing, Leviticus also refers to postpartum lochial bleeding as "the blood of purification" (Lev. 12:5; although the LXX translator renders the Hebrew as "in the blood of impurity"). Regardless, these Greek and Roman writers do not think that menstrual or postpartum blood is pure and healthy; rather, such writers make it clear that they believe menstrual blood to be noxious. For instance, the Hippocratic treatise titled *Diseases of Women* asserts that women experience all sorts of diseases due to menstrual blood,[29] and Aristotle believes that a menstruating woman can dim a mirror simply by gazing into it.[30] Why then do such writers refer to menstruation as cleansing? Soranus, a second-century CE medical writer, makes the reasoning apparent in his treatise *Gynecology*: "It is also called *catharsis*, since, as some people say, excreting blood from the body like excessive matter, it effects a purgation of the body."[31] Through the excretion of blood, the body purges itself of something that is impure and medically unhealthy. Elsewhere he claims that while menstruation is normal, it is unhealthy. This assertion fits within his larger conviction (one he purports to share with other contemporary doctors) that pregnancy, sex, and childbirth, while natural, are actually detrimental to women.[32] Plutarch portrays menstrual blood in a

---

25. Diogenes Laertius, *Lives of Eminent Philosophers* 8.33.

26. Theophrastus, *Characters* 16.9.

27. Censorinus, *The Birthday Book* 11.7.

28. Supplementum epigraphicum graecum ix.72.a.4. See, more broadly, Cole, "*Gynaiki ou Themis*," and Lennon, "Menstrual Blood in Ancient Rome." Cf. Macrobius, *Saturnalia* 1.23.13; 5.19.26.

29. *Diseases of Women* 1.62.

30. Aristotle, *Insomniis* 459b24–460a23.

31. Temkin, *Soranus' Gynecology* 1.19. For treatments of women's bodies, including genital discharges, see Dean-Jones, *Women's Bodies*; King, *Hippocrates' Woman*; Carson, "Dirt and Desire"; and Flemming, *Medicine and the Making of Roman Women*.

32. Temkin, *Soranus' Gynecology* 1.42; cf. 1.30.

similar way: "Monthly menstruation is indicative not of a quantity of blood, but of corrupt and diseased blood; for blood's unassimilated and excrementitious part has no position and no structure in the body."[33]

Third, and most pertinent, we have evidence that Greeks, too, prohibited menstruants from sacred space. For instance, a second-century BCE inscription from a temple in Megalopolis declares, "Let the one who wants to sacrifice enter the temple precincts, purified on the ninth day after childbirth, on the forty-fourth day after an abortion, on the seventh day after menstruating, seven days after bloodshed . . ."[34] Although postdating the Gospel writers, a second- or third-century CE stele from the cult of Mens also declares, "No one impure is to enter, but let them be purified from garlic and swine and women. When members have bathed from head to foot on the same day they are to enter. And a woman, having washed for seven days after menstruation. And (likewise) for ten days after (contact) with a corpse."[35] Like Leviticus, then, at least some Greeks and Romans believed that genital discharges, including menstruation, were impure and consequently precluded one from entering into sacred space. And at least one author assumes that it was commonly held that men should avoid having sex with menstruating women. If a menstruating woman was prohibited entry into sacred space, how much more a woman (or man) with an abnormal genital discharge?

These similarities notwithstanding, some Greek and Roman writers believed that menstruation contaminated in ways that differed from early Jewish thinking. Aristotle, as noted above, thought menstruating women dimmed mirrors. We see another example of this belief in the latter half of the first century or early second century CE.[36] Columella, a Roman agricultural writer, advises his readers not to permit menstruating women to approach certain crops and plants, since contact with them will kill the vegetation: "Care, however, must be taken that a woman is admitted as little as possible to the place where the cucumbers and gourds are planted; for usually the growth of green-stuff is checked by contact with a woman; indeed if she is also in the period of menstruation, she will kill the young produce merely by looking at it."[37] Soranus also thought that menstrual blood was detrimental to those who came into contact with it.[38] While these texts discuss menstruants specifically,

---

33. Plutarch, *Moralia* 651D.
34. See Te Riele, "Une Nouvelle Loi Sacreé en Arcadie."
35. Horsley and Llewelyn, *New Documents*, 6:920–21.
36. See Lennon, *Pollution and Religion*, 83; Dean-Jones, "Menstrual Bleeding"; and Schultz, "Doctors, Philosophers, and Christian Fathers."
37. Columella, *De re rustica* 11.50; cf. 11.38; cf. Pliny, *Natural History* 28.23.79.
38. Soranus, *Gynecology* 1.27–29.

it seems reasonable to infer that a woman who suffered a nonmenstruous discharge, especially a medically abnormal discharge, would be included here as well. The discharged blood would surely have been considered, in Plutarch's words, "corrupt and diseased." One can see in the writings of Columella, Pliny, and Soranus that some Greco-Roman writers linked menstrual blood to illness and even viewed it as a cause of death with regard to plant life.

Ancient Near Eastern and Greco-Roman literature demonstrate that Jewish ritual concerns over genital discharges were not some sort of oddity in the ancient Mediterranean world. While each culture inflected their purity concerns in distinctive ways, they all shared the belief that certain genital discharges rendered people impure and unfit for entrance into sacred space. What this evidence suggests is that while Mark may have had Leviticus 15 in mind, such purity concerns were not exclusively Jewish. And unlike many modern readers, Mark and his readers would have found nothing foreign about such purity concerns. D'Angelo draws an important conclusion from the ubiquity of these beliefs in the ancient Mediterranean world: "Such restrictions might well have been viewed by the early Christians not only as taught by Judaism but even more as universally comprehensible, as 'natural.'"[39]

The *Zavah* in the Second Temple Period

When we turn to Jewish ritual practices in the Greco-Roman period, it is therefore unsurprising that Jews continued to prohibit new mothers, menstruants, and male and female genital dischargers from entering into sacred space. But due in part to the tension between the differing legislation in Numbers 5 and Leviticus 15, we see multiple interpretations regarding the way to treat such people.

The Qumran community evidenced heightened concern regarding ritual purity. In part, this concern may have resulted from the community's conviction that it functioned as a temporary replacement for the Jerusalem temple. According to the *Temple Scroll*, which was composed during the latter half of the second century BCE, the *zav*, the menstruant, and the new mother needed to be quarantined within the city during the period of their impurity: "In four cities you shall establish a place in which to bury. And in each city, you shall make places for those contaminated with *lepra* and with sores and with scales so that they do not enter your cities and defile them; also for *zavim* and for women when they are in their menstrual impurity and after giving

39. D'Angelo, "Gender and Power," 85.

birth, so that they do not spread impurity among you with their menstrual impurity."[40] While the *Temple Scroll* does not mention the *zavah*, presumably the regulations that apply to the *zav* pertain also to the *zavah*: she too needs to be quarantined during her impurity. The explicit rationale that the author provides for this legislation is that such stipulations will safeguard against the possibility of these women defiling others around them. When one lives in close proximity to sacred space, any casual transfer of impurity has numerous implications. Were a man, for instance, to contract impurity unknowingly from a *zavah* or menstruant or new mother, he might bring this impurity into sacred space unwittingly. On the other hand, a man who came to Jerusalem to participate in cultic activities might contract ritual impurity from a woman in one of these states and learn of it. Since he would then be temporarily prohibited from entering into sacred space, he would suffer the inconvenience, financial and otherwise, of having to stay a day longer in Jerusalem before he could again become ritually pure enough to conduct his ritual practices in sacred space. Two columns earlier the *Temple Scroll* stipulates, "You shall make three places to the east of the city, separated from each other, to which shall come those suffering *lepra* and *zavim* and the men who have a seminal emission."[41] Similarly, another Qumran scroll devoted to purity regulations requires that the *zav* stay eighteen feet away from both pure communal food and any communal dwelling.[42] The author does not mention the *zavah* here, perhaps because he envisages a male-only community.[43] In these texts, then, we see legislation that looks closer to Numbers 5 than to Leviticus 15; the impurity of the *zavah* and others needs to be closely monitored and controlled so that it does not spread and infect sacred space or sacred food.

The Qumran community's views of impurity do not necessarily reflect broader Jewish perceptions of impurity. Nonetheless, Josephus demonstrates a similarly expansive understanding of how to deal with certain impurities.[44] In his *Jewish War* he states that the *zav* (Greek: *gonorroios*) and the *lepros* were entirely excluded from the city. Again, while he only mentions the male genital discharger, it is likely that this exclusion would apply to the female equivalent—the *zavah*. Menstruants, on the other hand, were permitted within the city but not within the temple precincts, an exclusion that applied

---

40. *Temple Scroll* (11Q19) XLVIII, 13–17. See J. Baumgarten, "Zab Impurity in Qumran."
41. *Temple Scroll* (11Q19) XLVI, 16–18.
42. 4Q274 1 I, 2–3.
43. As Hannah Harrington states, "The Scroll authors, like the Rabbis, assume that all of the purification procedures of the *zab* apply to the *zabah*" (*Purity Texts*, 99). On women at Qumran, see Wassen, *Women in the Damascus Document*; Schuller, "Women in the Dead Sea Scrolls"; and Schuller, "Women at Qumran."
44. So too Noam, "Josephus and Early Halakhah," 139.

to impure men as well, including impure priests.[45] This restriction of the impure person from sacred space—the temple and by extension, in some circumstances, the city of Jerusalem—also included a restriction of consumption of sacred food: "Neither those suffering *lepra*, nor the *zavim*, nor menstruous women, nor anyone who was otherwise impure were permitted to partake in the Passover feast."[46] Elsewhere, in an allusion to Numbers 5, Josephus maintains that Moses excluded the *lepros*, the *zav*, the menstruant, and the corpse-impure person from the city.[47] This text prohibits the menstruant not only from entering sacred space but also from entering the city of Jerusalem. Again, it is likely that Josephus would have treated the *zavah* in the same way that he treated the *zav*—she would be unable to enter into the city. While he alludes to Numbers 5, he modifies its regulations. The prescriptions of Numbers 5 apply only to Israelite life in the wilderness camp, but Josephus extends them to Jewish life settled in the land and the city of Jerusalem.

As noted above, Cohen argues that Numbers 5 represents "a utopian extension" of the regulations of Leviticus 15. What we see, then, both in Qumran purity codes and in Josephus, are Second Temple Jewish efforts to implement this utopian hope in a variety of ways. Those experiencing severe impurities not only must avoid sacred spaces but must also quarantine themselves so that they do not inadvertently pass impurity on to others who might come into close proximity to sacred space. Even later rabbinic literature attests to the fact that some rabbis restricted the movements of menstruating women: "The ancients did not eat with menstruating women."[48] While we cannot know what all Jews in the Second Temple period thought regarding the *zav* and *zavah*, it is clear that at least some believed that those suffering from these two impurities, much like those suffering from *lepra*, should be quarantined in order to eliminate or minimize the possibility of passing that contagion on to others.[49]

An Involuntary Purifying Power

It is within this context that we must read the story of the hemorrhaging woman and Jesus. As the preceding discussion demonstrates, many early readers of Mark 5 would have considered this woman to be ritually impure, and

45. Josephus, *Jewish War* 5.227.
46. Josephus, *Jewish War* 6.425–26, my translation.
47. Josephus, *Jewish Antiquities* 3.261–62.
48. Tosefta, *Shabbat* 1.14.
49. See Kazen, *Issues of Impurity*, 111.

many of them would have identified this woman with the *zavah* of Leviticus 15. For any followers of Jesus who were trying to understand his views on ritual impurity, the story would have been of considerable importance. Mark describes the woman in the following way:

> And there was a woman who had a discharge of blood [*en rhysei haimatos*] for twelve years. And she had endured much under numerous doctors and spent all she had, and gained no benefit, but had, in fact, grown worse. Hearing about Jesus and coming behind him in the crowd, she touched his clothing. For she told herself, "If I just touch his clothing, then I will be saved/healed." And immediately her flow of blood [*hē pēgē tou haimatos autēs*] dried up and she knew in her body that she had been healed of her affliction. And immediately, knowing in himself that power had departed from him, Jesus turned around in the crowd and asked, "Who touched my clothes?" And his disciples said to him, "You can see the crowd milling about you and yet you ask, 'Who touched me?'" And he looked to see who had done this thing. And the woman, frightened and trembling, knowing what had happened to her, came and fell before him and told him the whole truth. And he said to her, "Daughter, your faith has saved you. Go in peace and be healed from your affliction." (Mark 5:25–34)

Some scholars have attempted to dismiss the importance of Jewish ritual purity concerns for understanding this story. Charlotte Elisheva Fonrobert, for instance, argues that Mark leaves the woman's ethnicity unknown and concludes that modern scholars may be wrong to identify her as a Jew.[50] If she is right, *Jewish* ritual purity is not at issue here, although even the non-Jewish Greco-Roman world considered genital discharges to be impure. But Mark rarely makes explicit the ethnic identity of characters within his narrative. Since Jesus lived primarily within the boundaries of Galilee, it is safest to assume that the people in Mark's narrative are Jews unless Mark explicitly states otherwise. In fact, when Jesus does encounter a gentile woman, the Syrophoenician woman of Mark 7, Mark notes her ethnicity. Jesus's words to the woman emphasize this very point: except in extraordinary situations, Jesus's mission focuses on Jews (Mark 7:27). By this saying, Mark makes it abundantly clear that the people with whom Jesus has interacted previously are all Jewish.

Fonrobert also suggests that Mark is not concerned with the issue of ritual purity—only healing. She avers, "The narrative ambiguity keeps the possibility open that the woman's status of impurity according to the priestly regulation in Leviticus is of no interest to them, since they are primarily concerned with

---

50. Fonrobert, *Menstrual Purity*, 192.

the healing miracle."[51] In other words, because Mark uses the verb *to heal* instead of the verb *to purify*, he must not care about any purification element in the event. Simply put, this is unlikely. This claim fails to account for the evidence of stories such as 2 Chronicles 30, in which King Hezekiah calls for a massive celebration of the Passover at the Jerusalem temple only to find out that some participants had eaten the Passover meal despite being in a state of impurity. Hezekiah prays to God on their behalf and God heals (*iasato*) these people of their impurities (30:20). Likewise, the priestly legislation regarding *lepra* can also refer to healing when discussing an issue of ritual impurity (Lev. 14:3, 48; Num. 12:13). And since this woman had an *abnormal* genital discharge, Mark can rightly call her state an illness that requires healing.

In her discussion of the parallel account of the hemorrhaging woman in Matthew's Gospel (9:20–22), Amy-Jill Levine suggests another way that one can minimize the significance of ritual purity within the story. Although the Gospel writers mention that the woman has a flow of blood, they do not specify that the woman endures a genital discharge. She concludes, based on similar language in Greco-Roman medical texts, that the blood may have stemmed from other areas of the body.[52]

Informed readers would not interpret this story as simply any healing story, though; rather, they would read it as a story that relates particularly to the Jewish purity system. The opening words of Mark's account, "And a woman having a discharge of blood" (*kai gynē ousa en rhysei haimatos*), evoke the legal terminology of the Greek of Leviticus 15:25, which begins similarly: "And a woman, if she suffers a discharge of blood . . ." (*Kai gynē, ean rheē rhysei haimatos*). The reference to "her discharge of blood" (*hē pēgē tou haimatos autēs*) in Mark 5:29 may, similarly, allude to the legislation of childbirth impurity in Leviticus 12:7, which is the only text in the Septuagint that refers to a woman's flow of blood (*apo tēs pēgēs tou haimatos autēs*). Further, Thomas Kazen observes that Mark stresses the language of touch (Greek: *haptō*, cf. Mark 5:27, 28, 30, 31), which the legislation of Leviticus 15 also emphasizes.[53]

Finally, Mark's earliest readers, the authors of the Gospels of Matthew and Luke, read Mark's story in relation to Leviticus 15. Matthew, for instance, uses the participle "bleeding" (*haimorrhoousa*, Matt. 9:20), and in so doing

---

51. Fonrobert, *Menstrual Purity*, 192. Cf. Gundry, *Mark*, 288; Lührmann, *Das Markusevangelium*, 104; Loader, *Jesus' Attitude towards the Law*, 60; D'Angelo, "Gender and Power," 91; and Kazen, *Issues of Impurity*, 107.

52. A.-J. Levine, "Discharging Responsibility," 384. In relation to Luke, see also Weissenrieder, "Plague of Uncleanness?," 207–22.

53. Kazen, *Issues of Impurity*, 106.

evokes the language of Leviticus 15:33 LXX. And Luke changes Mark's phrase "her flow of blood" (*hē pēgē tou haimatos autēs*) to "her discharge of blood" (*hē rhysis tou haimatos autēs*, Luke 8:44), using the word *rhysis*, which the Septuagint translator uses ten times in Leviticus 15 for genital discharges (cf. the similar use of *rhysis* in Lev. 20:18 and Deut. 23:11). Therefore, Matthew and Luke demonstrate that early readers would have naturally identified this woman with the *zavah*. Further, Mark places this story of the bleeding woman within a story about a corpse and after a story about a demon-possessed man surrounded by various forms of impurity (as I will discuss in chap. 6). If Mark does not have impurity on his mind here, then the juxtaposition of these impurity stories is a remarkable coincidence.

These verbal correspondences between Mark 5 and Leviticus 12 and 15 undermine the claims of scholars who suggest that Mark was not concerned about purity issues in this story. At times it appears that what motivates these various arguments is the belief that if this story is concerned about impurity, then it inevitably demonstrates that Jesus and early Christ followers rejected the whole ritual purity system—especially as it related to women.[54] But Mark and his audience would have known that this woman endured impurity as a result of her medical condition.[55] Does acknowledging this fact necessitate that Jesus or Mark reject the ritual purity system? No.

Mark tells his readers very little about this woman. We know neither her name nor any other aspect of her identity apart from her condition: an unrelenting genital discharge. As Susan Haber observes, "The anonymous woman is described solely in terms of her physical affliction: a flow of blood that identifies her to the implied audience and marks her literary role in the narrative. She is the 'hemorrhaging woman,' not the 'impure woman.'" Nonetheless, Haber proceeds to emphasize the importance of impurity for the story: "Her hemorrhage carries with it an impurity that could not have been ignored either by Mark's audience or the society in which she lived. Her illness is explicit; her impurity is implicit."[56] In rabbinic terminology, she is a *zavah*, a woman who endures a long-standing, abnormal ritual impurity. As the legislation

---

54. One can see this concern made explicit, for instance, in D'Angelo, "Gender and Power," 91.

55. So too C. A. Evans, "'Who Touched Me?,'" 368; Holmén, "Jesus' Inverse Strategy," 19–20; and Wassen, "Jesus and the Hemorrhaging Woman," 643. Contrary to this is the view of Kazen, who maintains, "When [Mark] wishes them to consider purity issues he tells them—and then usually for the explicit purpose of bringing out theological and christological points. We may even question whether he really wishes his audience to consider such issues at all, or whether it is rather the details of his tradition that force him to provide necessary explanations for his relatively uninformed recipients" (*Issues of Impurity*, 108).

56. Haber, "A Woman's Touch," 173.

of Leviticus 15:25 LXX makes clear, "And a woman, if she has a discharge of blood [*ean rheē rhysei haimatos*] of many days, not in the time of her menstruation, or if she has a flow after her menstruation, then all the days of her flow she shall be impure, just as the days of her menstruation she will be impure." As long as she has this irregular discharge, she remains ritually impure to the same degree as a woman during menstruation. The significant difference, though, is that the menstruating woman's state of impurity lasts for a discrete period of time: seven days. The *zavah*'s state of impurity, on the other hand, is indefinite—it lasts as long as the discharge remains and then requires a subsequent seven-day period before the woman becomes ritually pure. In Mark's story, this woman has gone through a prolonged state of impurity with no end in sight—and this despite the best medical efforts of multiple doctors.

Jesus's Supposed Rejection of Impurity Laws

Numerous Christian interpreters have suggested that this story demonstrates Jesus's laxity toward and perhaps even disdain for the Jewish ritual purity system. Such scholars usually point to three details within the text as evidence for their conclusions: (1) the woman's supposed disregard for the need to dwell in seclusion or quarantine while she suffers from this impurity; (2) the woman's negligence in conveying impurity toward others—after all, she enters a large crowd where she no doubt makes contact with numerous people and also chooses to touch Jesus's clothing; and (3) Jesus's own disregard for ritual impurity as seen in his evident lack of concern that an impure woman has touched him. Such readings fundamentally misunderstand both the Jewish ritual purity system and the point of Mark's story.

First, many scholars argue that this woman should have been quarantined.[57] The fact that Mark depicts her walking in a crowd around Jesus demonstrates her own disregard for, and consequently Mark's indifference to, the fact that she might transmit impurity to others. As noted above, the *Temple Scroll* portrays the quarantine of women,[58] and Josephus claims that Moses prohibited menstruants from entering into the city of Jerusalem.[59]

While these texts seem to stipulate that those who bear particular kinds of impurities need to be isolated in certain contexts (in the wilderness camp, Jerusalem, or in all cities), such a requirement, as Cohen argues, was probably

---

57. For instance, Marcus, *Mark 1–8*, 357.
58. *Temple Scroll* (11Q19) XLVIII, 15–17.
59. Josephus, *Jewish Antiquities* 3.261.

idealistic in terms of the entire Jewish community. Perhaps some people or communities practiced such isolation, but we cannot know what all Jews thought of such an interpretation. Since Leviticus 15 does not include such legislation, undoubtedly a good number of Jews did not follow the expansionist vision of Numbers 5:2–3. In other words, some Jews may have thought that this woman should isolate herself from the broader society, but other Jews would have believed that such a woman did not need to undergo quarantine. Yet still others might have required isolation only when the woman came to a city or to the city of Jerusalem specifically. Different legal positions and practices likely existed, and proponents of each position would have been able to appeal to sacred scriptures to make their case. Perhaps some Jews thought that such a woman was guilty of neglecting the laws pertaining to dischargers, but we have no evidence that all Jews would have concluded the same thing. Thus the woman's presence among other people says nothing about her own law observance. Even more, her presence in public tells us nothing about Mark's view of the legislation pertaining to genital discharges. How, after all, can we be confident that this particular woman's actions tell us about Mark's Jesus and his views on the impurity associated with genital discharges?

But the woman not only moves around in public in a state of ritual impurity; she also deliberately touches Jesus despite her impurity. Consequently, William Loader concludes that the woman was guilty of "transgressing Torah," and Peter Trummer maintains that both the woman and Jesus are now impure and guilty (German: *schuldig*).[60] From his understanding of this woman's actions, Loader draws a larger conclusion about Mark and his community:

> It is even probable that for Mark menstruants were no longer considered unclean and that for him the issue is only the healing, not removing for the woman a hurdle which for Mark no longer had validity. Mark may have been aware of the way Jewish purity concerns would have had a bearing on various aspects of the story, but his silence is best interpreted on the basis that for him such requirements no longer matter. Theoretically it could mean that he acknowledges them and chooses to say nothing; but it is much more likely that it means that he no longer acknowledges their applicability. Ultimately, Mark's silences also imply that for him Jesus also gave such provisions no regard.[61]

These remarks reveal an unfortunate and widespread misunderstanding about ritual impurity. To contract ritual impurity is not to sin within Jewish

---

60. Loader, *Jesus' Attitude towards the Law*, 61, and Trummer, *Die blutende Frau*, 85. Cf. Sariola, *Markus und das Gesetz*, 70.

61. Loader, *Jesus' Attitude towards the Law*, 62.

thinking. The woman herself is neither guilty for being ritually impure nor guilty for touching a ritually pure person. What is more, the person who contracts a lesser degree of impurity through contact with a *zavah* is also not guilty. Ritual impurity has nothing to do with guilt *unless* one brings it into the wrong context—that is, into sacred space. Ritual impurity and moral impurity (sin) are two different categories, although they overlap at times, as some scholars have stressed. The woman who suffers a ritual impurity is not guilty of sin, but were this same woman to enter into the courtyard for women at the Jerusalem temple, she would wrongfully encroach upon holy space, bringing impurity into contact with the realm of the holy, and would thus become guilty of sin or moral impurity as well.[62] As Leviticus 15:31 states, "Therefore, you shall separate the people of Israel from their impurity, so that they do not die by their impurity by defiling my tent which is in their midst." The person enduring a ritual impurity does not sin when he or she comes into contact with and thereby passes a lesser form of that impurity on to another person.

Further, Mark's narrative stresses that it is the woman herself who initiates contact with Jesus, and even this is done tentatively—touching only his clothing. Whatever the story is about, it is clearly not focused on *Jesus's* beliefs about the Jewish purity system. The woman's contact causes an uncontrolled and unintended power to discharge from Jesus's body. In no way, then, does this story say anything about Mark's understanding of Jesus's motives or halakhic positions with regard to genital discharges.

This last point brings us to the final aspect of the story that people think demonstrates Jesus's indifference to ritual impurity: Jesus does not criticize the impure woman for touching and thereby conveying impurity to him. For instance, Adela Yarbro Collins claims that "the story portrays Jesus as relatively indifferent to the issue of the transmission of ritual impurity due to genital discharges." Similarly, Loader avers, "The conclusion is then inevitable: the Jesus of Mark no longer operates on the assumption that clean-unclean boundaries which the passage raises have validity."[63] A number of problems arise from such statements. First, we do not know whether this ritually impure woman would have conveyed impurity to another person through contact with her hand. According to Leviticus 15:11, a *zav* conveys impurity to other people through the hands unless he has washed his hands. As Milgrom states, "Cleansing the hands eliminates the communicability of the [*zav*'s] impurity by touch, temporarily. It is presumed that the [*zav*'s]

---

62. Cf. Josephus, *Jewish War* 5.199, 227.
63. A. Collins, *Mark*, 284, and Loader, *Jesus' Attitude towards the Law*, 62.

hands have been contaminated by contact with the genitals during mic-turition, and washing them removes their impurity momentarily."[64] If the washing of the *zav*'s hands keeps him from communicating that impurity through his hands to others, presumably the same procedure applies to his female counterpart, the *zavah*. And we do not know whether the hemor-rhaging woman of Mark 5 has washed her hands. Perhaps Mark and his readers simply would have assumed that a *zavah* would have washed her hands before entering into public space.[65]

But even if the woman has not washed her hands and instead conveys impurity to others through her hands, this communication of impurity is not sinful. Surely numerous impure people touched pure people on a regular basis in Jesus's day. Even if such encounters resulted in the transmission of impurity to the other person, this was neither deemed sinful nor viewed as abandonment of the Jewish ritual purity system. If these interpretations of Jesus's encounter with the hemorrhaging woman are based on false assump-tions, how should we read this particular story? If Mark does not intend to depict Jesus abandoning or rejecting the ritual impurity system, what major point does he intend the story to convey?

Jesus's Uncontrollable Discharge of Power

Mark's portrayal of the hemorrhaging woman highlights the fact that she has had this disease for twelve years. For over a decade, then, this woman has suffered a ritual impurity that, while not necessarily restricting her regular day-to-day movements, prevented her access to the Jerusalem temple and possibly even to the city of Jerusalem itself. Being impure, she could not enter into the court of women outside of God's temple. Most Jews surely would have viewed this restriction from the temple negatively; what an un-mitigated loss it was for this woman that she had not been able to go to the temple for twelve years and might never be able to go there again! As the psalmist exclaims,

> Better is one day in your courtyards
>   than a thousand elsewhere.

---

64. Milgrom, *Leviticus 1–16*, 920.

65. Thus Wassen concludes, "Mark ignored the subject matter of impurity for a very good reason: as he presents the story, the hemorrhaging woman does not impart any impurity" ("Jesus and the Hemorrhaging Woman," 660). Further, she suggests that there is an important difference between touching an impure person and being touched by an impure person (654). Only the former, she argues, conveys impurity.

[Better to be] a doorkeeper in the house of my God
than to dwell in the tents of wickedness. (Ps. 84:10 [v. 11 in
Hebrew])

If this woman was devoted to the Jerusalem temple, then she would have
longed to enter into the temple grounds to take part in the sacrifices, worship, and annual festivals that occurred within sacred space. Many of the
people who endured long-term *lepra* or males who experienced long-term
genital discharges would have also shared this desire. But to conclude from
this yearning that this woman or the *lepros* or the *zav* would desire the abolishment of the ritual purity system is incorrect. While the rules pertaining
to the *zav* and *zavah* excluded them from sacred space and, depending upon
which stream of Jewish purity thought they belonged to, may have put other
limitations on their actions and movements, such laws were set in place out
of both concern for God's presence and compassion for those suffering these
impurities. As Leviticus 15:31 states at the conclusion of the laws pertaining
to the *zav* and *zavah*, "Therefore, you shall separate the people of Israel from
their impurity, so that they do not die by their impurity by defiling my tent
which is in their midst."

This woman did not seek the abolishment of the ritual purity system;
rather, she sought the destruction of a disease that consigned her to a life of
long-term impurity. If those experiencing ritual impurities concurred with
the priestly rationale for their exclusion from the realm of the sacred, they
would not have resented the ritual purity system—it constituted, after all,
God's instructions to ensure that those enduring ritual impurities did not
die as a result of bringing those impurities into contact with holy space. It
is both unhelpful and inaccurate, therefore, to contrast a system of purity
and holiness (the Levitical purity system) with a system of compassion (the
Gospels' portrayals of Jesus), as does Marcus Borg: "Against the politics of
holiness, Jesus not only protested, but advocated an alternative core value
for shaping Israel's life—a politics of compassion."[66] Only through careful
instruction and subsequent legal observance could Israel hope to live in

66. Borg, *Conflict, Holiness, and Politics*, 15. In his second edition of this book, Borg
seeks to clarify that his reconstruction is not anti-Jewish, merely anti-elite: "The emphasis
upon holiness/purity was Jewish, but it was not Judaism. Instead, it was a form of Judaism
advocated by the elites and their retainers. Rather than representing Judaism or the Jews of
their day, they might fairly be seen as the oppressors of the vast majority of the Jewish people
in that time" (15). While we cannot know with certainty what the majority of nonelite Jews
thought about the ritual purity system, the diffusion of ritual baths throughout Judea and
Galilee suggests that many Jews of Jesus's day would not have agreed with Borg. See Miller,
At the Intersection of Texts.

such close proximity to its utterly holy God while continuing to endure a mortal existence that was frequently marked by ritual impurities. The proper separation of ritual impurity from the realm of the sacred was, simply put, a matter of compassion.

Yet in addition to being unable to enter into the temple precincts, this woman would have been unable to bear children. Cecilia Wassen rightly highlights this consequence of her medical condition: "There may be more to her illness than bleeding alone; since vaginal bleeding often is accompanied by infertility, the healing in question may also entail the restoration of the woman's fertility. Even if the woman is not medically infertile, her permanent state of impurity would prevent her from engaging in sexual intercourse, and hence render her incapable of conceiving a child."[67] The woman's ritual impurity affected numerous aspects of her life—from the religious and social realms to the relational, familial, and sexual realms. And as Peter Bolt notes, "Her barrenness is easily associated with death, by virtue of its being the death of the line, and, because it does not produce life, the barren womb is naturally described as being dead, or destroyed."[68] Bolt points to Euripides's *Andromache*, in which Hermione says to Andromache, whom she believes has cursed her, "My womb is perishing unfruitful because of you."[69] But even beyond being barren, the woman, because of her condition, could be perceived as particularly close to death. For instance, Hippocratic medical literature states, "The following diseases are uncertain with regard to mortality: pneumonia, ardent fever, pleurisy, phrenitis, angina, staphylitis, splenitis, nephritis, hepatitis, dysentery, a haemorrhage in a woman [*gynaiki rhoos haimatōdēs*]."[70] One can also find similar associations between barrenness and death in Jewish texts:

> R. Joshua b. Levi said: A man who is childless is accounted as dead, for it is written, Give me children, or else I am dead. And it was taught: Four are accounted as dead: A poor man, a [*lepros*], a blind person, and one who is childless. A poor man, as it is written, for all the men are dead [which sought thy life]. A [*lepros*], as it is written, [And Aaron looked upon Miriam, and behold, she had [*lepra*]. And Aaron said unto Moses . . .] let her not be as one dead. The blind, as it is written, He hath set me in dark places, as they that be dead of old. And he who is childless, as it is written, Give me children, or else I am dead.[71]

67. Wassen, "Jesus and the Hemorrhaging Woman," 644.
68. Bolt, *Jesus' Defeat of Death*, 171.
69. Euripides, *Andromache* 157.
70. *Diseases* 1.144.
71. Babylonian Talmud, *Nedarim* 64b; cf. *Exodus Rabbah* 1.34.

The woman who has had a dead womb for twelve years is dead no longer; she is now able to have children. (So, too, in the next chapter, we will examine a father whose twelve-year-old child is given back to him.)

The laws related to the *zavah* provide an essential context within which to read Mark's portrayal of Jesus's encounter with the hemorrhaging woman. It is possible, as Joel Marcus has argued, that this woman believes that she "must come into physical contact with a healer in order to be cured by him. But she is unclean, and her touch defiles, and therefore there is a danger that any physical contact she may have with the healer will annul his miracle working power and wreck the whole effort."[72] Such a dilemma might have fueled the woman's fears—would touching heal her, or would it make Jesus impure? If the latter, her secretive approach *might* lead to Jesus's entry into sacred space while unknowingly enduring a ritual impurity. But the woman overcomes her fear. She is convinced that whatever power resides in Jesus is a force more potent than the condition that has plagued her for a dozen years. And the woman's confidence is rewarded, for when she touches Jesus's garment, her disease is healed.

Candida Moss has provided a helpful reading of this story in light of Greco-Roman conceptions of male and female bodies. The woman's body is leaky, wet, and porous. Upon contact with Jesus's clothing, though, her body dries up and becomes hard: her discharge of blood dries up (*exēranthē*, Mark 5:29).[73] This woman who suffers from a strong form of ritual impurity, an abnormal discharge of vaginal blood, comes into indirect contact with Jesus and leaves healed of her disease. Now that her body has been healed, she will again, after undergoing the rites of purification like the *lepros* of Mark 1 was supposed to, be able to enter into sacred space, consume sacred food, have sex, and possibly bear children.

In a way that parallels the woman who has an uncontrolled discharge of blood leaking from her body, Mark portrays Jesus experiencing an uncontrolled discharge from his own body. The woman's furtive touch of Jesus's clothing causes a discharge of power to depart from his body and to enter into hers. Whereas some, if not all, of Mark's initial readers might have expected the woman's ritual impurity to flow out of her and into Jesus, thereby contaminating him, Mark depicts Jesus's power streaming out of him and into the woman. Instead of a defiling force moving from one body to another, Mark portrays a force or power moving from Jesus to the woman, healing her of this long-suffered, impurity-inducing condition.

---

72. Marcus, *Mark 1–8*, 366. So too Haber, "A Woman's Touch," 183.
73. Moss, "Man with the Flow of Power."

Again, this depiction of Jesus portrays something unexpected. Whoever Jesus is, even contact with his garment can provoke an unconscious flow of healing power from his body. Such power (*dynamis*) emanating or leaking out of Jesus's body through mere contact with his clothing (with, of course, the woman's trust) demonstrates that Jesus's body contains some sort of contagious holiness. Jesus is the holy one of God (Mark 1:24)—he is a force of holiness that opposes the forces of impurity. As Horace Jeffery Hodges and John Poirier observe, "The dynamism of Jesus' holiness is a closer parallel to the dynamism of the holiness present in the inner sanctuary that the high priest enters on the Day of Atonement than the holiness of the high priest himself."[74] Contact with Jesus's clothing is analogous to contact with a variety of holy objects within the tabernacle or temple. After all, contact with the altar or certain tabernacle furnishings or even certain offerings renders an object holy (Exod. 29:37; 30:29; Lev. 6:10–11, 27). In fact, Mark's title for Jesus, the holy one of God, parallels Leviticus 21:23 LXX, which refers to the tabernacle as *to hagion tou theou*, which is the neuter form of Mark's title for Jesus—*ho hagios tou theou*. (It also evokes 2 Kings 4:9, where a wealthy Shunammite woman tells her husband that Elisha is a holy man of God—*anthrōpos tou theou hagios houtos*.) Whereas these tabernacle/temple instruments and offerings render other things holy though, Mark's Gospel portrays Jesus's holiness removing the conditions that give rise to ritual impurities in others. Contact with Jesus, the holy one of God, causes a discharge of holiness to surge out of Jesus—a holiness that overpowers the source of impurity in the one touching Jesus. Just as the tabernacle and its accoutrements exercise no will in sanctifying objects that come into contact with them, Mark portrays Jesus's body automatically and involuntarily purifying those who touch him in faith. In contrast, when Jesus presumably wants to heal others in his hometown of Nazareth, their lack of confidence constrains his power (Mark 6:1–5).

At the end of the story, Jesus has healed a woman who has suffered a twelve-year disease and impurity. From this fact, many scholars conclude that Mark intends to portray the abolishment of the ritual purity system. But is this accurate? Again, no. Were Mark intending to demonstrate that either Jesus or Mark's community no longer cared about ritual purity and had rejected the entire system, he should have portrayed Jesus telling the woman that of course she could touch him and that her illness did not make her impure. Jesus should have then encouraged the woman, and all who were classified as impure due to genital discharges—the *zav*, the *zavah*, the parturient, the menstruant, and those who have had sexual intercourse—to go up to the temple

---

74. Hodges and Poirier, "Jesus as the Holy One," 172. Cf. Holmén, "Jesus' Inverse Strategy."

and participate in the temple cult in spite of their sundry genital discharges. And he could have declared to all of them that the categories of purity and impurity were no longer, or perhaps had never been, valid. This instruction would have signaled quite clearly to all that Jesus rejected the entire system. Some modern readers might prefer this alternate account, but Mark portrays Jesus unwittingly healing the woman of the condition that makes her ritually impure. Again, there is an implicit essentialism at play in Mark's thinking: Jesus's body is ontologically holy, oozing holiness even apart from any effort or intention on his part and destroying a real force or power in the woman's body—the disease that makes her ritually impure.

Premised on essentialism

As was the case with the *lepros* in the preceding chapter, such healing and purification have no clear precedent in priestly literature. Leviticus does not envisage the possibility that a person—be it a priest or layperson—might actually cause the *zav* or *zavah* to become pure through a miraculous healing of their underlying medical conditions. But the unprecedented nature of this purification does not mean that Mark aims to abolish the ritual purity system. Instead, Mark intends to show that a new and previously unheard-of source of powerful holiness has entered into a world mapped by the categories of purity and impurity, holiness and profaneness. Jesus, the holy one of God, represents such an overwhelming force of holiness that those who suffer even the most enduring forms of ritual impurities find themselves dried up, healed, and purified. The woman is now in the precise position envisaged in Leviticus 15:28: purified of her discharge.

Leviticus goes on to say that while such a woman is purified of her discharge, a lingering seven-day ritual impurity remains and is removed through washing and waiting. Unlike in his treatment of the man with *lepra*, here Jesus does not explicitly tell the woman to wash and wait. Perhaps Mark assumes that his readers know Leviticus 15 and will conclude that the woman did just this. Or perhaps he thinks that his depiction in Mark 1:44 of Jesus commanding the *lepros* to go offer what is necessary for purification implies that Jesus would have said the same thing to the woman here. Regardless, Jesus does not intend to destroy the ritual purity system; rather, his body naturally destroys the source of ritual impurities.

Matthew on Genital Dischargers

Unlike his treatment of *lepra*, in which he adds extra material to what he takes from Mark, Matthew discusses only this one woman with a genital discharge. Yet Matthew's account of the hemorrhaging woman makes a few small but notable modifications to the story found in the Gospel of Mark. First,

Matthew changes Mark's phrase "in a flow of blood" (*en rhysei haimatos*) to the participle "bleeding" (*haimorrhoousa*, Matt. 9:20). In doing so, Matthew alludes to the language of Leviticus 15:33 LXX, since the verb occurs only here and in Matthew 9:20 in Jewish texts written in Greek.[75] He also omits any reference to her efforts to seek help from doctors, thereby abbreviating the story. Additionally, he depicts the woman touching the fringe (*kraspedon*) of Jesus's garments not merely the garment as in Mark 5:27. Here Matthew may be dependent upon Mark's later reference to the fringe of Jesus's garment functioning as a point of contact in other of healings (Mark 6:56; cf. Matt. 14:35–36; 23:5). In portraying her actions in this way, Matthew's account contains a parallel to later rabbinic literature, which portrays children grabbing hold of Honi the Circle Drawer's fringe in order to ask for rain.[76]

This reference to the fringe of Jesus's garment casually underlines Jesus's obedience to the legal requirement that Jewish men wear fringes (Greek: *kraspeda*; Hebrew: *tzitzit*) on their garments to remind them of God's commandments (Num. 15:37–39; Deut. 22:12). In potential support of this interpretation is the claim in Numbers that in helping one focus on God's commands instead of on the lust of one's own heart and eyes, the fringe enables one to be holy. As the Sifre to Numbers later states, "The commandment regarding fringes serves to add to the holiness of Israel."[77] Jesus's fringe, then, is a sign and perhaps an extension of his holiness and is therefore a particularly appropriate point of contact for the woman to access the power of Jesus's purifying holiness.

Finally, Matthew removes Mark's claim that Jesus did not know who had touched him and gives Jesus's intentionality a role in her healing; only after he turns toward her and tells her that her confidence has healed or saved her does the woman undergo healing (Matt. 9:22). While Jesus's body emits an involuntary force in Mark, in Matthew Jesus willingly chooses to heal the woman. Matthew emphasizes Jesus's intentions and thinking in a way that demonstrates once again his desire to remove illnesses associated with ritual impurity.

Luke on Genital Dischargers

As I discussed in chapter 1, Luke portrays Mary, Joseph, and Jesus going up to Jerusalem to undergo purification after Jesus's birth in accordance with

---

75. As A.-J. Levine ("Discharging Responsibility") notes, the verb also occurs in the Hippocratic corpus.

76. Babylonian Talmud, *Ta'anit* 23b.

77. *Sifre Numbers* 115.

the laws of Leviticus 12. Apart from this narrative, Luke only retells Mark's story of Jesus and the hemorrhaging woman, without adding any further encounters with genital dischargers.

Following Mark, Luke claims that the woman had spent all her money on doctors, who were unable to heal her (Luke 8:43). Following Matthew, though, Luke also stresses that the woman touched only the fringe (or *tzitzit*) of Jesus's garment.[78] After this one detail, Luke follows Mark's account quite closely. In particular, he portrays the woman's healing occurring immediately upon touching the fringe of Jesus's clothing: "The flow of her blood stopped" (8:44). Additionally, Luke follows Mark in portraying Jesus's ignorance about who touched him. In this regard, it appears that Luke chooses to show Jesus's power, which streams out of him without any intention on his part, rather than choosing to follow Matthew, who showcases Jesus's knowledge. In fact, Luke builds upon Mark's account of Jesus's unreflectively powerful body, for elsewhere he portrays groups of people trying to touch Jesus because power automatically emanates out of Jesus's body and heals any who touch him (Luke 6:19). Like Mark, then, Luke uses the story of the woman with a ritually impure discharge to present Jesus's body as unconsciously and naturally discharging a holy power to those who touch him.

Conclusion

Mark believed it necessary for Christ followers to hear a story about Jesus's encounter with a woman who had been hemorrhaging for twelve years. The placement of her story within the story of the deceased twelve-year-old girl, as I shall argue in the following chapter, links both of their stories together in significant ways. Contrary to the many claims of Christian interpreters over the centuries, the Jesus depicted in the story does not abandon or reject the Jewish ritual purity system. In fact, Jesus doesn't *do* anything intentional prior to or during the woman's contact with him. The woman's hesitancy reflects her own doubts about whether touching Jesus will result in her healing and move her closer to a state of ritual purity, or whether it might result in Jesus becoming impure. But her confidence in Jesus's power overcomes her fears, and she covertly touches Jesus's garments. Through this contact, Jesus's body involuntarily emits a discharge of power that purifies the woman of her long-standing impure discharge. When Jesus determines what has happened, his words commend the woman's confidence in his power over her

---

78. Some manuscript witnesses to Luke (e.g., Codex Bezae and the Old Latin) lack the reference to Jesus's fringe.

fears regarding the power of her illness and the impurity it creates: "Daughter, your confidence has saved you. Go in peace/wholeness and be healed of your affliction" (Mark 5:34). Again, Jesus does not dismiss the reality of her condition prior to meeting him. Instead, he acknowledges it. Only someone with a real condition could exhibit such faith or confidence in Jesus's ability to overcome it. The Jesus whom the Synoptic writers portray is one whose body naturally opposes and overwhelms the most persistent and abnormal of genital discharges, conditions that even the doctors are powerless to address.

In the previous chapter, I focused on Mark's account of Jesus healing a man with *lepra*. There I argued that Mark's central point in that story is to stress Jesus's desire to purify a ritually impure man. In that story, Mark addresses the concern that Jesus and his followers no longer care about the Jewish ritual purity system. The story serves to teach its readers just how concerned Jesus was with ritual impurity—any hint of indifference to impurity resulted in his anger. In Mark's story of the hemorrhaging woman (and Luke's retelling of it), on the other hand, Jesus's will is entirely irrelevant. Mark emphasizes the woman's hesitant confidence, which stirs her to touch Jesus's clothing without his permission or foreknowledge. At the woman's touch, and without his consent, Jesus's power emanates from his body and purifies the woman from her long-lasting, impurity-inducing disease. The story of the hemorrhaging woman gives readers the impression that Jesus is innately, one could say ontologically, opposed to ritual impurity and that his body, like a force of nature, inevitably will destroy impurity's sources.

CHAPTER 5

Jesus and the Dead

In the previous two chapters, I examined Jesus's interactions with those suffering from *lepra* and with a woman suffering from a twelve-year genital hemorrhage. I argued that the Gospel writers depict Jesus healing the underlying conditions that cause ritual impurity, thus paving the way for the ritually impure person to undergo the rites of purification. The stories depict Jesus seeking to destroy the root causes of ritual impurity. As Jacob Milgrom and others have argued, these ritual impurities were associated with mortality and death. What, then, of death itself?

Each of the canonical Gospels, including the Gospel of John, portrays Jesus's encounter with corpses.[1] Every time Jesus encounters a corpse, it returns to life. In fact, we see the Gospel traditions about corpses become more dramatic over time: the later the tradition, the greater the physical distance between the corpse and Jesus, and the greater the temporal distance between Jesus's interaction with the corpse and the person's actual time of death. Modern readers generally focus on the miraculous nature of raising the dead, and with good reason—such accounts, if true, are remarkable displays of power. Ancient readers would have agreed. But both early Jewish and non-Jewish readers who knew the Jewish law would have read these stories within the context of the Jewish ritual purity system, since corpses were the third and final source of ritual impurity. For this reason, we must pay careful attention to the priestly legislation pertaining to corpse impurity.

1. Cf. *Infancy Gospel of Thomas* 9.3, where the child Jesus raises one of his dead playmates.

Corpse Impurity in Priestly Thinking

> He who touches the corpse of any person shall be impure seven days; he shall purify himself with the water on the third day and on the seventh day, and so be pure; but if he does not purify himself on the third day and on the seventh day, he will not become pure. Whoever touches a corpse, the body of any person who has died, and does not purify himself, defiles the tabernacle of Yhwh, and that person shall be cut off from Israel; because the water for impurity was not thrown upon him, he shall be impure; his impurity is still on him. (Num. 19:11–13)

Like other sources of ritual impurity, the corpse conveys impurity through direct physical contact: if one touches a corpse, one becomes contaminated. But the remaining legislation shows how corpse impurity differs from, and is also much stronger than, other forms of ritual impurity:

> This is the law when a person dies in a tent: everyone who comes into the tent, and everyone who is in the tent, shall be impure for seven days. And every open container, which has no cover fastened upon it, is impure. Whoever is in the open field and touches one who is slain with a sword, or a dead body, or a bone of a person, or a grave, shall be impure for seven days. (Num. 19:14–16)

Unlike any form of ritual impurity in Leviticus, corpses contaminate even without coming into direct contact with people or objects; merely being in the same tent as a corpse renders one ritually impure for a seven-day period.[2] Similarly, coming into contact with a grave would convey impurity to a person. The corpse, then, emits a strong force of impurity, one that fills enclosed spaces and radiates upward out of the ground under which the corpse is buried.

Additionally, the one who touches a corpse contracts an impurity that lasts for a period of seven days. The length of this contracted impurity is the same as for a new mother (at least the initial stage after the birth of a male child; Lev. 12:1–5), a menstruant (15:19), a *zav/zavah* (15:13, 28), and a *lepros* (14:8). In priestly thinking, then, a person who touches a corpse is considered as impure as someone whose body endures the *sources* of impurity, and that person has a stronger impurity than one who comes into contact with ritually impure people (cf. 14:46; 15:7–11, 19–23, 27; 22:6).[3] Such a

---

2. As we saw in chap. 2, later Jewish legal experts believed that ritual impurity due to *lepra* could be conveyed without physical contact.

3. One exception is the seven-day impurity that a man incurs for having sexual intercourse with a menstruant (Lev. 15:24). As Jonathan Magonet explains, "The act of intercourse creates a single entity, 'one flesh,' and both are equally affected by the status of uncleanness of the other"

long-lasting *secondary* impurity demonstrates the strength of the corpse's *primary* impurity. Unlike all other sources of impurity, the corpse is, to use a later rabbinic term, a "father of fathers of impurity": the impurity it conveys makes the corpse-impure person also contagious. The person who has contracted impurity from a corpse becomes a "father of impurity"; such people convey a lesser degree of corpse impurity to others. Thus, those who contract corpse impurity endure a long-lasting and contagious secondary impurity.

Furthermore, the purification rites for those who experience corpse impurity differ from the rites that purify other ritual impurities. As Numbers 19:12 stipulates, corpse-impure people must bathe twice—on the third and on the seventh day of their impurity. It also requires that ashes from a red heifer be mixed with water and sprinkled upon them on the third and seventh days of their state of impurity:

> For the impure [the priests] shall take some ashes of the burnt offering, and running water shall be added in a vessel; then a pure person shall take hyssop, and dip it in the water, and sprinkle it upon the tent, and upon all the furnishings, and upon the persons who were there, and upon him who touched the bone, or the slain, or the corpse, or the grave; and the pure person shall sprinkle upon the impure on the third day and on the seventh day; thus on the seventh day he shall purify him, and he shall wash his clothes and bathe himself in water, and at evening he shall be pure. (Num. 19:17–19)

Simply put, corpses were the most powerful source of impurity in the priestly ritual purity system. But again, despite the strength of corpse impurity, Jews did not believe that contracting it was sinful or even something one necessarily ought to avoid. Numbers 19 makes it clear that for the common person, corpse impurity only became a problem if it was not dealt with through the divinely given means of ritual purification. Failure to undergo purification results in the defilement of God's sacred space, an egregious fault that leads the priestly writer to apply the *karet* penalty to the guilty person—cutting him or her off from Israel.[4]

Finally, priestly literature emphasizes the distinctiveness of corpse impurity by prohibiting certain people from contracting it. For instance, Leviticus 21 forbids a priest from becoming corpse impure through anyone but his close family members—his parents, his siblings, and his children (Lev. 21:1–3; Ezek.

("But If It Is a Girl," 151). In other words, having become one flesh, the man too endures the primary impurity of the woman, not a secondary impurity.

4. Even here, later Jews suggested ways to deal with corpse impurity if a person failed to undergo the rites of purification in a timely manner. Josephus, for instance, claims that such a person can offer two lambs to deal with this impurity. See *Jewish Antiquities* 3.262.

44:25). The legislation states that the priest can defile himself on behalf of his deceased sister only if she is unmarried and a virgin. Further, it may imply that the priest cannot defile himself on behalf of his deceased wife.[5] Since priests serve within sacred space, they must take considerable precautions not to acquire a seven-day impurity that would exclude them from service in this realm. The same legislation prohibits the high priest from contracting corpse impurity even for his closest family members (Lev. 21:11). Likewise, in Numbers the priestly writer stipulates that a man who has taken a Nazirite vow cannot contract corpse impurity for anyone (Num. 6:6–8).

Corpses in Ancient Near Eastern Thought

Ancient Israelites were not the only people in antiquity to believe that corpses conveyed impurity. If any culture was unique, it might have been the Egyptians, since within Egyptian literature we have evidence that one needed to purify oneself *before* entering a tomb.[6] So impure were corpses in Zoroastrian thinking, for instance, that they were not buried, because corpses dishonored the earth.[7] Although we have evidence of early Persian-period burials of rulers, the bodies were enclosed in stone tombs, which prevented the spread of corpse impurity. Neither were corpses cremated, since they polluted fire, which Zoroastrians considered holy.[8] Instead, corpses were left out for animals and the weather to decompose.[9] Upon the death of an animal or human, the corpse-demon possessed the corpse and polluted it.[10] Once the bones had been cleansed of flesh, they were placed in ossuaries, which would contain their corpse impurity.[11] Similar to some Jewish thinking, any animal or human that died in a tent or house rendered the entire structure impure.[12] Contact with corpses required a ten-day purification process.

Greek and Roman literature also provide ample evidence of a widespread belief in death impurity. Here I will cite representative texts chronologically in order to establish how widespread and long-standing this belief was. According to Fabian Meinel, the "historical evidence suggests that pollution became

5. On this passage, see Carmichael, "Death and Sexuality."
6. On death and burial in ancient Egypt, see Assmann, *Death and Salvation.*
7. *Vendidad* 1.13; 3.8–13.
8. *Vendidad* 1.17.
9. Cf. Herodotus, *Histories* 1.140.
10. *Vendidad* 5.27–28; *Gizistag Abāliš* 6.3.
11. See Fong, "Purity and Pollution." On purity and impurity more broadly in Zoroastrian thinking, see Choksy, *Purity and Pollution in Zoroastrianism.*
12. *Vendidad* 8.2–3.

a real issue [in Greek society] only after Homer."[13] Although our knowledge of the work is fragmentary and depends on a second-century CE chrestomathy attributed to Proclus, the seventh-century BCE epic *Aethiopis* mentions the purification of the Amazonian Penthesilea after she involuntarily killed Hippolyta, as well as the purification of Achilles after he killed Thersites.[14] As in priestly thinking, the legislation of Solon, the sixth-century BCE Athenian politician, prohibited anyone who had come into contact with a corpse from entering sacred space, and for five days subsequent to the body's removal, members of the priestly caste in Coan were excluded from any building that had housed a corpse.[15] According to Martin Nilsson, if a person died in a sanctuary, the body had to be removed and the sanctuary purified.[16]

In the fifth century BCE, Euripides depicts the goddess Artemis departing from Hippolytus as his death approaches, saying, "Farewell: it is not lawful for me to look upon the dead or to defile my sight with the last breath of the dying. And I see that you are already near that misfortune."[17] Artemis's abandonment of Hippolytus at the point of his death may appear insensitive, but the fact that the gods kept their distance from death was, in the words of Robert Parker, "a truism of Greek theology."[18] Euripides begins his play *Alcestis* with this same motif, depicting Apollo leaving the palace of Admetus to avoid encountering the figure of Death: "And I, to avoid the pollution of death in the house, am departing from this palace I love so well."[19] Relatedly, Thucydides claims that in 426 BCE the Athenians purified the sacred island of Delos, which housed an important temple to the god Apollo, by removing all sepulchers and forbidding anyone to die or give birth on it.[20]

In the fourth century BCE, Theophrastus describes the superstitious person in the following way: "He refuses to step on a gravestone, view a corpse or visit a woman who has given birth, and says it's the best policy for him not to incur pollution."[21] Such mockery might suggest that the educated or civilized

---

13. Meinel, *Pollution and Crisis*, 2.

14. *Aethiopis* argument 1.

15. Parker, *Miasma*, 38, 52.

16. Nilsson, *Geschichte der Griechischen Religion*, 1:102. On the dead and death more broadly, see 1:95–104. See also Wächter, *Reinheitsvorschriften im griechischen Kult*, 43–63, and Parker, *Miasma*, 32–48. Thucydides mentions that temples were filled with dead bodies during a plague but makes no mention of any purification rites, not because there were no such rites but presumably because they lay outside of his narratival interests (*History of the Peloponnesian War* 2.52.1–3).

17. Euripides, *Hippolytus* 1437–39.

18. Parker, *Miasma*, 33.

19. Euripides, *Alcestis* 22–23; cf. *Iphigenia at Taurus* 380–82.

20. Thucydides, *History of the Peloponnesian War* 3.104.1–2.

21. Theophrastus, *Characters* 16.9.

person did not believe that corpses or birth defiled, but Theophrastus derides the superstitious person's *fear* of contracting ritual impurity, not necessarily the belief in its existence. Regardless, the evidence demonstrates that such thinking about ritual impurity was widespread. For instance, a fourth-century sacral law from Cyrene requires that if a woman miscarries an articulated fetus, then both the house and those in it are polluted in the same way that they would be after death.[22] Likewise in the fourth century, Plato insists that priests and priestesses cannot approach any tomb, but he stipulates one exception: they can attend the funeral of an examiner.[23] In this one instance, though, they can do so because the corpse will not defile them.

In the late fourth or early third century BCE, Menander portrays servants within the house of someone who has died communicating with those outside via water channels. This statement presumes that when a death occurs in an Athenian house, its occupants are restricted in their access to others due to ritual pollution.[24] And Robert Garland points to a second-century BCE inscription from the island of Lesbos that stipulates that family members must purify themselves after a funeral and then wait twenty days before entering areas dedicated to the gods.[25]

I noted above that Thucydides mentions the island of Delos needing to be kept pure of corpse contamination. Such a belief persisted for centuries, as Strabo's claims in the first century CE attest—the inhabitants of Delos transported their deceased to a nearby island so that they might keep Delos free from corpse contamination.[26] This practice fits with wider thinking about sacred space, as evidenced in the Greek sacral laws inscribed at the entrance of sanctuaries, which frequently state that a person should "enter pure from wife and childbed and mourning."[27] As in Jewish priestly thought, proximity to sexual intercourse, birth, and death precluded one from the realm of the sacred precisely because the gods avoided impurity.

Roman society also held the corpse to be impure.[28] For instance, the *Twelve Tables* bans burials and cremations within the *pomerium*, the religious boundary that marked off the city of Rome from the territories it controlled.[29] Again, this desire to contain and restrict corpse contamination was rooted in Roman

---

22. Rhodes and Osborne, *Greek Historical Inscriptions 404–323 BC*, 106, no. 97.

23. Plato, *Laws* 12.947.

24. Menander, *The Shield* 465.

25. R. Garland, *Greek Way of Death*, 45.

26. Strabo, *Geography* 10.5.5.

27. N. Robertson, "Concept of Purity," 195.

28. On death pollution in Roman thought, see Lindsay, "Death-Pollution and Funerals"; Edwards, *Death in Ancient Rome*; and Lennon, *Pollution and Religion in Ancient Rome*, 136–66.

29. *Twelve Tables* 10.1; cf. Cicero, *Laws* 2.58.

theology, which envisaged the immortal gods keeping their distance from death, an axiom that Plutarch articulates in the first century CE: the god Osiris "is far removed from the earth, uncontaminated and unpolluted and pure from all matter that is subject to destruction and death."[30]

Writing in the second century CE, Lucian of Samosata claims that the Galli, the eunuch priests of the goddess Cybele, do not enter a sanctuary on the day that they see a corpse. They undergo purification the next day and can then enter into sacred space, while others must wait thirty days and then shave their heads before they can enter a temple.[31] Also writing in the second century CE, Aulus Gellius relates the various laws pertaining to the priests of the god Jupiter, noting that one can read them in the third-century BCE writings of Fabius Pictor. Among these laws is a prohibition against coming into proximity with a corpse: "He never enters a place of burial, he never touches a dead body; but he is not forbidden to attend a funeral."[32] Such prohibitions for priests were common in the Greco-Roman world and parallel Leviticus 21:1–11.[33]

Related to Theophrastus's mockery of people's fear of contracting ritual impurity, the third-century BCE Stoic philosopher Chrysippus, according to Plutarch, rejected the idea that corpses contaminated. Plutarch states that Chrysippus suggested that there was nothing wrong with going from the childbed or the deathbed directly to a sacred space, since nature itself taught, via the behavior of animals, that such actions did not pollute the gods.[34] Plutarch also observes that the ninth-century BCE Spartan legislator Lycurgus "did away with all superstitious fear connected with burials, granting the right to bury the dead within the city, and to have the tombs near the shrines. He also abolished the pollutions associated with death and burial."[35] Finally, with possible support from Cicero,[36] Plutarch claims that Numa, the second king of Rome, attempted to teach the Romans that corpses did not pollute.[37]

Nonetheless, the wide variety of evidence surveyed here suggests that the majority of Greeks and Romans believed that corpses were impure, that they contaminated those who came into contact with them, and that such

---

30. Plutarch, *Isis and Osiris* 382F.

31. Lucian, *Syrian Goddess* 52; cf. Lucian, *Phalaris* 1.12. Although some scholars question whether Lucian was the author of *Syrian Goddess*, they still date it to the second century CE. See here Dirven, "Author of *De Dea Syria*."

32. Aulus Gellius, *Attic Nights* 10.15.24–25.

33. R. Garland, *Greek Way of Death*, 45.

34. Plutarch, *Moralia* 1044F–45A.

35. Plutarch, *Sayings of Spartans* 238D.

36. See Cicero, *Laws* 2.58.

37. Plutarch, *Roman Questions* 23; cf. 79.

people required purification before they could enter into sacred spaces. Frequently, the nature of corpse impurity placed further restrictions on various priestly castes since they worked in sacred spaces. What this evidence from both Greece and Rome suggests, then, is that concern over corpse impurity was a widespread phenomenon in the Mediterranean world. When Jews restricted access to sacred space, they were participating in assumptions that were diffusely shared with their non-Jewish contemporaries. Consequently, when the Gospel writers portrayed Jesus coming into contact with corpses, even gentile readers who were unfamiliar with the Jewish law would have understood Jesus to be interacting with ritual impurity. All ancient readers would have naturally connected Jesus's encounters with corpses to ritual impurity.

The Second Temple Jewish Expansion of Corpse-Impurity Legislation

At times, Second Temple Jewish literature expands upon the priestly legislation pertaining to corpse impurity. I will not provide here a full account of all these changes but will show some of the ways in which Jews of the period strove to contain corpse impurity. One of the key texts from the period is the *Temple Scroll* from Qumran.[38] In this work, the author admonishes his readers to bury the dead properly: "And you will not do as the gentiles do, who bury their dead in any place—even in the middle of their houses. Instead, you will separate places in the midst of your land where you will bury your dead. In four cities you will establish a place for burial."[39] The author of this work requires that the dead be buried in designated areas— necropolises—instead of on people's familial property, claiming that Israel should not imitate the gentiles, who bury their dead in their houses. In fact, he expresses his desire that Israel should build only one cemetery for every four towns in order to minimize the places that emit corpse impurity. This legislation seems to be an application of Numbers 5:2–3, which excludes the corpse impure from the wilderness camp: "Command the sons of Israel that they send out from the camp every *lepros*, every *zav*, and everyone who is impure by a corpse—both the male and the female you shall send outside, you shall send them out of the camp so that they do not make impure their camps in the midst of which I dwell." By limiting the places where one can incur corpse impurity and by making it evident to all people that corpses lie buried where they do, the author hopes that fewer people

---

38. See Schiffman, "Impurity of the Dead," and Berlejung, "Variabilität und Konstanz."
39. *Temple Scroll* (11Q19) XLVIII, 11–14.

will find themselves inadvertently contaminated by corpses and therefore limited in their access to the Jerusalem temple. In other words, the *Temple Scroll* seeks to minimize and control contact with corpses in order to provide greater access to sacred space. While it was not considered sinful for the average Jew to contract corpse impurity, and at certain times was even required, the *Temple Scroll* provides additional legislation to curtail incidental corpse contamination.

A different sort of expansion pertains to corpse-impurity legislation. The *Temple Scroll*, for instance, requires anyone contracting corpse impurity to bathe not only on the third and seventh day but also on the first day.[40] This expansion might have been unique to Qumran, since we have no evidence of a first-day bathing ritual elsewhere.[41] Such a rite would have permitted the corpse-contaminated person to dwell in profane space and eat nonsacred food, but it would not have allowed access to sacred space and things.

Additionally, both the Septuagint and Qumran literature understand the reference to a tent in Numbers 19 to apply not only to tents but also to permanent structures. The LXX translates *tent* (Hebrew: *ohel*) as *house* (Greek: *oikos*), and the *Damascus Document* and the *Temple Scroll* also refer to a house (Hebrew: *bayit*), not a tent.[42] The latter work, in fact, considers the whole house to be impure—the floor, roof, and walls—a possibility that one might infer from the requirement to sprinkle the tent with the ashes of the red heifer (Num. 19:18).[43] Consequently, the house itself must be purified seven days after the corpse is removed:

> If a man dies in your cities, the whole house in which the deceased dies will be impure for seven days; everything in the house and everything which goes into the house will be impure for seven days; and all food upon which wa[t]er is spilt shall be impure; every drink will be impure; and the clay vessels will be impure and everything in them will be impure for every pure person; and the open (vessels) will be impure for every Israelite person, all the drink that is in them. [. . .] And the day when they remove the dead person from it, they will purify the house of every stain of oil, and wine, and dampness from water; they will scrub its floor, its walls, and its doors; with water they will wash its hinges, and its jambs, and its thresholds, and its lintels. The day when the dead

40. *Temple Scroll* (11Q19) XLIX, 17; cf. Num. 19:12.

41. Werrett (*Ritual Purity*, 140) points to Philo, *Special Laws* 3.206–7, as evidence of a first-day bathing ritual elsewhere, but Philo says nothing explicit about such a rite, whereas he does mention bathing on the third and seventh days. On first-day purifications, see Milgrom, "First Day Ablutions," and Kazen, *Issues of Impurity*, 63–89.

42. *Damascus Document* XII, 18; *Temple Scroll* (11Q19) XLIX, 5–10.

43. So too Werrett, *Ritual Purity*, 141.

person is brought out from it, they will purify the house and all its utensils, the mills, and the mortar, and all the utensils of wood, iron and bronze, the sacks, and the skins.[44]

Similarly, Josephus claims, "After the funeral the house and its inhabitants must be purified."[45] And in early rabbinic literature, as one can see throughout Mishnah tractate *Ohalot*, the rabbis consider a house to be included within the category of a tent; it is something made by humans and is therefore susceptible to impurity.[46]

Finally, the *Temple Scroll* addresses a delayed miscarriage, a situation that was likely all too common in antiquity. What should be done in the case of a pregnant woman whose fetus has died but still remains in her uterus? The author believes that in such an instance the woman conveys that impurity as though she were a corpse herself: "And if a woman is pregnant and her child dies in her womb, all the days that he is dead within her she will be impure like a grave; every house which she enters will be impure with all its utensils for seven days; and everyone who comes into contact with her will be impure until the evening; and if someone enters the house with her, that person will be impure for seven days."[47] Such legislation contrasts with later rabbinic claims that the woman who has a delayed miscarriage remains ritually pure.[48] For the rabbis, a midwife contracts a seven-day ritual impurity if she touches the miscarried fetus during a vaginal inspection, but the mother herself remains pure. The underlying logic of the Qumranic position is this: if touching a corpse makes one impure for seven days, then a woman who contains within her body a corpse must at least endure a seven-day ritual impurity. As Jonathan Magonet puts it, "If any entity can be considered to be a 'single flesh' made up of two persons, it is a mother bearing a child."[49] Even more, the *Temple Scroll* understandably concludes that since a real force of impurity resides in the fetus and since the fetus and the woman are analogous to a corpse and a grave, the pregnant woman must also emit corpse impurity like a grave as long as the fetus remains within her. Here the *Temple Scroll* might also depend upon the words of Jeremiah 20:17: "[Cursed be that man] because he did not kill me in the womb; so that my mother would have been to me a grave."

---

44. *Temple Scroll* (11Q19) XLIX, 11–14; cf. *Damascus Document* XII, 17–18.
45. Josephus, *Against Apion* 2.205, my translation.
46. Cf. *Sifre Numbers* 129.
47. 1Q19 L, 10–13.
48. Mishnah, *Hullin* 4.3; cf. Babylonian Talmud, *Hullin* 72a.
49. Magonet, "But If It Is a Girl," 151.

Although we can see various early Jewish expansions on the laws regarding corpse impurity in Numbers, Jews in the Second Temple period nonetheless considered burying the dead to be a noble and compassionate action. The book of Tobit, for instance, begins with Tobit declaring that he walks in the ways of truth and righteousness, doing many charitable deeds (Tob. 1:3). Among the deeds of charity that he lists, he includes the fact that he frequently buries the bodies of deceased Jews (1:17–19; 2:7–9) even though his actions incur the ire of Sennacherib, the king of Assyria. To care for and bury the dead, to ensure that the deceased do not lie abandoned and unburied, was a hallmark of Jewish piety. In the first century CE, both Josephus and Philo claim that Moses commanded Jews to bury the dead and to make sure that no one was left unburied.[50] And as a rule, close relatives should perform these burial rites.[51] In fact, one of Josephus's primary pieces of evidence of the impiety of the Zealots in the Jewish Revolt was their practice of leaving their dead enemies unburied.[52] Such disregard for corpses diverged from the general Jewish practice of attending to the dead. So vital was proper and timely burial that early rabbis claimed that when one's dead relative remained unburied, one was exempt from the requirements to recite the Shema or to wear *tefillin*.[53] Other versions of this passage add the sweeping claim that such a person is exempt from *all* the responsibilities of the law, a sentiment that the Babylonian Talmud preserves: "A mourner, as long as his dead is lying before him, is exempt from reading the Shema and *Tefillah* and from all the commandments prescribed in the Torah."[54]

Burying the dead was one thing, but Josephus suggests that living among them was quite another. In 20 CE, Herod Antipas, ruler of Galilee and son of Herod the Great, built the city of Tiberias on the western shore of the Sea of Galilee in honor of the Roman emperor Tiberius. Despite the city being located in what Josephus calls the best part of Galilee, Antipas experienced difficulties trying to convince Jews to settle there. This reluctance to populate Tiberias stemmed from the fact that the city was built on a graveyard.[55] As Josephus relates, Antipas had to compel people to dwell there because they were hesitant to live in a place where they would remain in a constant state of corpse impurity—a place that would require them first to leave their hometown and then go through a seven-day ritual purification before they could worship in the Jerusalem temple.

50. Josephus, *Against Apion* 2.211; Philo, *Hypothetica* 7.7.
51. Josephus, *Against Apion* 2.205.
52. Josephus, *Jewish War* 4.317.
53. Mishnah, *Berakhot* 3.1 (according to the Kaufmann Codex).
54. Babylonian Talmud, *Semahot* 48b.
55. Josephus, *Jewish Antiquities* 18.36–38.

Jesus and the Dead

When modern readers encounter stories of Jesus raising the dead, they are struck by the miraculous nature of such deeds—and rightly so. Ancient readers would have been struck by this as well. But given the survey of texts above, it is likely they would have also connected such actions to various ritual purity systems, which almost always ascribed impurity to human corpses. Again, a failure to read these revivification stories within the context of the Jewish ritual purity system effectively removes Jesus from the world of the first century and transplants him to our own world. These various laws pertaining to corpse impurity, then, illuminate a number of different stories in the Gospels, including the story of Jairus's twelve-year-old daughter in Mark 5 (which both Matthew and Luke retell), the story of the dead son of a widow in Luke 7, and the story of Jesus's dead friend Lazarus in John 11. They also, as I shall discuss, help us better understand a number of Jesus's sayings.

The Corpse in Mark

According to Mark, a synagogue ruler by the name of Jairus approached Jesus to ask him to heal his deathly ill daughter: "My daughter is at the point of death. Come and place your hands on her so that she might be saved and live" (Mark 5:23). As with the *lepros* discussed above in chapter 3, so it is with Jairus: his conviction that Jesus's touch alone would save his daughter from death demonstrates his remarkable confidence in Jesus's power. The story of the hemorrhaging woman, which I examined in the preceding chapter, interrupts this story about Jairus's daughter, but once Mark resumes it, his readers find out that the twelve-year-old girl has in fact died before Jesus could touch her. Despite this news, Jairus, Jesus, and three disciples—Peter, James, and John—continue to Jairus's house. Mark depicts Jesus entering the house, thereby appearing to contract corpse impurity. Since the corpse impurity fills the entire structure, all who enter into the house become contaminated by the corpse of the young girl.

Amy-Jill Levine says of this story, "The text, of course, says nothing about corpse uncleanness,"[56] arguing that to connect this story to ritual impurity would be an over-reading. But the conclusion Levine draws from this silence is unwarranted. First, as the survey above demonstrates, most readers in the Greco-Roman world would have assumed the presence of corpse contamination in the story, and those familiar with Jewish customs and scriptures would have associated it with Numbers 19. Second, Mark (and following

---

56. A.-J. Levine, "Discharging Responsibility," 385.

him, Matthew and Luke) places the story of this little girl around the story of the hemorrhaging woman, connecting two women who endure two different ritual impurities. This is either a rather singular coincidence or the result of Mark's intentional effort to focus on ritual impurity. Given the fact that the entirety of Mark 5 contains numerous impurities (impure *pneumata*, impure pigs, impure graveyards, a hemorrhaging woman, and a corpse), the latter seems more likely.

Once again, there is nothing unlawful or sinful about Jesus contracting corpse impurity from the dead girl. While a priest or the high priest or a Nazirite might face restrictions, Jesus does not. Consequently, his entering into a house containing a corpse says nothing about his view of the ritual purity system. After all, the mourners whom Jesus first encounters when entering the house have also become ritually impure; surely they are not guilty of disregarding the laws of corpse contamination. Further, since he has already entered into a house that is permeated by corpse impurity, the fact that he touches the girl's dead body does not signal any disdain for the law. Physical contact with a corpse is no more defiling than being in an enclosed structure with a corpse.

Mark states that after removing the mourners, Jesus takes the dead girl's hand and says, "*Talitha koum*"—an Aramaic phrase meaning, "Little girl, arise!" (Mark 5:41). At these words, the girl arises and begins to walk, to the amazement of all. Again, the purity legislation assumes that the body of a dead person will convey impurity to the pure—Jesus *should* have become impure. Yet Jesus's encounter with the dead girl ends with her alive and walking. Jesus's touch and words revivify her. The girl's body has been separated from the source of her impurity—death. This revivification is both miraculous and previously unimagined in priestly laws pertaining to corpse impurity.

Jesus's Death and Corpses in Matthew

Matthew modifies Mark's account of the daughter of Jairus and supplements Mark's treatment of Jesus and corpses. Most importantly, with regard to Jairus's daughter he heightens the father's confidence in Jesus's power over the forces of death. In Matthew's version, Jairus first approaches Jesus *after* his daughter has died, asking that Jesus not merely heal his daughter but in fact raise her from the dead (Matt. 9:18; Luke, by contrast, follows Mark here).

Matthew also adds another story in which Jesus revivifies the dead, this revivification happening at the time of Jesus's crucifixion: "And again crying out in a loud voice, Jesus gave up the *pneuma*. And, behold, the curtain of the temple was torn in two from top to bottom. And the earth shook and the rocks were split, and the tombs were opened and many bodies of the holy ones who had fallen asleep were raised. And, coming out of the tombs after [Jesus's] resurrection, they entered into the holy city and appeared to many people" (Matt. 27:50–53). This story, unique to Matthew's Gospel, suggests that the precise moment of Jesus's death results not only in the torn curtain of the temple, which Mark mentions (Mark 15:37–38), but also in an earthquake that cracks open both rocks and tombs and, most notably, in the revivification of numerous corpses.[57] Incidentally, Matthew's depiction suggests that while the corpses come back to life at the moment of Jesus's death, they only exit their tombs three days later. Matthew does not tell his readers what they did in the interim.[58]

In the death of Jesus, people who had apparently become irreversibly impure in death were raised and therefore set on the path to purity. Priestly language and concepts run throughout Matthew's story. The deceased were themselves holy but dwelled in a place of impurity. And Jesus's death, the moment when the forces of impurity appeared to overwhelm Jesus himself, results in the holy ones undergoing the first step toward purification while in their tombs and then coming out of these places of impurity in order to enter into the holy city of Jerusalem. Jens Herzer helpfully notes that Matthew's Gospel elsewhere refers to the tombs of dead prophets and righteous people, tombs toward which the Pharisees and scribes showed great honor (Matt. 23:29–33).[59] According to Matthew 23, though, the Pharisees and scribes were the offspring of those who murdered the prophets and righteous. The holy ones whom God raised at Jesus's death, then, may be those unjustly murdered by their fellow kinspeople. Jesus's own unjust death at the hands of his compatriots unexpectedly results in the revivification of Israel's holy martyrs. What this raising of the holy ones signifies is that Jesus's own martyrdom is more efficacious than the death of these earlier holy ones. Matthew, consequently, presents life-giving power still connected to Jesus even in his death.

57. The first-century BCE Roman poet Virgil claims that at the death of Caesar Augustus there was darkness and an earthquake that destroyed many graves (*Georgica* 1.466–97). Were ancient readers to connect Matthew's depiction of Jesus's death to Virgil's depiction of Caesar's death, they would note one striking difference: Jesus's death results not only in miraculous portents but also in life to the dead.

58. Dale C. Allison Jr. describes the passage as "a piece of primitive Christian tradition based upon Ezek. 37:1–14 and Zech. 14:4–5" (*End of the Ages*, 45–46), while Timothy Wardle shows the way in which the passage can be read in light of Isa. 52:1–2 ("Resurrection and the Holy City").

59. Herzer, "Riddle of the Holy Ones," 152–53. Note also the resurrection of the holy ones in *1 Enoch* 51.2.

What is most shocking about this portrayal is that at the very moment that the forces of impurity seem to have finally beaten Jesus, at the precise instant that Jesus becomes a corpse and presumably a source of corpse contamination, holy power emanates out of him and into the abode of death—tombs—to snatch away bodies who were themselves sources of ritual impurity. Whereas corpses usually emit some miasma of impurity, Jesus's corpse appears to emit a miasma of holy power that selectively revivifies long-dead saints. This holy discharge is wide-ranging, traveling from Jesus's corpse at Golgotha to and through Jerusalem. It is also unspeakably powerful, reaching deep into the bowels of death to give life to those who have been long dead. Matthew narrates in dramatic fashion how Jesus's crucifixion is ultimately a victory over death itself.

While Matthew relates no further instances of Jesus interacting with corpses, he does transmit a lengthy polemical speech in which Jesus castigates the scribes and Pharisees for what he calls hypocrisy: "Woe to you, scribes and Pharisees, hypocrites! For you are like plastered tombs, which appear beautiful on the outside, but are full of the bones of the dead and of all impurity on the inside" (Matt. 23:27). Matthew's Jesus alludes to the common Jewish practice of whitewashing tombs to set them apart from their surroundings so that people would not unwittingly walk among or upon them,[60] thereby unknowingly becoming corpse impure. He denounces his opponents for not being what they seem. They appear pure and righteous on the outside—white as snow—yet they are actually full of impurities due to their lawlessness—that is, their moral impurity (Matt. 23:28). He does not criticize the Pharisees for being punctilious observers of the law, or "legalists" as Protestant theology often calls them; rather, he censures their hypocrisy and their *lack* of lawful, righteous living. The Pharisees simply are not righteous enough according to Jesus.[61]

In order to illustrate his accusation regarding the moral impurity of the Pharisees, Jesus uses ritual purity practices associated with corpses. But one should not conclude from Matthew's metaphorical use of corpse impurity that he has abandoned the literal meaning of corpse impurity. Previously Israel's prophets had used the language of ritual impurity to illustrate Israel's sins (e.g., Lam. 1:17; Ezek. 36:17; Zech. 13:1) without intending to diminish the significance of ritual impurity itself. The indictment assumes that those reading Matthew's Gospel know and probably even observe this custom. For

---

60. See Mishnah, *Sheqalim* 1.1; Mishnah, *Ma'aser Sheni* 5.1; Mishnah, *Mo'ed Qatan* 1.2.
61. Compare the similar claim in Matt. 5:20, as well as the discussion of Thiessen, "Abolishers of the Law."

the metaphor to succeed, one must assume, as does Matthew's Jesus, that tombs truly convey ritual impurity.

Matthew, then, both retains and adds to the material on corpse contamination found in Mark's Gospel. Like Mark, Matthew does not suggest that Jesus has rejected the ritual purity legislation pertaining to corpses. Rather, both Jesus's words and his deeds demonstrate his indebtedness to this system of thought.

Jesus and Corpses in Luke's Gospel

Luke, as I have noted above, preserves Mark's story of Jairus's daughter, but he omits Matthew's startling story about the dead being raised at the precise moment of Jesus's death. Nonetheless, he adds one additional story about Jesus encountering a corpse:

> And shortly after, [Jesus] went into a city called Nain, and his disciples and a large crowd went with him. As he came near to the gate of the city, a man who had died was being carried out—this man was the only son of his mother, who was herself a widow. And a large crowd from the city was with her. And seeing her, the Lord had compassion upon her and said to her, "Do not weep." And he came and touched the bier, and those who carried it stood still. And he said, "Young man, I say to you, arise!" And the dead man sat up and began to speak. And Jesus gave him to his mother. And fear seized all, and they were glorifying God, saying: "A great prophet has arisen among us!" and "God has visited his people!" And this word concerning him went out into the whole of Judea and the entire surrounding area. (Luke 7:11–17)

Many of my earlier remarks regarding Jairus's daughter are equally applicable to Luke's account of the young dead man. But here, unlike in the case of Jairus's daughter, Jesus *inadvertently* encounters a dead body. Amplifying the pathos of the situation, Luke informs his readers that the dead man was young and was the only son of his widowed mother. His death, therefore, has left his mother without any immediate male supporters. For this reason, Luke stresses that Jesus has compassion on the woman. But such compassion is not, contrary to what many Christian readers think, something Luke intends to contrast with legalism; rather, it is the fulfillment of the Jewish law, which repeatedly emphasizes care for the widow.[62]

---

62. See Exod. 22:22; Deut. 10:18; 24:19–21; 27:19; Job 24:21; 31:16–18; Pss. 94:6; 146:9; Isa. 1:17; Jer. 7:6; 22:3; Ezek. 22:7; Zech. 7:10; Mal. 3:5; Sir. 35:17; *2 Enoch* 42.9; *4 Ezra* 2.20. Such laws have ancient Near Eastern precedents as well. For instance, *Laws of Ur-Namma* (LU) Prologue: "I did not deliver the orphan to the rich. I did not deliver the widow to the mighty"

As in Mark 5, Jesus appears to contract ritual impurity. But unlike in Mark 5, Luke's Jesus does not touch the corpse, only the bier upon which the corpse lies. He then speaks to the corpse: "Young man, I say to you, arise!" Jesus's contact with the bier and his words to the man are enough to bring him back from the dead. In fact, the man comes to life and has enough *pneuma* in him to begin to speak immediately. So powerful is the holiness within Jesus that even his indirect contact with the corpse through the bier suffices to bring a young man back to full life.

Consequently, the details of Luke's story magnify Jesus's power over death. In Mark, Jesus was on the way to heal a girl who was on the verge of death; Mark's story implies that Jesus raised the girl from the dead just after she died. Matthew's rewriting of the same story pushes the girl's death slightly further into the past; her father approaches Jesus only after she has died. Nonetheless, Jesus still encounters her corpse while it rests in the house, and only shortly after her death. Luke's story of the raising of the young girl follows Mark in depicting her as dying shortly before Jesus's arrival (Luke 8:40–42). But in the story of the young man, the man has been dead for some time, since Jesus encounters his corpse as it is being moved for burial. Further, unlike in the account of Jairus's daughter in all three Synoptic Gospels, Jesus does not need to touch this corpse to bring it back to life. And even though the powers of death have had considerable time to destroy the body of the young man, Jesus is able to call him back to health and life.

Luke contains one final story that impinges upon our understanding of Jesus's view of corpse impurity: the story commonly known as the parable of the good Samaritan. Here the story does not detail Jesus's actions as they relate to corpses, but it does signify Luke's depiction of Jesus's teachings that relate to this form of impurity. When a legal expert asks Jesus what he must do to inherit eternal life, Jesus responds by asking the man what the law states. This response demonstrates that, for Luke, Jesus acknowledges the law's authority in addressing such questions. The man replies by quoting both Deuteronomy 6:5 and Leviticus 19:18: "You shall love Yhwh your God with all your heart, and with all your soul, and with all your strength, and with all your mind, and [you shall love] your neighbor as yourself." Luke has taken a story from Mark and Matthew in which Jesus provides this answer (Mark 12:28–34; Matt. 22:34–40; in both accounts the man approves of Jesus's answer) and instead puts these words in the mouth of Jesus's interlocutor.

(trans. Roth, *Law Collections from Mesopotamia*). See also Hallo, *Context of Scripture*, 1:100 (1.43), where the high steward Rensi is described as a father to the orphan, a husband to the widow, and a brother to the rejected woman.

Luke's Jesus agrees with the man's answer, but the man asks a follow-up question about Leviticus 19:18: "Who is my neighbor?" To answer this question, Jesus tells a story about a priest, a Levite, and a Samaritan, who all encounter a man lying on the side of the road. Beaten and robbed, the man appears to be dead. The priest and the Levite, both of whom were on their way down to Jericho from the city of Jerusalem (that is, they were not going up to the temple in Jerusalem but moving away from it!), cross to the other side of the road and leave the man unattended. In contrast, a Samaritan man approaches him, tends to his wounds, and then pays for his stay in an inn while he convalesces.

This story has engendered numerous Christian attacks upon Judaism, the temple, and the ritual purity system.[63] Surely, so the thinking behind such polemics goes, this story demonstrates that Jews, perhaps especially the priestly and religious elite, have interpreted the law in such a way that it discourages them from pursuing actions of compassion and mercy. Of course, this story *is* about the proper interpretation of the law, but it does not pit compassion against law observance. As Richard Bauckham observes, "Jesus is here represented by Luke as engaged in the kind of discussion about the correct interpretation of the law which was a normal feature of discussion among religious teachers in first-century Judaism."[64] But this is precisely the point: the entire narrative stresses the way that Luke's Jesus believes himself to be adhering to the Jewish law.

But the Jewish law, like any legal code, contains potential interpretive issues that might complicate proper application. In the first century BCE, for instance, the Roman lawyer and politician Cicero acknowledged this legal quandary: "A controversy arises from a conflict of laws when two or more laws seem to disagree."[65] What happens when obedience to one law results in the breaking of another law? How does one adjudicate between the two laws to determine which should be kept and which should be broken? Cicero answers this question in the following way: "In the first place, then, one should

63. For some of these derogatory depictions, see A.-J. Levine, *Misunderstood Jew*, 144–49, and A.-J. Levine, *Short Stories by Jesus*, 71–106.

64. Bauckham, "Scrupulous Priest," 475–76. Contrary to Amy-Jill Levine (*Misunderstood Jew*, 145; *Short Stories by Jesus*, 93), Bauckham asserts that this story is also about ritual impurity, even though Jesus says nothing explicit about it: "Commentators who refuse to acknowledge that a purity issue is at stake because purity is not specifically mentioned in the parable have failed to enter imaginatively the first-century Jewish world, in which confronting a priest with a dying man on a deserted road could scarcely fail to raise the issue of corpse-defilement for any informed hearer" ("Scrupulous Priest," 477). My treatment here is dependent on Bauckham's fine article.

65. Cicero, *On Invention* 2.49.144.

compare the laws by considering which one deals with the most important matters, that is, the most expedient, honourable or necessary. The conclusion from this is that if two laws (or whatever number there may be if more than two) cannot be kept because they are at variance, the one is thought to have the greatest claim to be upheld which has reference to the greatest matter."[66]

A couple of more general moral examples: Should one steal food in order to feed one's starving family? Would it be right to lie in order to protect someone from being murdered? Cicero's answer would suggest that the weightier matters (preservation of life, in these cases) take precedence over the lighter ones. We see this legal logic at work at Qumran. For instance, some texts address the question of whether a corpse-impure person ought to undergo the final water purification if the seventh day happens to fall on a Sabbath. Their legal answer: no.[67] Later rabbis also frequently ask such questions. For example, does one set aside the Sabbath in order to circumcise a male infant on the eighth day after his birth in accordance with Genesis 17:12–14 and Leviticus 12:3? Their legal answer: yes.

In the case of Jesus's story, the conflict arises due to two laws. As noted above, according to priestly literature, priests were prohibited from contracting corpse impurity from anyone but the closest family members: a mother, a father, a son, a daughter, a brother, and a virgin sister (Lev. 21:1–3; cf. Ezek. 44:25). This prohibition meant that a priest could not touch, bury, or attend the funeral of a dead person, apart from close blood relatives. But according to Deuteronomy 21:23, when a person's body is hung from a tree, it must be buried on that same day. In later Jewish thinking, this commandment was understood to imply that one must bury the dead on the day of their death. Thus, as observed above, Tobit finds and apparently personally buries murdered Israelites whose bodies had been abandoned without burial (Tob. 1:17–19; 2:3–9; 12:12–13). And in the first century CE, Josephus notes that Moses commanded Jews not to let anyone lie unburied, a claim that Philo also makes.[68]

In exceptionally rare circumstances these two divine commandments might come into conflict, a situation that Luke's Jesus constructs in his answer to the lawyer. Given the commandment to bury the dead, what was a priest to do if he discovered a neglected corpse in need of burial? Should he contract corpse impurity in order to bury the dead body in obedience both to this reading of Deuteronomy 21:23 and to the priestly command to love one's

66. Cicero, *On Invention* 2.49.145.
67. 4Q251 1–2 6; 4Q265 6 5–6.
68. Josephus, *Against Apion* 2.211; Philo, *Hypothetica* 7.7.

neighbor (Lev. 19:18)? Or should he avoid the corpse and corpse contamination in obedience to the legislation of Leviticus 21:1–3? For that matter, what was a priest to do if he discovered a body that, as in Jesus's story, might or might not be a corpse? Should he risk corpse impurity on the off chance that the person is still alive and could be saved? This is the legal conundrum that Jesus's story assumes.

Both choices, contracting impurity in order to bury the dead (and thus showing love to one's neighbor) and priestly avoidance of corpse impurity, are aspects of law observance. In fact, both commandments spring from priestly literature: the love commandment from Leviticus 19:18 and the prohibition against priests contracting corpse impurity from Leviticus 21:1–3. Given this (presumably infrequent) situation, which law should be observed and which should be set aside? How does one obey God and God's law in such a situation? As Bauckham again argues, "Resolving such cases by deciding which law takes precedence in no way implies that a law is invalid or can be ignored. It is a necessary task in the interpretation of the law. The parable is thus inviting its audience to make an halakhic [that is, legal] judgment."[69]

Regarding this judgment, Bauckham suggests that there are three possibilities for what the Jews of Jesus's (or Luke's) day might have concluded:

1. All Jews believed that a priest should avoid corpse impurity in such a situation.

2. All Jews believed that a priest should contract corpse impurity to bury the man.

3. Jews debated which law took precedence in this situation.[70]

He proceeds to argue that while we do not have evidence from the Second Temple period, early rabbinic literature helps us answer this question. The

---

69. Bauckham, "Scrupulous Priest," 480.

70. Amy-Jill Levine argues that Levites did not need to follow Lev. 21:1–3 and that the Levite in Luke's story therefore cannot be concerned about contracting corpse impurity (*Short Stories by Jesus*, 92–93). This may be, but I know of no Second Temple or early rabbinic text that makes this issue clear one way or another. In fact, the Mishnah claims that when Herod Agrippa came to the temple court, the Levites began to sing (Mishnah, *Bikkurim* 3.4; cf. *Pesahim* 5.7; *Sukkah* 5.2; *Middot* 1.1). Thus, while Lev. 21 does not specifically address Levites, any Levites who functioned as cultic personnel (and not all did) might have been under the same sorts of restrictions with regard to corpses as regular priests. If they were required to serve in sacred space in their capacity as Levites, they likely observed the same regulations pertaining to impurity. Finally, Mishnah, *Nega'im* 14.4 notes that both Nazirites (Num. 6:18) and Levites (Num. 8:7) are required to shave (admittedly, those with *lepra* need to as well). Perhaps from this shared requirement, some Jews concluded that Levites needed to avoid corpses just like Nazirites were commanded (Num. 6:6–7). See the similar argument of Sanders, *Jewish Law*, 56–57.

Mishnah, for instance, addresses the question of the *Mēt Mitzvah*, the rabbinic term for the law pertaining to an unburied and neglected corpse. The assumption of this law is that Jews *must* as a rule contract corpse impurity to attend to a neglected corpse. But it also acknowledges that such a law conflicts with the law that prohibits high priests from contracting corpse impurity on behalf of anyone, including close relatives (Lev. 21:11; cf. 21:1–3), and the law that prohibits the person who has taken a Nazirite vow from contracting corpse impurity even for a close family member (Num. 6:6–7). It therefore envisages a similar situation to the one that Luke's Jesus sets up. What should a high priest or a Nazirite do if they happen upon an unburied, abandoned corpse? The rabbis imagine the following scenario: "And they [that is, a high priest and a Nazirite] are walking on a road and they find a neglected corpse . . ."[71] What should be done? The rabbis appear divided. According to the Mishnah, Rabbi Eliezer, a first-century CE rabbi, claims that the high priest should defile himself but that the Nazirite should not.[72] In contrast, the Sages claim that the Nazirite should contract corpse impurity but that the high priest should not.[73] The later commentary on this passage asserts that Eliezer and the Sages differ on which of the two is supposed to defile himself in the (highly unlikely!) event that the two men are walking together and stumble upon an unburied corpse. What this later commentary suggests, then, is that earlier rabbis agreed that the Nazirite and the high priest were to defile themselves in such a situation *if* they were alone. But if they were together, there was a debate about which of the two men ought to defile himself so that the other person might remain in a state of purity and holiness.[74] In other words, the question really revolves around whose state of purity takes precedence in such an unlikely event.

This rabbinic debate is of relevance for Jesus's story, for it assumes one central thing: both lay Israelites and regular priests *must* defile themselves in order to bury such a corpse. This is precisely the scenario that Luke's Jesus presents in his story. Neither the priest nor the Levite is a high priest or a Nazirite, so according to the (later) legal argumentation of the rabbis, they are obligated to defile themselves (a) to check if the man is alive and (b) to bury him if he is not. This legal opinion probably existed at the time that

71. Mishnah, *Nazir* 7.1.
72. Cf. Babylonian Talmud, *Megillah* 3b; Babylonian Talmud, *Zevahim* 100a.
73. Cf. Mishnah, *Nazir* 6.5.
74. Babylonian Talmud, *Nazir* 47b. An exception to this view (that the high priest or Nazirite must defile himself on behalf of the unburied dead): if the high priest would have to neglect circumcision or the offering of the paschal lamb, two laws that stipulate that lack of observance results in being cut off from Israel, then he must not defile himself for the dead (Babylonian Talmud, *Nazir* 48b).

Luke wrote his Gospel, but we cannot know how widespread such an interpretation was. It is possible (although far from certain) that the Sadducees or the Qumran community held a different legal position on this question.[75] Again, we see here the importance of acknowledging that Jews disagreed with one another at times on how to interpret and live out the Jewish law. Luke's Jesus enters into this debate with his own position: he sets love of neighbor, as shown by one's concern to bury neglected corpses, over the requirement that a priest not defile himself for the dead. Or put differently, Jesus argues that the laws of Leviticus 19:18 and Deuteronomy 21:23 take legal precedence over the law of Leviticus 21:1–3.

While the rabbis do not explicitly connect the commandment to bury the dead to the commandment to love one's neighbor, other rabbinic texts stress that the call to love one's neighbor in Leviticus 19:18 is the greatest principle of the law. For instance, in the late first or early second century CE (if we can trust later rabbinic claims), Rabbi Akiva avers that Leviticus 19:18 is the greatest principle of the law.[76] In fact, both Luke and Mark actually portray other first-century Jews agreeing that the love of neighbor was one of the two most important commandments in the Jewish law (Luke 10:27; Mark 12:32–33).[77] But such legal argumentation shows, contrary to what some Christian interpreters think, that Jesus does not attack some sort of Jewish legalism here. Again, Bauckham puts it well: "In helping the wounded man he is obeying the commandment. His compassion is not some kind of alternative to legalism; it is what the commandment to love one's neighbour requires of him."[78]

Such a story, which emphasizes Jesus's preference for neighbor love over concern about a priest contracting corpse impurity for a stranger, has no doubt given rise to Christian claims that compassion or love of neighbor is opposed to ritual impurity. But it would be a rare instance in which such laws

75. See the suggestion of Mann, "Jesus and the Sadducean Priests."

76. *Sifra Leviticus* 19.18; *Genesis Rabbah* 24.7; and Jerusalem Talmud, *Nedarim* 9.3–4. For other efforts to distill the 613 commandments of the law of Moses to one (or a few) principles, see Babylonian Talmud, *Makkot* 24a; *Berakhot* 63a; and *Shabbat* 31a.

77. Dale C. Allison Jr. states, "That the New Testament cites the pivotal verse of Lev. 19, the famous 19:18, more than any other line from the Torah, surely suggests the chapter's popularity. Jewish sources likewise favor this encapsulating commandment" (*Constructing Jesus*, 352). He points to numerous early texts in support of this claim: Sir. 13:15; *Jubilees* 7.20; 20.2; 36.4, 8; *Damascus Document* VI, 20; 1QS V, 25; *Testament of Reuben* 6.9; *Testament of Issachar* 5.2; *Testament of Gad* 4.2; *Testament of Benjamin* 3.3–4; Matt. 5:43; 19:10; Mark 12:31, 33; Rom. 12:9; 13:9; Gal. 5:14; James 2:8; *Gospel of Thomas* 25; *Didache* 1.2; *Gospel of the Nazarenes* fragment 16; *Sibylline Oracles* 8.481. On the love command, see now Akiyama, *Love of Neighbour*.

78. Bauckham, "Scrupulous Priest," 486. Again, see Fredriksen, "Compassion Is to Purity."

would conflict. Beyond that, as I have reiterated throughout this book, the ritual purity system is animated by compassion and neighbor love—priestly literature excludes impure people from sacred spaces in order to protect their lives, not to ruin or hurt them. The purity system itself, at least as many Jews conceived of it, aimed to preserve what is holy (life) and to limit the forces of impurity (death).

What is more, the Samaritan's actions result in less ritual impurity not more. In Jesus's story, a priest or Levite who contracts corpse contamination in order to see whether the man is still alive does so with the result that he either (a) preserves the life of the beaten man and therefore saves the world from one more corpse and its concomitant, never-ending ability to pollute or (b) buries the man's remains, thereby honoring and loving the dead man, and marks the burial site so that other people do not unwittingly contract corpse contamination. Either scenario inevitably leads to *less* corpse impurity. This outcome is something that scholars have not previously observed. Exercising compassion does not undermine the ritual purity system; it ultimately confirms it. This story, like the previous stories discussed in this chapter, essentially raises a source of ritual impurity from the dead back to life, enabling these people to enter into a state of ritual purity. In Jesus's case, actual corpses come back to life. In the story of the priest, Levite, and Samaritan, the Samaritan saves the beaten man from certain death and raises a soon-to-be corpse back to life and health again.[79]

79. The Gospels of Matthew and Luke attribute a saying to Jesus that relates to death, although not to the impurity caused by death: "Another of his disciples said to him, 'Lord, first let me go and bury my father.' But Jesus said to him, 'Follow me, and let the dead bury their own dead'" (Matt. 8:21–22). Luke modifies this story in two ways. First, he does not call the man one of Jesus's disciples, since the man does not actually follow Jesus. Second, Luke's Jesus adds to the command to let the dead bury the dead by stipulating that this person should go and proclaim the kingdom of God (Luke 9:56–60). But as I have mentioned, two scriptural precedents suggest that certain people should not contract corpse impurity even for a father: the high priest and the Nazirite (Lev. 21:11; Num. 6:7). In both instances, the holiness of the high priest and the holiness of the Nazirite preclude them from tending to the dead and assume that others will bury the dead. This saying of Jesus likewise assumes that others will bury the dead. It is possible, then, that Matthew and Luke intend to depict Jesus extending this heightened state of holiness to those who follow him. While Matthew does not make it explicit, Luke suggests that the action of proclaiming the kingdom of God is more important than burying one's father. Whereas later rabbis claim that tending to the dead takes precedence over saying the Shema and possibly over all other duties of the Torah, Jesus's argument suggests that some duties are more important than even burying one's deceased father. In other words, Jesus makes a halakhic argument. One would need to accept two premises here to find Jesus's logic convincing: (1) that he and his followers were correct about the kingdom of God and (2) that proclaiming this kingdom took precedence over burying one's father.

Interestingly, the Mishnah states that a *ḥaber*, a rabbinic colleague, should not pollute himself on account of the dead (Mishnah, *Demai* 2.3). This statement makes no room for provisions,

The Gospel of John and the Revivification of Lazarus

Although the majority of this book examines the Synoptic Gospels, it is important to consider Jesus's raising of Lazarus in John 11. Unlike the Synoptic Gospels, the Gospel of John makes no mention of Jesus healing those suffering *lepra* or those enduring an impurity due to genital discharges. And on Jesus's treatment of demons—what the Synoptic writers at times refer to as impure *pneumata*—John also remains silent. The fact that John does not deal with any of these sources of impurity might suggest that he has abandoned all concern for ritual impurities—except for the story of Jesus raising Lazarus from the dead.

Given the considerable differences between the Gospel of John and the Synoptic Gospels, scholars have long debated whether John knew of these other Gospels. While one's position on this question does not affect the interpretation of the story of Lazarus, I am convinced that John knew one or more of the Synoptic Gospels[80] and believe his account of the raising of Lazarus heightens the already considerable drama of the previously discussed resuscitations. First, Lazarus has been dead for some time and has been buried in the tomb for three days (John 11:17); he has been dead three days longer than the young man in Luke 7. John stresses this fact, for when Jesus demands that the tombstone be rolled back, Martha emphasizes the length that Lazarus has already been dead—his body will be giving off the unpleasant odor of a decomposing corpse (John 11:39). It is possible that John wants the reader to conclude that Lazarus's soul has now departed his body, as evidenced by the decaying state of his body. Such a belief is attested in later rabbinic literature, which states that in the late third century CE, Rabbi Levi argued that the soul of a person hovers near the body after death for three days. But after three days the body begins to disintegrate, and the soul leaves the body.[81] Second, unlike the young girl, whom Jesus touches directly, and the young man, with whom Jesus makes contact via the bier, John portrays Jesus standing at a considerable distance from the dead body of Lazarus. Consequently, it would be impossible for Jesus to contract corpse impurity in this account. Further, Jesus's words alone ("Lazarus, come out!") bring the dead man back to life (11:43–44).

---

such as for the death of one's close family member, and is therefore similar to Jesus's statement. For some rabbis at least, the duty of studying Torah takes precedence over care for the dead. Ultimately, what these debates and statements pertain to is not whether the Jewish law should be obeyed or broken but how to order the various laws that make up the Jewish law rightly.

80. The classic statement against John's knowledge of the Synoptic Gospels remains Gardner-Smith, *St. John and the Synoptic Gospels*. But see the various arguments in Denaux, *John and the Synoptics*, and Keith, "'If John Knew Mark.'"

81. *Leviticus Rabbah* 18.1.

John, too, portrays a Jesus that, in one instance, encounters someone who is ritually impure. Intentionally or otherwise, then, John builds upon trends seen in both Matthew and Luke: Jesus's power over death traverses both space and time. The dead, buried, and even decaying body of Lazarus is still subject to the holy power of Jesus, who is able to call this person out of death and into life, out of impurity into purity.

Jewish Antecedents to Jesus's Treatment of Corpses

The story of the raising of Jairus's daughter depends upon two stories about Elijah and Elisha. In the first, the prophet Elijah brings back to life the son of the widow of Zarephath (1 Kings 17:17–24), while in the second, Elisha raises the son of a Shunammite woman (2 Kings 4:32–37). In fact, both stories stress that Elijah and Elisha make extensive contact with the corpses of these young boys. Elijah lies on top of the boy three times, while Elisha lies upon the Shunammite's son once and places his mouth, eyes, and hands upon the mouth, eyes, and hands of the corpse. Such close contact results in both boys coming back to life. Clearly neither Elijah nor Elisha worried about contracting corpse impurity. And the author tells us nothing about whether they undergo ritual purification after this physical contact.[82]

Both prophets represent powerful forces of life that contest death. In fact, Elisha's power is so contagious that even in death he reaches out to heal. According to 2 Kings 13, some Israelites were burying one of their dead when a band of Moabites attacked. In their haste to escape, the Israelite men cast the dead man into the grave of Elisha, where his corpse comes into contact with Elisha's bones. Upon touching Elisha's bones, the dead man returns to life. This story is rather surprising, since nothing within priestly legislation (or anything else in Jewish scriptures) suggests that a corpse can give life to another corpse. Nonetheless, neither any ancient Jew nor any modern commentator interprets this story to suggest that the author of 2 Kings has rejected the ritual purity system. Whatever the precise meaning of these peculiar stories, no one concludes that their author (or Elijah or Elisha) intended to abolish the ritual purity system or the temple cult. But if Elijah's and Elisha's behavior elicit no such interpretation, why do so many scholars understand Jesus's similar actions to suggest such an abolishment of the ritual purity legislation? The answer appears to be that modern Christian presuppositions constrain our thinking about what Jesus and his earliest followers must have thought about ritual impurity.

82. One could also point to the priest/prophet Ezekiel, whom God brings into the heart of the valley of corpse remains (Ezek. 37).

Conclusion

All four Gospels contain accounts of Jesus interacting with corpses. These writers include these stories because they want to portray Jesus overcoming death in a way that anticipates his own resurrection from the dead. Yet the writers of these Gospels and their initial readers inhabited a world that almost universally perceived corpses to be defiling. In Jewish ritual purity thinking, corpses were the strongest sources of defilement, conveying impurity not only through contact but also through proximity, whether in a structure or through overhang. And the impurity that corpses conveyed was both long-lasting (seven days) and itself contagious to others. Unlike modern readers, ancient readers who encountered these stories of Jesus raising the dead would have naturally thought about them within the context of ritual impurity.

Mark and Luke portray Jesus raising a girl by taking her by the hand and calling her back to life shortly after she has died. Matthew also portrays Jesus raising this girl, although in Matthew's retelling, the girl has been dead for a slightly longer period of time. In Luke's account of the widow's son, even more time intervenes between the young man's death and his encounter with Jesus. Additionally, Jesus does not make direct contact with the corpse, but his holy power moves from the funeral bier, which he touches, into the man's corpse. In this way, Jesus's power is infectious even at a distance, just like a corpse's pollution infects at a distance. Finally, we see Jesus's holy power emanating from his body and giving life on more than one occasion, even though no physical contact has occurred. In this regard, Jesus's power parallels (and overcomes) a corpse's ability to pollute at a distance. In John, Jesus raises Lazarus even though Lazarus has been dead for days and lies at some physical distance from Jesus. And in Matthew's crucifixion narrative, Jesus's holy power is able to raise the dead, even at the point of his own death—even further removed both physically and chronologically than the corpses in these other stories. Despite the fact that corpse contamination was the strongest form of impurity in Jewish purity thought, the Gospel writers depict Jesus repeatedly overcoming it. The only conclusion that one can draw from such portrayals is that the Gospel writers were convinced that Jesus was a source of holiness that was even more powerful than death itself.

CHAPTER 6

Jesus and Demonic Impurity

The preceding chapters examined Jesus's interactions with those who were ritually impure: those with *lepra*, a woman with a genital discharge, and corpses. With regard to these ritual impurities, Jesus performed deeds of power that are not envisaged in priestly literature but have precedents in depictions of Elijah and Elisha. The Gospel writers, though, portray another form of impurity with which Jesus interacts, but it is one that priestly literature does not discuss: demonic or pneumatic impurity.[1] In order to understand these stories, it will be instructive to look at the demonic in Jewish scriptures, the ancient Near East, early Judaism, and the Greco-Roman world more broadly so that we do not encounter the demons of the Gospels with modern conceptions that distort our understanding of these stories.

The Demonic in Jewish Scriptures

Belief in demons was widespread in the ancient Near East, yet priestly literature makes no explicit mention of their existence or any pollution that is associated with such entities. From this silence Jacob Milgrom argues that although Israel's purity thinking shared many commonalities with other ancient Mesopotamian purity systems, the priests stripped the demonic from their own worldview. In contrast to their surrounding culture, which was pervaded by belief in both malevolent and benevolent entities, Israel's priests demythologized the world. Priestly thinking, according to Milgrom, "posits

---

1. See Kazen, *Jesus and Purity Halakhah*, 300–341.

the existence of one supreme God who contends neither with a higher realm nor with competing peers. The world of demons is abolished; there is no struggle with autonomous foes, because there are none. With the demise of the demons, only one creature remains with 'demonic' power—the human being."[2]

A cursory reading of priestly literature demonstrates that Milgrom is, in general, correct. And yet even within Leviticus, traces of the demonic linger. Most significantly, Yom Kippur, the Day of Atonement, requires the use of two goats, one devoted to Israel's God and one devoted to Azazel (Lev. 16:8, 10, 26). This contrast between Azazel and YHWH might lead one to infer that the legislation of Leviticus 16 views Azazel as some sort of divine being. Further, the text locates Azazel in the wilderness (16:10), a place identified elsewhere as the haunt of demons (e.g., Isa. 13:21; 34:14). Milgrom argues that the goat sent into the wilderness is a relic of a pagan sacrifice to a demon named Azazel, a vestige that the priestly writer demythologizes and incorporates into priestly ritual practices. While this suggestion may be true, it requires us to believe that an originally demonic figure is demythologized in priestly thinking only to be remythologized in later Jewish literature.[3] Additionally, if the priests did not think of Azazel as a demonic figure, it seems ill-advised for them to mention this name within a broader culture that would have. Nonetheless, they did mention it, suggesting that they were not entirely averse to demonology.

The rite of the jealous husband (Num. 5:11–31) may provide further evidence of the demonic in priestly literature, since it contains a procedure in case a *ruaḥ* (spirit) of jealousy incites a husband to suspect his wife of adultery. Whether this *ruaḥ* should be understood in demonic terms is unclear though.[4] So too the rite of the ashes of the red heifer may be based upon an apotropaic effort to defend against the demonic.[5]

On the other hand, Leviticus and Numbers are the literary products of the priestly caste—one particular group of elites in Israel. Milgrom may be

2. Milgrom, *Leviticus: A Book of Ritual and Ethics*, 9. Milgrom here follows the earlier arguments of Kaufmann, *Religion of Israel*, 103–4. For a convincing argument that the priestly writer did not discuss demonology because, like the broader ancient Near East, he did not think that demons threatened the tabernacle or temple, see Cranz, "Priests, Pollution and the Demonic."

3. E.g., *1 Enoch* 8.1; 9.6; 10.4–8; 13.1; 54.5; 4Q203 7 I, 6; *Apocalypse of Abraham* 13.4–9; *3 Enoch* 4.6; *Pirqe Rabbi Eliezer* 46. See Orlov, *Dark Mirrors*.

4. At least in later rabbinic tradition some viewed this *ruaḥ* as demonic and impure (Babylonian Talmud, *Sotah* 3a). But see the treatment of Feinstein, *Sexual Pollution*, 43–47.

5. See Milgrom, *Leviticus 1–16*, 270–78, as well as the later claims of Yoḥanan ben Zakkai in, for instance, *Pesiqta of Rab Kahana* 7.4. Cf. *Pesiqta Rabbati* 14.14; *Numbers Rabbah* 19.8.

correct to conclude that the priests suppressed (or at least did not focus on) the demonic in their expositions of the purity system, but this fact does not mean that all ancient Israelites dissociated purity and impurity from the realm of the demonic.[6]

Outside of priestly literature, Jewish scriptures refer to the existence of demonic beings on a number of occasions. For instance, the Deuteronomistic Historian mentions evil *ruḥot* (spirits) in passing, apparently assuming the existence of and widespread belief in the demonic. In recounting the life of Israel's first king, Saul, the Historian states that after God's *ruaḥ* abandoned Saul, an evil *ruaḥ* came and tormented him (1 Sam. 16:14–23 [Greek: *pneuma*]).[7] This contrast between God's *ruaḥ* and an evil *ruaḥ* indicates a force distinct from Israel's God. While David succeeds in soothing Saul, the evil *ruaḥ* becomes hell-bent on destroying David, compelling Saul to try to kill him (18:10–11, 25; 19:1, 9–17). The narrative makes apparent, nonetheless, that even this oppressive demonic force ultimately serves Israel's God (18:10–11; 19:9–10).

Not only do demons afflict people, but they also deceive them, as the Historian makes clear through the words of the prophet Micaiah: "And YHWH said: 'Who will deceive Ahab so that he will go up and fall at Ramoth-gilead?' . . . Then a *ruaḥ* came forward and stood before YHWH, saying: 'I will deceive him.' And YHWH said to it, 'How?' And it said, 'I will go out and be a lying *ruaḥ* in the mouth of all his prophets.' And [God] said, 'You shall deceive and succeed—go out and do so!'" (1 Kings 22:20–22). This prophetic account of the heavenly throne room portrays God seeking a servant to ensure God's will—to convince King Ahab to go up to Ramoth-gilead to fight against the king of Syria. God intends for Ahab to die through this deceit. A lying *ruaḥ* rushes to do God's bidding, using the false words of Israel's prophets to convince Ahab that God has promised him success in his military venture. The result: Ahab listens to the deceitful words of the *ruaḥ* given voice by the false prophets and goes up to Ramoth-gilead, where he dies in battle. The fact that the Chronicler, who may have been of Levitical or priestly descent, incorporates this same story into his history of Israel (2 Chron. 18:18–23)

6. So too D. Wright, *Disposal of Impurity*, 4. More broadly, Karel van der Toorn concludes, "By comparison with the wealth of documentation on demons from Mesopotamia, the Hebrew Bible has little to offer on demons. This does not imply that the ordinary Israelite was less concerned about the danger of demonic activities than his contemporaries from surrounding cultures" ("Theology of Demons," 62). Van der Toorn examines three texts, (Deut. 32:23–24; Isa. 34:14; Hab. 3:5) that refer to demons known from Mesopotamian literature. Cf. Dietrich, Loretz, and Sanmartín, *Die keilalphabetischen Texte* 1.5 ii 24; 1.14 i 18–19; and 1.15 ii 6.

7. Cf. *Liber antiquitatum biblicarum* 60.1–3; *Psalms Scroll*[a] XXVII, 10.

suggests that at least some of those who were of priestly descent were open to the existence of the demonic.[8]

One final reference to a *ruaḥ* in the Deuteronomistic History bears mentioning. When the Assyrian king Shalmaneser besieges Jerusalem, Isaiah prophesies that God will send a *ruaḥ* to the king so that he will hear rumors of his homeland that will cause him to lift the siege and return home, where he will die (2 Kings 19:7; cf. Isa. 37:7). Each of these stories presents such beings as under the control of God and as attempting to deceive or kill humans. Even as it acknowledges the existence of malevolent divine beings, then, the Deuteronomistic History also emphasizes that they serve Israel's God. Consequently, the work shows the way that the Israelites, priests or otherwise, could, in the words of Milgrom, posit "the existence of one supreme God who contends neither with a higher realm nor with competing peers"[9] *and* believe in the existence of numerous demons. Ultimately, as Paula Fredriksen puts it, ancient monotheism, both Jewish and non-Jewish, "spoke to the imagined architecture of the cosmos, not to its absolute population."[10] Ancient monotheism did not preclude the existence of numerous divine beings; rather, it required only that there be one supreme God who ruled over all other gods.

The evil *ruḥot* of the Deuteronomistic History may shed light on a passage from Zechariah that is of relevance to our discussion of Jesus and the demonic. According to the prophet, God promises the following: "'And on that day,' says Yhwh of hosts, 'I will cut off the names of the idols from the land, so that they will be remembered no more. And I will also remove from the land the prophets and the *ruaḥ* of impurity'" (Zech. 13:2). While it is possible to interpret the phrase "*ruaḥ* of impurity" as referring to an internal human disposition, it is also conceivable that the prophet here envisages some divine malevolent force, a force perhaps associated with the idols he mentions,[11] that Israel's God will purge.[12] If so, the passage demonstrates again that a priest (Zech. 1:1) believed in the demonic.

8. Ralph W. Klein, for instance, suggests that the author was a member of the temple personnel (*1 Chronicles*, 17). I will not wade here into the debate about whether an originally pro-Levitical document was later redacted by a pro-priestly editor (e.g., De Vries, *1 and 2 Chronicles*, 191–96). The point remains: the work is the product of those who labored in the temple.

9. Milgrom, *Leviticus: A Book of Ritual and Ethics*, 9.

10. Fredriksen, "Mandatory Retirement," 241.

11. The LXX translator of Psalms, for instance, seems to identify idols with demons in his decision to translate the Hebrew for "idols" (*elilim*) as *daimonia* (Ps. 95:5 LXX; 96:5 Masoretic Text). Cf. the apostle Paul's remarks in 1 Cor. 8:4–6; 10:18–21.

12. In the first century CE, for instance, Rabbi Eliezer uses this same terminology and contrasts it with the holy *ruaḥ* of God (*Sifre Deuteronomy* 173). See Lange, "Considerations concerning the 'Spirit of Impurity.'" On the larger difficulties surrounding the interpretation of the word *ruaḥ*, see Lilly, "Conceptualizing Spirit."

Demons in the Ancient Near East

As Milgrom notes, Israel's neighbors had a robust demonology. One of the most important demonological works, the sixteen-tablet book known as *Udug-hul* (Evil Demons), shows how early and widespread was the belief that the demonic could possess people. This work contains materials dating from the Old Akkadian (2300–2200 BCE) to the Seleucid period (300–200 BCE), thus demonstrating the long-standing fears that many people in the ancient Near East had of the demonic.[13] For instance, one apotropaic text from this composite work states,

> Do [not say, "let me] stand [at the side]."
> [Go] out, [evil Udug-demon,] to [a distant place],
> [go] away, [evil Ala-demon], to [the desert].[14]

Here we see, like in Leviticus 16, the association between the demonic and the wilderness, as well as a spell to exorcise the demonic presence. Another text portrays the possession of a man and the rite needed to remove the demon from the man's body:

> Go, my son, Asalluhi,
> Pour water in an *anzam*-cup,
> And put in it tamarisk and the innuš-plant.
> (He recited the Eridu [incantation]). Calm the patient, and bring out
>   the censer
> and torch for him,
> so that the Namtar demon existing in a man's body, may depart from it.[15]

Yet another illuminating text describes the nature of the demonic in the following terms:

> Neither males are they, nor females,
> They are winds ever sweeping along,
> They have not wives, engender not children,
> Know not how to show mercy,
> Hear not prayer and supplication.[16]

13. For an overview, see Sorenson, *Possession and Exorcism*, and Geller, *Forerunners to Udug-Hul*. See also Geller, *Evil Demons*.

14. *Udug-hul* 8.73–75, in Geller, *Forerunners*, brackets in the original.

15. *Udug-hul* 7.669–74, in Geller, *Forerunners*, brackets in the original. See *Šurpu* 5.6.1–16, in Reiner, *Šurpu*, which also speaks of demon possession.

16. *Cuneiform Texts from Babylonian Tablets in the British Museum* 16, plate 15, v. 37–46; Jacobsen, *Treasures of Darkness*, 12–13.

We see a similar preoccupation with the demonic in Zoroastrian literature, which is notoriously difficult to date. Later incorporated into the seventy-two-chapter *Yasna*, the seventeen hymns of the *Gathas* portray the dualistic worldview of Zoroastrian thinking:

> Yes, there are two fundamental spirits, twins which are renowned to be in conflict. In thought and in word, in action, they are two: the good and the bad. Furthermore, when these two spirits first came together, they created life and death.[17]

This statement belongs to what scholars believe is the oldest material within the *Yasna*. Importantly, it associates the bad spirit with the creation of death. In a later stratum of the *Yasna* we see an expansion of this thinking:

> I foreswear the company of the wicked Daevas . . . and the followers of Daevas, of demons and the followers of demons, of those who do harm to any being by thoughts, words, acts or outward signs.[18]

Similarly the *Vendidad*, a Zoroastrian compendium on evil spirits that contains material compiled over a wide range of time, claims that *Angra Mainyu*, the destructive spirit, is the source of 99,999 diseases that trouble humanity.[19] Thus the demonic is the font of both disease and death among humanity—a veritable death force opposed to *Ahura Mazda*, the higher spirit, creator, and force of life, whom Zoroastrians worshiped. In a manner comparable to the Israelite priestly thinking discussed in chapter 5, Zoroastrians considered corpses defiling. But in a manner distinct from Israelite priestly literature, Zoroastrian thinking connected corpse impurity to the demon Drug Nasu:

> If a man alone by himself carry a corpse, the Nasu rushes upon him, to defile him, from the nose of the dead, from the eye, from the tongue, from the jaws, from the sexual organs, from the hinder parts. This Drug Nasu falls upon him, [stains him] even to the end of the nails, and he is unclean, thenceforth, forever.[20]

All of these Zoroastrian texts associate the demonic with the realm of impurity and death. A saying preserved in the tenth-century CE work known

---

17. *Yasna* 30.3–4, in Insler, *Gāthās of Zarathustra*.
18. *Yasna* 12.4–5, in Boyce, *Textual Sources*.
19. *Vendidad* 22.2; 2.29.
20. *Vendidad* 3.14, in Darmesteter and Mills, *Zend-Avesta*.

as the *Dēnkard* encapsulates Zoroastrian thinking: "Purity is this: separation from demons."[21] Such a sentiment suggests that although Zoroastrian texts do not refer to demons as impure, the "impure spirit" terminology of Zechariah 13:2 was an apt description of the demonic.

The Demonic in the Greco-Roman World

Almost all ancient Jews thought that demons were malevolent and opposed to both God and humanity. Such a belief, though, was not necessarily the case outside the Jewish world. In *Inventing Superstition*, Dale Martin documents the way people in the Greco-Roman world perceived the demonic. While the philosophers generally viewed demons as benevolent, many people appeared to view them as malicious.[22] Consequently, one must be careful not to introduce a negative meaning of the term into non-Jewish Greco-Roman texts unless the context requires it.

A couple of examples of positive references will suffice. For instance, the fifth-century BCE Greek tragedian Euripides says that the newly deceased Alcestis is now a "blessed *daimōn*."[23] Similarly Plato's *Symposium* preserves the belief that "the whole of the daimonic is between divine and mortal." The belief that these beings exist and bridge the ontological and spatial gap between the gods and humanity was widespread. *Daimones* were thought to be messengers who traversed the heavens and the earth: "Interpreting and transporting human things to the gods and divine things to men; entreaties and sacrifices from below, and ordinances and requitals from above: being midway between, it makes each to supplement the other, so that the whole is combined in one."[24] We see this belief as early as Homer,[25] but Plutarch claims that Hesiod "was the first to set forth clearly and distinctly four classes of rational beings: gods, demigods, heroes, in this order, and last of all, men."[26] Plato claims that the *daimonion* is incapable of falsehood.[27] And Dio Cassius, clearly intending to pay a compliment, asks who is more *daimonic* than Augustus, who is a lower divinity.[28]

21. *Dēnkard* 576, in Choksy, *Purity and Pollution in Zoroastrianism*, 112.

22. Martin, *Inventing Superstition*, x. Likewise Petersen: "No uniform concept of the *daimon* existed in the ancient Greek culture" ("Notion of Demon," 24).

23. Euripides, *Alcestis* 1003.

24. Plato, *Symposium* 202E.

25. Homer, *Iliad* 1.222. See also Aphrodite in *Iliad* 3.420; 5.438–41.

26. Plutarch, *Moralia* 415B–C.

27. Plato, *Republic* 382E.

28. Dio Cassius, *Roman History* 53.8.1.

Plutarch provides what was likely the learned description of the demonic in the first and second centuries CE:

> Plato and Pythagoras and Xenocrates and Chrysippus, following the lead of early writers on sacred subjects, allege [*daimones*] to have been stronger than men and, in their might, greatly surpassing our nature, yet not possessing the divine quality unmixed and uncontaminated, but with a share also in the nature of the soul and in the perceptive faculties of the body, and with a susceptibility to pleasure and pain and to whatsoever other experience is incident to these mutations, and is the source of much disquiet in some and of less in others. For in [*daimones*], as in men, there are diverse degrees of virtue and of vice.[29]

Plutarch's description implies that not all *daimones* are benevolent; like humans, some are more virtuous (or vice ridden) than others. Nonetheless, Plutarch laments the fact that many of his contemporaries viewed the demonic fearfully—as malevolent and destructive superhuman forces. Such a belief he calls *deisidaimonia*—often translated into English as "superstition," though it essentially refers to the fear of the *daimonic* and was clearly widespread enough to draw Plutarch's scorn. In fact, similar mockery occurs much earlier in the fourth or third century BCE in Theophrastus's *Characters*.

Unsurprisingly many of the people who feared demons looked for relief through exorcistic rites, since the connection between the demonic and death was prevalent in the Greco-Roman world.[30] Already in Hesiod we see the belief that *daimones* are the transformed dead men of the golden age who roam upon the earth.[31] Euripides presents Hercules, who has just overcome Death, as boasting, "I closed in conflict with the Lord of [*daimonōn*]."[32] While these beings might not be malevolent, they nevertheless fall under the power of death. Reminiscent of the book of Tobit, a Roman imperial-period inscription blames a demon for the death of a young woman about to be married: "Dorotheos her father buried Theodosia, aged eighteen, his only child and a virgin. She was about to be married (but) on the twentieth day of the month Tybi you took her, evil *daimōn*, you who did not fatefully spin for her a return back (home) as she expected."[33] In his collection of *Sayings of Spartans*, Plutarch recounts a story of a demon haunting a grave

29. Plutarch, *Moralia* 360D–E; cf. 362E.
30. Ferguson, *Demonology*, 41.
31. Hesiod, *Works and Days* 121–39.
32. Euripides, *Alcestis* 1140; cf. 843–44.
33. Horsley and Llewelyn, *New Documents*, 4:221–29.

mound,[34] and a magical papyrus claims that *daimones* dwell in the region of corpses.[35]

This repeated association of death with the demonic developed into one stream of demonology that attributed to demons deadly intentions. Plutarch summarizes this fear in the following way: "Mean and malignant *daimones*, in envy of good men and opposition to their deeds, try to confound and terrify them, causing their virtue to rock and totter, in order that they may not continue erect and inviolate in the path of honour and so attain a better portion after death than themselves."[36] Even Homer, who usually associates the demonic with the benevolently divine, portrays a man lying ill and under demonic attack.[37] In his tragedy the *Persians*, Aeschylus attributes military defeat to "some destructive power or evil demon."[38] Similarly, the fifth-century tragedian Sophocles states that the garment stained with Nessus's blood afflicted Heracles, and he calls this affliction a demon: "It has clung to my sides and eaten away my inmost flesh, and lives with me to devour the channels of my lungs. Already it has drunk my fresh blood, and my whole body is ruined, now that I am mastered by this unspeakable bondage. . . . Again a spasm of torture has burned me, it has darted through my sides, and the ruthless devouring malady seems never to leave me without torment. . . . For again it is feasting on me, it has blossomed, it is launched."[39] The second-century CE geographer Pausanias speaks of the demon of a man who was stoned to death and who returned to kill others.[40] Even Plutarch, who laments the fear of demons, claims that the *daimōn* of Caesar sought revenge upon those who murdered him.[41] While Peter Bolt suggests that "the Stoics generally avoided the δαιμ- [demonic] vocabulary,"[42] any lacuna in Stoic writing on the subject, if Plutarch can be believed, is due more to the vicissitudes of history in preserving Stoic writings than to an actual absence from Stoic thinking. He avers of Stoic thinking, "The philosophic school of Chrysippus thinks that *daimonia* stalk about whom the gods use as executioners and avengers upon unholy and unjust men."[43]

---

34. Plutarch, *Sayings of Spartans* 236D.
35. *Papyri Graecae Magicae* 4.446, in Betz, *Greek Magical Papyri*; cf. 8.81.
36. Plutarch, *Dion* 2.
37. Homer, *Odyssey* 5.396.
38. Aeschylus, *Persians* 354.
39. Sophocles, *Trachiniae* 1053–89.
40. Pausanias, *Description of Greece* 6.6.8.
41. Plutarch, *Caesar* 69.
42. Bolt, "Jesus, the Daimons and the Dead," 80.
43. Plutarch, *Moralia* 277A, alt.

Despite this common belief in the malevolence of demons, we have little evidence of exorcistic or apotropaic efforts to curtail their influence. The best examples come from the *Greek Magical Papyri*, which date from second century BCE to fifth century CE and come from Egypt. One, which will require more careful examination when we turn to Jesus, contains the following spell: "I adjure you [*exorkizō*], *daimōn*, whoever you are. . . . Come out [*exelthe*], *daimōn*, whoever you are, and withdraw from so-and-so, quickly, quickly, now, now. Come out [*exelthe*], *daimōn*, since I fetter you with unbreakable adamantine fetters, and I hand you over into the black chaos into destruction."[44] While we cannot date this text with certainty, we also have the claims of the second-century CE sophist Philostratus, who portrays an exorcism in his biography of Apollonius, a Pythagorean philosopher who lived in the first and early second century CE.[45] Lucian of Samosata also discusses the work of an exorcist:

> "You act ridiculously," said Ion, "to doubt everything. For my part, I should like to ask you what you say to those who free possessed men from their terrors by exorcising the [*daimonōntas*] so manifestly. I need not discuss this: everyone knows about the Syrian from Palestine, the adept in it, how many he takes in hand who fall down in the light of the moon and roll their eyes and fill their mouths with foam; nevertheless, he restores them to health and sends them away normal in mind, delivering them from their straits for a large fee. When he stands beside them as they lie there and asks: 'Whence came you into his body?' the patient himself is silent, but the [*daimōn*] answers in Greek or in the language of whatever foreign country he comes from, telling how and whence he entered into the man; whereupon, by adjuring the [*daimona*] and if he does not obey, threatening him, he drives him out."[46]

This popular-level belief in the malevolence of the demonic contributes to the background of the Gospel writers' portrayals of Jesus, since as Everett Ferguson claims, "An important factor in the Christian success in the Roman world was the promise which it made of deliverance from demons."[47]

Second Temple and Rabbinic Demons

In comparison to ancient Near Eastern and Zoroastrian literature, priestly literature remains circumspect regarding the demonic. But an incipient expan-

44. *Papyri Graecae Magicae* 4.1239–41, 1243–48, in Betz, *Greek Magical Papyri*.
45. Philostratus, *Life of Apollonius* 4.12.
46. Lucian, *The Lover of Lies* 16.
47. Ferguson, *Demonology*, 129.

sion of demonology occurs already in the work of the various LXX translators. For instance, whereas the Hebrew of Psalm 96:5 states that the gods of
the nations are idols (*elilim*), the LXX translator of this verse says that "the
gods of the nations/gentiles are demons" (*daimonia*, Ps. 95:5 LXX). We can
see this same connection between idols and demons in the way that other
LXX translators connect the worship of foreign gods to demons (e.g., Deut.
32:17; Ps. 105:37 LXX; Isa. 65:3).

At the same time, early Jewish writings evince a veritable explosion of
demonology. The book of Tobit, for example, portrays an evil demon named
Asmodeus. According to the author, Asmodeus torments a woman named
Sarah out of jealous love for her by repeatedly killing anyone she marries prior
to the consummation of the marriage (Tob. 3:8).[48] These seven suspicious
deaths lead Sarah's maids to accuse her of being a black widow and drive
her to contemplate suicide. Instead, she prays to God, who sends his angel
Raphael to deliver her from this demonic stalker and to give her in marriage
to Tobias (3:17). Raphael instructs Tobias to burn the heart and liver of a
fish in the bridal chamber so that the resulting incense will drive the demon
away from Sarah. This apotropaic act expels Asmodeus all the way to Egypt,
freeing Sarah and Tobias to consummate their marriage and produce offspring
who will continue their lineage. It is possible that the name of this demon
betrays the author's knowledge of Zoroastrian demonology, since Asmodeus
might be connected to the Persian *Aeshma-daeva*, the demon of rage.[49] If so,
Tobit provides confirmation that Zoroastrian demonology influenced Jewish thinking and perhaps functioned as a catalyst in the outburst of Jewish
demonology. Relatedly, the *Genesis Apocryphon*, which dates to either the
third or early second century BCE, depicts Abraham exorcising the demons
that torment Pharaoh and the Egyptians with plagues after Pharaoh attempts
to take Sarah for his wife.[50]

According to the book of *Jubilees*, after God cleanses the earth of the violence that had built up prior to the flood, Noah realizes that demons continue
to influence his offspring. He warns his sons that he can see demons seducing
them and worries that they will return to their violent ways after his death.[51]
Noah's unease is confirmed shortly thereafter, as impure demons begin to
lead his sons astray from God in order to destroy them. Seeking help, his sons

48. Cf. Babylonian Talmud, *Berakhot* 54b.
49. So Haupt, "Asmodeus." On Asmodeus within the narrative of Tobit, see Owens, "Asmodeus." Later rabbinic literature demonstrates knowledge of the burning of incense to drive
demons away but condemns the practice (Babylonian Talmud, *Sanhedrin* 65a).
50. *Genesis Apocryphon* XX.
51. *Jubilees* 7.26.

report that these demons are deceiving them, blinding them, and killing their sons.[52] After Noah beseeches God to deliver them from demonic oppression, God responds by binding the majority of the demons, but he leaves one-tenth of them to Mastema, the prince of demons.[53] Although God has curtailed their activities, they remain bent on destroying humanity: "And the prince, Mastema, acted forcefully. . . . And he sent other spirits to those who were set under his hand to practice all error and sin and all transgression, to destroy, to cause to perish and to pour out blood upon the earth."[54]

In the prologue to *Jubilees*, Moses prays that the spirit of Beliar would not rule over Israel but that God would give the Israelites an upright and holy spirit.[55] This contrast between the spirit of Beliar and a *holy* spirit likewise suggests that the forces of Beliar are impure. The author may have considered these demons to be impure because they were the hybrid offspring of angels and humans. As Loren Stuckenbruck observes, "Giants, precisely *because they are composite creatures*, the products of a union between angels and human women, are inherently corrupt or impure."[56] This innate impurity, then, is comparable to the innate impurity of certain animals in Jewish thinking.[57]

The "Book of Watchers," now preserved in *1 Enoch*, contains a similarly expansive demonology. According to the author the sexual relations between the watchers of heaven (that is, angels) and women result in the birth of giants.[58] This mixture between heavenly and terrestrial beings, an offensive transgression of cosmic boundaries, leads to mutant offspring who turn to violence against humans and animals, consuming even blood.[59] At their death, these violent giants turn into evil spirits and continue in their violent behavior toward all: "The spirits of the giants oppress each other; they will corrupt, fall, be excited, and fall upon the earth, and cause sorrow. They eat no food, nor become thirsty, nor find obstacles. And these spirits shall rise up against the

---

52. *Jubilees* 10.1–2.
53. *Jubilees* 10.9.
54. *Jubilees* 11.5.
55. *Jubilees* 1.20–23.
56. Stuckenbruck, "Giant Mythology and Demonology," 335, emphasis original. See also VanderKam, "Demons in the Book of *Jubilees*." Such thinking would fit with earlier Mesopotamian conceptions of the demons as the misformed spawn of the god of heaven, fit neither for heaven nor for earth. As van der Toorn states, "Demons are cosmological accidents, anomalous births, the misfits of creation. Their inherently evil nature is a moral defect, congenital, all the more terrifying because of the combination with supernatural powers" ("Theology of Demons," 68).
57. So too Wahlen, *Jesus and the Impurity of Spirits*, 36.
58. *1 Enoch* 7.2; 9.8–9; 15.3–4; cf. Gen. 6:1–4; *Jubilees* 5.1.
59. *1 Enoch* 7.3–5; cf. Gen. 9:4.

children of the people and against the women, because they have proceeded forth (from them)."[60]

The original angels who cohabited with women, while not called "evil spirits" or "demons," surely belong within this realm; the "Book of Parables" lists these fallen angels, along with their various crimes against humanity. For instance, Yeqon and Asb'el were the cause of the angelic descent and commingling with women; Gader'el taught humans the "blows of death" and gave them weaponry; Pinem'e taught humans to write, a skill that the author believes is the cause of mortality; and Kasadya taught humans how to abort fetuses, among other things.[61]

Since both *Jubilees* and Enochic literature were influential for the Qumran community, it is not surprising to find a similar interest in the demonic in other texts discovered at Qumran. For instance, one text discusses ringworm and the priest's examination of the person affected, mentioning the entrance of a *ruaḥ* into the person's body.[62] A few columns after discussing the two *ruḥot* that govern humanity—the *ruaḥ* of holiness and light and the *ruaḥ* of impurity and darkness[63]—the *Community Rule* contains the words, "I will not keep Belial [the evil *ruaḥ*] in my heart."[64] This passage depicts two different *ruḥot*, one holy and one impure, as dynamic powers that oppose each other and do so using human bodies as the battleground.

Similarly, a Psalms scroll contains a prayer of deliverance that voices the following plea: "Forgive my sin, YHWH, and purify me from my iniquity. Give me a *ruaḥ* of faithfulness and knowledge. . . . Let neither Satan nor an impure *ruaḥ* rule over me; let neither pain nor the evil desire possess my bones."[65] In a reference to the mixed offspring of the angels and women (cf. Gen. 6), *4QIncantation* speaks of "all the *ruḥot* of the bastards" (that is, these mixed offspring) and "the *ruaḥ* of impurity."[66] In a fragmentary Aramaic text that contains an exorcism (*4QExorcism ar*), we see the physical indwelling of evil *ruḥot*, both male and female, who enter into the flesh of people and inflict physical torments upon them. This hostile pneumatic invasion requires an exorcism spell to remove the demonic presence from the sufferer.[67] In a fragmentary scroll known as *Apocryphal Psalms*ᵃ, we

---

60. *1 Enoch* 15.11–12. See Stuckenbruck, "'Angels' and 'Giants' of Genesis 6:1–4."

61. *1 Enoch* 69.4–15.

62. 4Q273 4 II, 10.

63. E.g., 1QS IV, 21–22.

64. 1QS X, 21.

65. 11Q5 XIX, 13–16.

66. 4Q444 2 I, 4.

67. On this text, see Penney and Wise, "By the Power of Beelzebub." Penney and Wise reconstruct the first line of column 1 to read "[Beel]zebub."

see the earliest attestation to the belief that Israel's King Solomon was a powerful exorcist:

> [. . .] Solomon, and he call[ed. . .]
> [. . . the *ru*]*ḥot* and the demons, [. . .]
> [. . .] These are [the de]mons, and the Pri[nce of Mastem]ah
> [. . . w]ho [. . .] the aby[ss . . .][68]

The text continues with an incantation to use against a demon of the night:

> Of David. Ag[ainst . . . An incanta]tion in the name of YHW[H. Invoke at an]y time.
> the heave[ns. When] he comes against you in the nig[ht,] you will [s]ay to him:
> Who are you, [oh seed of] man and of the seed of the ho[ly] ones?
>   Your face is a face of
> [dec]eit, and your horns are horns of a dr[ea]m. You are darkness and not light
> [injus]tice and not justice. [. . .] the prince of the host. YHWH [will bring] you [down]
> [to the] deepest [Sheo]l, [he will shut] the bronze [ga]tes through [which n]o
> light enters.] . . .[69]

In discussing the eschatological battle between the forces of God and the forces of Belial (the sons of light and the sons of darkness), the *War Scroll* declares, "Cursed be Belial for his hateful plan, may he be damned for his sinful rule. Cursed be all the [*ruḥot*] of his lot for their evil plan, may they be damned for their deeds of filthy impurity. For they are the lot of darkness but the lot of God is for [everlast]ing light."[70] Numerous writings from Qumran, then, show the way in which the current cosmos is an arena within which God and the forces of Belial, the forces of holiness and impurity, do battle. At the eschaton God and the sons of light will vanquish Belial and the sons of darkness once and for all. Again, we see a vigorous belief in one supreme God coexisting with the belief in innumerable demonic forces.

The first-century Alexandrian Jewish philosopher Philo also discusses the demonic. In his interpretation of the myth of Genesis 6, in which angels

---

68. 11Q11 II, 2–5.
69. 11Q11 V, 4–11. On the exorcism here, see Puech, "11QPsApᵃ," and Puech, "Les deux derniers psaumes davidiques."
70. 1QM XIII, 4–6.

come to earth and have sexual intercourse with women, he states that what the philosophers call demons, Moses calls angels. These beings, according to Philo, are souls that hover in the air.[71] For Philo, like many non-Jews, demons can be either good or bad.[72] Perhaps in part indebted to the LXX, Philo claims that Balak took the prophet Balaam to a pillar erected to a demon,[73] thereby identifying foreign gods with lower gods, which he calls demons, an identification seen elsewhere in his writings.[74]

Josephus's historical writings contain a number of references to demons. In his rewriting of the Deuteronomistic History, Josephus mentions the demonic attacks upon King Saul,[75] but he adds that this demon sought to suffocate Saul. Elsewhere, he combines the term "demon" with "evil *pneuma*."[76] In his *Jewish War* he claims that Herod's son Alexander boasted that he would seek vengeance on his father on behalf of the demons of Hyrcanus and Mariamne, whom Herod had killed.[77] These rumors led Herod to kill his two sons, Alexander and Aristobulus, whose demons then haunted the palace.[78] Thus, for Josephus, demons are the spirits of the dead who linger among the living with malicious intent, a belief he states concisely in *Jewish War*: demons are "the *pneumata* of wicked men which enter the living and kill them unless aid is forthcoming."[79] Elsewhere he asserts that God gave Solomon the ability to help those tormented by demons and claims that such an ability has persisted down to Josephus's own day in, among others, a man named Eleazar.[80] Like in *Jubilees* and *1 Enoch*, Josephus associates the demonic with the spirits of those who have died, although he believes them to be the spirits of humans, not of the giants of Genesis 6. Like other Second Temple Jewish writers apart from Philo, Josephus believes that such beings are universally hell-bent on violence and trying to kill humans.

In the testamentary literature of Second Temple Judaism we see an emphasis on the fact that when God's kingdom comes, Satan will be no more.[81] The *Testament of Benjamin* promises that *impure pneumata* and beasts will

---

71. Philo, *On Giants* 6.
72. Philo, *On Giants* 16.
73. Philo, *On the Life of Moses* 1.276.
74. E.g., Philo, *On the Decalogue* 54; Philo, *On the Virtues* 172.
75. Josephus, *Jewish Antiquities* 6.166; cf. 1 Sam. 16:14–16.
76. Josephus, *Jewish Antiquities* 6.211.
77. Josephus, *Jewish War* 1.521.
78. Josephus, *Jewish War* 1.599, 607; cf. *Jewish Antiquities* 13.317, 415, 416.
79. Josephus, *Jewish War* 7.185.
80. Josephus, *Jewish Antiquities* 8.45–49.
81. E.g., *Testament of Moses* 10.1.

flee those who do what is good.[82] According to the *Testament of Simeon*, Simeon's desire to kill Joseph sprang from a *pneuma* of jealousy sent by the prince of deceit.[83] Simeon counsels his sons to beware of the *pneuma* of deceit and envy—clearly a personified evil, since he claims that if one flees to God, the evil *pneuma* will run from him.[84] By avoiding envy, Simeon's sons will trample the *pneumata* of deceit under their feet and rule over wicked *pneumata*.[85] And according to the *Testament of Levi*, all evil *pneumata* attack Israel, and a *pneuma* of fornication attacks the Jerusalem temple in order to pollute it—but an angel of God protects them from such polluting onslaught.[86] Most expansively, Dan instructs his children in the following words:

> And now fear the Lord, my children, be on guard against Satan and his [*pneumata*]. Draw near to God and to the angel who intercedes for you, because he is the mediator between God and men for the peace of Israel. He shall stand in opposition to the kingdom of the enemy. Therefore the enemy is eager to trip up all who call on the Lord, because he knows that on the day in which Israel trusts, the enemy's kingdom will be brought to an end. This angel of peace will strengthen Israel so that it will not succumb to an evil destiny. But in Israel's period of lawlessness it will be the Lord who will not depart from her and therefore she will seek to do his will, for none of the angels is like him.[87]

Finally, Pseudo-Philo refers to a demon with the term "impure *spiritus*."[88] Here too we see that one of the chief goals of the demonic is to lead astray: in this case, the priest Eli thinks that the voice calling to Samuel in the night might be an evil and impure *spiritus* who intends to deceive Samuel.

This brief overview of the demonology of Second Temple Jews shows that, apart from Philo, Second Temple Jewish writers stress that demonic beings are always evil. What motivates these beings is a desire to deceive, injure, and destroy humans.

Although rabbinic literature postdates the writing of the Synoptic Gospels, a concise examination of the way the rabbis conceived of the demonic will also prove helpful when we turn to the Gospels.[89] The Babylonian Talmud, for instance, repeatedly insists that demons exist and are intent on destroying

---

82. *Testament of Benjamin* 5.2.
83. *Testament of Simeon* 2.7; cf. Gen. 37:20.
84. *Testament of Simeon* 3.1–5; cf. 4.7–9.
85. *Testament of Simeon* 6.6; cf. *Testament of Levi* 18.10–12.
86. *Testament of Levi* 5.6; 9.9.
87. *Testament of Dan* 6.1–6.
88. *Liber antiquitatum biblicarum* 53.3.
89. See Rosen-Zvi, *Demonic Desires*, and Ronis, "'Do Not Go Out Alone at Night.'"

people. Consequently, the rabbis recommend that people do not go out at night, because "Igrath the daughter of Mahalath [the queen of demons], she and one hundred eighty thousand destroying angels go forth, and each has permission to wreak destruction independently."[90] Furthermore, they associate the demonic with a host of dangerous animals, calling demons "agents of death."[91] The rabbis also connect the demonic with cemeteries. Certain people, they claim, fast and spend the night in a cemetery so that an impure *ruaḥ* will rest upon them to help them foretell the future.[92] Evil *ruḥot* also work to deprive people of their right minds.[93] Finally, such demons enter into people in order to compel sin.[94]

Although priestly literature may be circumspect about the existence of demons, the rabbis connect the demonic to the very center of the priestly world: the tabernacle. If later rabbinic ascription can be trusted, Rabbi Yoḥanan of the first century CE made the following claim: "Before the Tabernacle had been erected the demons were wont to vex mankind in this world. From the moment when the Tabernacle was erected, and the Shechinah took up its residence here below, the demons were exterminated from the world."[95] What such a claim suggests is that the demonic is intrinsically opposed to God and God's holy presence. Ultimately, the two cannot coexist, and through the establishment of the tabernacle and a newly created safe space for God to dwell on earth, God drives the demonic out of this world.

↳ Which implies what
about 2T Tabernacle?

Jesus and the Impure Demons

Instead of examining every story of the demonic in the Gospels, I will highlight some key themes before turning to two exorcism accounts in Mark. First, the Gospel writers repeatedly portray the demonic as a hostile force bent on physically tormenting and afflicting people. They also associate demons with illnesses, causing, among other things, people to be deaf and mute (e.g., Mark 9:25).[96] The Gospel writers do not portray demons tempting humans, although Satan is one exception (Mark 1:13; 8:33; Matt. 4; Luke 4; 13:16; 22:3); rather, they focus on the destructive and debilitating physical power

90. Babylonian Talmud, *Pesahim* 112b.
91. Babylonian Talmud, *Semahot* 47b.
92. Babylonian Talmud, *Sanhedrin* 65b; cf. Babylonian Talmud, *Niddah* 17a; Babylonian Talmud, *Hagigah* 3b.
93. Babylonian Talmud, *Eruvin* 41b.
94. *Sifre Deuteronomy* 318.
95. *Numbers Rabbah* 12.3.
96. See Machiela, "Luke 13:10–13," and Wassen, "Impurity of the Impure Spirits."

that demons wield over human bodies. Additionally, the hostility they show to humans has no explicit connection to divine judgment for sinful behavior. Humans are the weak victims of the demonic; they crave release but are unable to find help until they encounter Jesus (cf. Matt. 12:43–45).

The Holy One of God and Impure Pneumata in Mark

The Gospel of Mark introduces Jesus abruptly; unlike Matthew and Luke, Mark gives readers no infancy narrative to contextualize the life of Jesus. He thrusts him onto the public scene—beginning with John's baptism of Jesus and Jesus's forty-day sojourn in the wilderness. After returning from the wilderness, Jesus calls a few disciples—Simon, Andrew, James, and John—and begins teaching at the synagogue in the Galilean village of Capernaum. Mark asserts that Jesus's teaching impresses the people due to the authority (*exousia*) that accompanies it. As evidence of this authority, Mark presents Jesus's first deed of power in his public mission—a confrontation between Jesus and an impure *pneuma*:

> And immediately there was in their synagogue a man in an impure *pneuma*.[97] And he cried out, "What have you to do with us, Jesus of Nazareth? Have you come to destroy us? I know who you are, the holy one of God." But Jesus rebuked him, saying, "Be quiet, and come out of him!" And the impure *pneuma*, shaking him and crying out with a loud voice, came out of him. And they were all amazed, so that they asked among themselves, saying, "What is this? A new teaching—with authority he commands even the impure *pneumata*, and they obey him." And, immediately, news of him spread out through the surrounding region of Galilee. (Mark 1:23–28)

This encounter between Jesus and the man with an impure *pneuma* begins Jesus's public work in the Gospel of Mark. "Mark consciously places this striking set piece near the outset of Jesus' public ministry," Joel Marcus observes, "just as Matthew leads his Gospel off with the Sermon on the Mount,

97. The Greek reads *anthrōpos en pneumati akathartō* and is therefore ambiguous. Does the man exist *within* the realm or body of an impure *pneuma*, or does he *have* an impure *pneuma*? Rightly to my mind, Joel Marcus reads the preposition *en* locatively: "This picture of 'a man in an unclean spirit,' enclosed by that which contaminates him, is horrifying" (*Mark 1–8*, 192). In fact, as Marcus argues, the language of 1:23–24 suggests that the man and the demon have merged into one intermixed being: "The man's personality has been so usurped by the demon that the demon has, as it were, swallowed him up. The fusion of the man's identity with that of the demon is underlined by the grammar of the passage" (*Mark 1–8*, 192). This would suggest something akin to the ancient Stoic theory of *krasis*, in which *pneuma* and other forms of matter are melded together.

Luke with the inaugural sermon in the Nazareth synagogue, and John with the wedding feast at Cana."[98] Mark's Jesus presents himself to the people as the one who drives out impure *pneumata*—demons, as Mark calls them elsewhere (e.g., Mark 7:25–30).

The terminology Mark uses in this story connects demonic forces to the larger theme of this book: three times he uses the adjective *impure* (*akathartos*) in reference to the *pneuma* that envelops this man. In contrast, the man calls Jesus *the holy one* (*ho hagios*) of God. This same Jesus, Mark informs his readers through the words of John the Immerser, will immerse people not with water but *in* the holy *pneuma* (1:8) and is himself equipped with the *pneuma*, who then drives him into the wilderness (1:10–12).[99] Mark 1 sets the holy one of God, armed with the holy *pneuma*, against a man who is currently in an impure *pneuma*. The opening language of Mark's Gospel, then, is reminiscent of the language that is central to priestly concerns: "You are to distinguish between the holy and the profane, the impure and the pure" (Lev. 10:10). As Milgrom has argued, while holy and profane are opposites, and pure and impure are opposites, only the holy and the impure are forces in priestly thinking—forces that are opposed to one another. When the impure comes into contact with the holy, it is customary for the holy to withdraw. With this dynamic in mind, we can see the way that Mark dramatically introduces Jesus to his readers: the holy one of God confronts a powerful pneumatic force of impurity.[100]

This contact between the holy and the impure cannot occur without consequences. The impure *pneuma* notes this fact, asking a question that often occurs in the context of conflict: "What have you to do with us?" (e.g., Judg. 11:12; 2 Sam. 16:10; 1 Kings 17:18; 2 Kings 3:13; 2 Chron. 35:21). What will happen between Jesus and the man in an impure *pneuma*? The man has his own concerns: "Have you come to destroy us?" Of this reference to "us," Clinton Wahlen notes, "The impure spirit seems to be speaking on behalf of an entire host of demons, afraid that Jesus will destroy them all," but it is equally plausible that since the *pneuma* and man are in essence fused, the *us* refers to both the man and the *pneuma*.[101] The answer, as it turns out, is both yes and no. Jesus silences the impure *pneuma*—commanding it to leave the

98. Marcus, *Mark 1–8*, 190.

99. Matthew will clarify that it is the *pneuma* of God (Matt. 3:16), while Luke stresses that it is the holy *pneuma* who descends upon Jesus, fills him, and then sends him into the wilderness (Luke 3:22; 4:1).

100. Lührmann, *Das Markusevangelium*, 51.

101. Wahlen, *Jesus and the Impurity of Spirits*, 91. See also Stuckenbruck, "Satan and Demons."

man, which it does. The fusion of the impure *pneuma* and the man has been undone: the demon is destroyed and the man saved. In this opening story, then, we see the holy one of God meet and expel the forces of impurity. The holy *pneuma* that has come down upon Jesus and animates him is more powerful than the impure *pneuma* that inhabits the man.

This initial story sets the tone for the rest of Mark's portrayal of Jesus. Repeatedly Jesus interacts with and overcomes the demonic, the impure forces that torment humans. Upon hearing this report of Jesus, people begin to bring their sick and demon possessed to Jesus, and he heals illnesses and drives out demons (Mark 1:32–34; cf. Matt. 8:16–17; 9:32–34; 17:14–20).[102] People bring their demon possessed to Jesus, but Jesus also travels all over Galilee proclaiming the kingdom and casting out demons (Mark 1:39). When he encounters the demon possessed, the impure *pneumata* fall down before him and identify him as the son of God (3:11). He even casts demons out from afar (Mark 7:25–30; cf. Matt. 15:22–28). And the holy one of God empowers his disciples, giving them the authority to cast out demons as well (Mark 3:15; 6:7; cf. Matt. 10:1).

Binding the Strong Man

Yet Jesus's success in casting out demons does not meet with universal approval. According to Mark, some scribes from Jerusalem dismiss Jesus's apparent power as itself a nefarious demonic plot: "He is possessed by Beelzebul, and by the ruler of demons he casts out demons" (Mark 3:22). In other words, as Mark clarifies, they accuse Jesus himself of having an impure *pneuma* (3:30), of being demonically empowered to trick people into following him. Although Beelzebul is not known from early Jewish traditions,[103] a second-century Christian work, the *Testament of Solomon*, refers to him as the ruler of demons.[104] One can see this idea—that a person might appear to have mastery over demons only through the subterfuge of demons—in (Pseudo-)Eusebius, who preserves the accusation that Apollonius, a noted first-century CE wonder-worker, "drives out one demon with the help of another." The purpose behind such exorcisms is for the first demon to leave only to be secretly supplanted by a second one.[105] In this case, the exorcist is the equivalent of a double agent for the demonic.

---

102. Ferguson argues that this passage demonstrates that "demon possession is distinguished from physical and mental illness, although belonging to the same general category of disorders" (*Demonology*, 4–5), but see Machiela, "Luke 13:10–13."

103. Baal-zebub (LXX: *baal-myia*), though, is a regional god of Ekron according to 2 Kings 1. The later Christian *Acts of Pilate* equates the two names.

104. *Testament of Solomon* 3.5–6; 6.1–2; 16.3.

105. Eusebius, *Against Hierocles* 26; cf. Origen, *Against Celsus* 1.6.

In response to this charge, Jesus asks, "How can Satan cast out Satan?" He then continues with a parable: "If a kingdom is divided against itself, that kingdom cannot stand. If a house is divided against itself, that house cannot stand. If Satan has risen up against himself and is divided, then he cannot stand, but is coming to an end" (Mark 3:23–26). Building on the idea of Satan's house, he asserts that only if one binds "the strong man," a term referring to Satan, can one plunder his house. Mark portrays Jesus doing this very thing.

In Mark 5, Jesus crosses the sea to go to the Decapolis—a region of ten cities that was predominantly but not exclusively gentile. His first encounter with a person in gentile territory parallels the story of the demon-possessed man in the synagogue (Mark 1:21–28). Here another man in an impure *pneuma* greets Jesus as he disembarks from his boat. Mark's description of the man is chilling: He was "a man in an impure *pneuma*, who lived among the tombs. . . . No longer was anyone able to bind him—not even with a chain" (5:2–3). Multiple negatives in the Greek stress people's inability to control this man: no longer (*ouketi*), no one (*oudeis*), not even (*oude*). While in English a double negative makes a positive, and more than two negatives just makes for confusion, piling negative on negative in Greek makes the point emphatic. Mark informs his readers that in the past people had tried to bind this man with both fetters for his feet and chains for his hands, but he had repeatedly broken these bonds apart. Simply put, no one was strong enough to subdue him. Consequently, the man roamed among the tombs both day and night, screaming and injuring himself with stones.

Providing some context will enable modern readers to appreciate the artistry of Mark's portrayal of this man. First, the fact that Mark depicts the man as dwelling among tombs both day and night signifies this man's state of mind. Later rabbinic literature, for instance, stresses that a man who spends the night in cemeteries is not of sound mind.[106] At the end of the story, Mark informs readers that this man is now both clothed and in his "right mind," confirming that he was previously unsound of mind (5:15). Given the numerous connections noted above between the dead and the demonic, it is unsurprising that people frequently portrayed demons haunting cemeteries.[107] Thus the cemetery has become the natural habitat for this man in an impure *pneuma*.

Further, while physically restraining a person sounds horrific and inhumane, this man's community was attempting to do the only thing it could:

106. E.g., Tosefta, *Terumot* 1.3; Babylonian Talmud, *Hagigah* 3b.
107. E.g., Plato, *Phaedo* 81D; Plutarch, *Sayings of Spartans* 236D.

confine the man in order to prevent him from hurting himself and, according
to Matthew, others (Matt. 8:28). Instead, the chains they used were too inef-
fectual for this strong man, leaving him free to wander the mountains and
injure himself. Mark deftly characterizes the man's situation in the direst
of terms. And yet this strong man falls at Jesus's feet and begs Jesus not to
torment him. The interaction between the two, which I have rearranged in
chronological order, is enthralling:

> JESUS: Come out of the man, impure *pneuma*!
>
> MAN: What have you to do with me, Jesus, son of the highest God? I
> adjure you by God, do not torment me!
>
> JESUS: What is your name?
>
> MAN: My name is Legion, for we are many.
>
> *The man then begs Jesus not to cast him out of the region.*
>
> MAN: Send us into the pigs.
>
> *Jesus permits them to enter into the pigs.*
>
> *The demon-possessed pigs drown themselves in the sea.*

The impure *pneuma* does not immediately leave the man when Jesus commands it to do so, though Mark conceals this fact by the way he orders the
interaction. Instead, it asks Jesus the same question that the impure *pneuma*
of Mark 1 asks: "What have you to do with me?" Jesus's first effort to exorcise this impure *pneuma* fails. While Luke retains Jesus's failed exorcism
(Luke 8:29), Matthew omits this detail (Matt. 8:28–32) and in fact ampli-
fies the power Jesus displays by doubling the number of demon-possessed
men.

Further, and again in a way that parallels Mark 1, the demon identifies
and names Jesus: "Jesus, son of the highest God." In the context of exorcisms, knowing and using the name of another person enables one to have
power over that person. Thus the demon here attempts to gain power over
Jesus by identifying him and then adjuring him by God not to torment him.
The verb *to adjure* (*horkizō*) occurs in exorcistic contexts and is usually used
by the exorcist on the demon.[108] As we saw above, one magical papyrus contains the following charm: "I adjure [*exorkizō*] you, *daimōn*, whoever you
are. . . . Come out [*exelthe*], *daimōn*, whoever you are, and withdraw from
so-and-so, quickly, quickly, now, now. Come out [*exelthe*], *daimōn*, since I

---

108. See Bauernfeind, *Die Worte der Dämonen*, 3–10, and Kee, "Terminology of Mark's
Exorcism Stories."

fetter you with unbreakable adamantine fetters, and I hand you over into the black chaos into destruction."[109] This spell contains the same language as Mark, as well as a reference to chaining the demon, which is reminiscent of the chains that failed to bind the man prior to Jesus's arrival. The demon tries to gain mastery over Jesus by adjuring him, but Jesus turns the tables on it, demanding to know *its* name. The demon divulges his name: *Legion*—a Roman military term for a unit of about five thousand soldiers—revealing the vast number of demons that afflict this man and give him his overwhelming strength.[110] The battle between Jesus and the impure, then, appears unevenly matched—five thousand demons against one holy one of God. And yet the legion of demons begs for permission to enter into the nearby herd of pigs so that they can remain in the region (or in Luke's account, keep themselves out of the abyss). Nonetheless, the herd of pigs thwarts their desire by rushing out of the region and into the sea, where they drown.

The narrative begins with a man in an impure *pneuma*, living among the tombs, of unsound mind, and whose nearest neighbors are a herd of pigs. While Mark does not make it explicit, to anyone attuned to the purity systems of early Jewish thinking, impurity saturates the entire scene: impure *pneumata*, tombs that house impure corpses (cf. Num. 19), and impure pigs (cf. Lev. 11 and Deut. 14).[111] The man's encounter with Jesus, though, results in the man's deliverance from all of these sources of impurity; the impure *pneumata* have left him and entered the pigs, who promptly drown both themselves and the impure *pneumata*. The man himself is now in his right mind and so no longer dwells among the tombs or does harm to his own body.

This story serves as the narrative fulfillment of Jesus's words to his detractors in Mark 3, where he asserts that no one is able (*ou dynatai oudeis*) to enter the house of a strong man (*ischyros*) unless one first binds (*deō*) the strong man and then plunders his house. In Mark 5 we meet the strong man whom no one is able to bind (*oudeis edynato auton dēsai*). No one is strong enough (*ischyō*) to subdue him, until Jesus arrives. Jesus plunders the house of these demons and steals their possession—the man—from their control. As Peter Bolt concludes,

109. *Papyri Graecae Magicae* 4.1239–41, 1243–48, in Betz, *Greek Magical Papyri*. Cf. *Damascus Document* XIII, 10: "He will undo all the chains that bind them, so that neither harassed nor oppressed will be in his congregation."

110. Although I do not take up this issue here, I agree with those scholars who believe that the name *Legion* reflects Mark's anti-Roman sentiment. Cf. Myers, *Binding the Strong Man*, 192–94. Nonetheless, the story cannot simply be demythologized and made to feel familiar by limiting its meaning to a criticism of empire and colonialism.

111. Mishnah, *Bava Qamma* 7.7 forbids Jews from raising pigs. See also Jerusalem Talmud, *Ta'anit* 4.5; Babylonian Talmud, *Bava Qamma* 82b.

This incident constitutes the supreme exorcism in the Gospel of Mark. Jesus' unanswered riddle to his opponents had suggested that no-one can plunder the strong man's house, "unless he first binds the strong man" (3.27). . . . By means of these allusions to 3.27, the subjugation of this unbindable strong man suggests another dimension to the readers: Jesus' riddle is finding an answer and *the* strong man is being subdued. As Jesus banishes the legion of *daimones* and delivers the man from the tombs, the "prince of the *daimones*" suffers a major defeat.[112]

Blasphemy of the Holy Pneuma

The connection between Mark 3 and Mark 5 demonstrates the centrality of this story to Mark's Gospel and its significance for properly identifying Jesus. Mark 3 focuses on the question of who Jesus is and from where he derives his authority and power. Jesus's own family believes him to be out of his mind. The scribes, similarly, believe him to be demon possessed, performing powerful deeds by the authority of the leader of demons—Beelzebul. While Mark does not define what he means by "scribes," it appears that they were an educated class in Jewish society that was of Levitical or priestly descent.[113] If this identification is correct, their opinion of Jesus was crucial, for they represented a learned legal and cultic authority to the masses. And in their opinion, the source of Jesus's authority over the demonic was itself impure.

With this assessment the scribes are working to distinguish between holy and profane, impure and pure, as God commanded them in Leviticus 10:10. And yet, according to Mark, they have gotten things confused. As Mark makes clear, Jesus receives the holy *pneuma* at his baptism and then baptizes others in that holy *pneuma* (1:8). And the impure *pneuma* that Jesus first encounters refers to him as the holy one of God. For Mark and his readers, the scribes have erroneously identified the forces of holiness with the forces of impurity. While Jesus's mission purifies and gives life, the scribes have mistakenly associated it with impurity, the demonic, and ultimately deceit and death. For this reason, Jesus warns his audience that those who blaspheme the holy *pneuma*, by equating the holy *pneuma*'s work with impurity, make a fatal mistake. They have confused the holy with the impure, life with death, and in so doing, they have aligned themselves with death and against life. While Matthew and Luke modify the Markan material, the fact that they also frequently mention Jesus's interactions with the demonic shows that such an understanding of

112. Bolt, *Jesus' Defeat of Death*, 146–47.
113. See Schwartz, *Studies in the Jewish Background*, 89–101; Sanders, *Judaism*, 170–82; and Schams, *Jewish Scribes*.

Jesus's actions continued to resonate with later Christ followers.[114] In fact, both of them add to Mark's defense of Jesus (Mark 3), that Jesus's exorcism of demons is the preeminent sign of the coming of God's kingdom and of the end of Satan's rule over humanity (Matt. 11:26–28; Luke 11:18–20).

Conclusion

The purification mission of Jesus in the Synoptic Gospels extends beyond the three sources of ritual impurity (*lepra*, genital discharges, and corpses) mentioned in priestly literature to demonic sources of impurity as well. The demonic realm is no longer free to plague humanity unopposed, something that Mark's first portrayal of an exorcism demonstrates: "What have you to do with us? Have you come to destroy us?" (Mark 1:24). And in the exorcism of the strong man, the demons beg Jesus not to torment them (Mark 5:7; Luke 8:28). This request is deeply ironic, for the demonic impulse, as both Jewish and non-Jewish literature frequently stress, is to torment and kill humans (cf. Matt. 15:22; Acts 19:16; 2 Cor. 12:7). Matthew's account of the exorcism of the strong man suggests that the demonic forces know they will be tormented at some point but believe that Jesus has come to do so prematurely: "Have you come here to torment us before the time?" (Matt. 8:29). The demons thought that they had free rein on earth to do as they pleased, yet the Gospel writers portray Jesus's invasion of the world to take it back from the demonic and to establish God's kingdom.

In this sense, Jesus's actions in the Synoptic Gospels parallel later rabbinic depictions of Israel's tabernacle, which also expelled demons from the earth. *Pesiqta of Rab Kahana*, for instance, avers regarding the reading of Psalm 91, "Once the Tent of Meeting was set up, demons came to an end in the world. But R[abbi] Yoḥanan said: Why need I draw such proof at such a remove in Scripture when I may draw it from the passage in hand? The Lord bless thee, and keep thee (Num. 6:24)—keep them from demons, of course."[115] A similar statement appears in *Numbers Rabbah*: "Before the Tabernacle had been erected the demons tormented humanity in this world. From the moment when the Tabernacle was erected, and the Shekinah took up its residence below, the demons were exterminated from the world."[116] Although both texts are

---

114. As Dale C. Allison Jr. puts it, this evidence suggests "not only that Jesus was an exorcist but also that he and others saw his ministry as a successful combat with the forces of Satan" (*Constructing Jesus*, 18). On the other hand, Allison notes that the *Gospel of Thomas* contains no mention of the demonic (133), an observation that applies also to the Gospel of John.

115. *Pesiqta of Rab Kahana* 1.5.

116. *Numbers Rabbah* 12.3.

significantly later than the Synoptic Gospels, it is tantalizing that *Pesiqta of Rab Kahana* claims that Rabbi Yoḥanan, who lived in the late first century CE (roughly the same time that the Gospel writers constructed a similar picture of Jesus), knew this tradition. Jesus's presence on earth introduces a power of holiness within the terrestrial realm that is both radically opposed to and stronger than the demonic. If some contemporaries of the Gospel writers were ascribing this same function to Israel's tabernacle (and by extension to the Jerusalem temple), since it housed the holy God of Israel, then the Gospel writers might have been implying that the holiness of Israel's God was housed in the person of Jesus in a way that actualized God's control over the demonic forces that plagued humanity.

CHAPTER 7

Jesus, Healing,
and the Sabbath Life

In the preceding chapters, I argued that the Gospel writers do not portray Jesus rejecting the ritual purity system or denying the reality of ritual purity. Instead, they consistently portray Jesus acting in ways that make sense only if he believes that ritual impurity from corpses, genital discharges, and *lepra* is something real and tangible. They are as real to the Jesus of the Gospels as the demons who populate the Gospel narratives. The miracles he performs are predicated on the assumption that impurities are powerful forces within nature and therefore require an equally real and even more powerful form of holiness to remove their sources. The Gospel writers declare that Jesus is this powerful force of holiness—the holy one of God. Every person who has a condition that makes them ritually impure for an undefined period of time leaves Jesus's presence healed of the condition that created ritual impurity.

Such an argument, though, suggests that common treatments of Jesus and the Jewish law need to be reconsidered. The Jesus of the Gospels does not reject the system of ritual purity or abandon all concern for ritual impurity; rather, Jesus systematically roots out the sources of ritual impurities when he encounters them. Given this fact, it is clear that while he may be doing something quite unexpected (if not entirely novel; again, recall Elijah and Elisha) in dealing with these conditions, the Gospel writers believed that Jesus thought the priestly categories of holy and profane, pure and impure, were themselves both real and relevant. For this reason, Jesus removes the sources of these impurities, restoring people to the path to purity, thereby allowing them to have greater access to the realm of the holy.

Whereas no character within the narrative worlds of the Gospels ever accuses Jesus of disregarding ritual impurity derived from *lepra*, genital discharges, or corpses, we have a number of stories in which people reproach Jesus for his observance of the Sabbath. How can the authors of the Synoptic Gospels portray Jesus's enduring concern for ritual purity while at the same time recounting stories of him breaking the Sabbath? Were they convinced that Jesus kept one aspect of the Jewish law while abandoning another?[1] Does Jesus's behavior on the Sabbath show that he rejects the idea of holy and profane, considering all days to be equally good days to work? In short, does the so-called holy one of God show blatant disregard for the sacred by profaning holy time? Again, this is implausible. After all, the Gospels repeatedly depict Jesus attending the synagogue on the Sabbath, as was customary among his Jewish contemporaries (Mark 1:21; 3:1–2; 6:2; Matt. 12:9–10; Luke 4:16, 31; 6:6; 13:10).[2]

Nonetheless, according to the Gospel writers, Jesus frequently encountered criticism over his approach to observing the Sabbath, repeatedly facing accusations of breaking it as a result of his willingness to heal people on this day of rest. In Mark, Jesus's first public deed of power occurs on the Sabbath in a synagogue in the Galilean town of Capernaum (Mark 1:21–28; cf. Luke 4:33–37). I examined this story in chapter 6, but note here that according to both Mark and Luke, this exorcism occasions no immediate criticism despite the fact that it took place on a Sabbath.[3] Instead, all who witness it marvel at Jesus's teaching and authority over demons—he commands them and they obey (Mark 1:27). This initial story in Mark's Gospel is, nonetheless, indicative of and perhaps sets the stage for every Sabbath controversy that follows. Except for one incident, which we will look at first, the only Sabbath activities over which Jesus faces criticism are *healing* deeds. Both Matthew and Luke preserve these controversy stories but modify them in some notable ways. To understand these accusations, modern readers need to familiarize themselves with Sabbath laws to get a sense of the legal debates that existed around how best to observe the Sabbath.

---

1. Numerous scholars are convinced that the Synoptic Gospel writers intended to portray Jesus's rejection of Sabbath observance. See, for instance, Yang, *Jesus and the Sabbath*. Similarly, Willy Rordorf concludes, "It is a misunderstanding to hold that Jesus did not attack the Sabbath commandment itself, but only the casuistical refinements of the Pharisees" (*Sunday*, 63).

2. Cf. Philo, *On the Embassy to Gaius* 156. See here Ryan, *Role of the Synagogue*.

3. So too J. Meier, *A Marginal Jew*, 4:252, and Sariola, *Markus und das Gesetz*, 113.

The Sabbath in Jewish Scriptures

Laws pertaining to the Sabbath occur throughout Jewish scriptures. Exodus 16 contains the first explicit commandment for humans to rest on the seventh day of the week. Here, at the inception of Israel's wilderness wanderings, God provides food in the form of manna from heaven for the Israelites. On the sixth day of the week, Moses commands them to gather twice as much manna as normal, saying, "This is what YHWH has commanded: 'Tomorrow is a day of solemn rest, a holy Sabbath to YHWH; bake what you desire to bake and boil what you desire to boil, and all leftovers put aside to be preserved until the morning'" (Exod. 16:23). In spite of this clear injunction, a number of Israelites go out on the Sabbath to collect more manna, only to find none. God responds to this disobedience: "How long will you refuse to obey my commandments and instructions? Behold, YHWH has given you the Sabbath. Therefore, on the sixth day he gives you two days' worth of food; everyone should stay where you are; do not leave your place on the seventh day" (16:28–29). God gives Israel two tangible signs of the holiness of the Sabbath here. First, no manna descends from heaven on the seventh day. Second, unlike any other day, manna from the preceding day does not go bad, even though it is kept overnight (16:24; cf. 16:20). In essence, the rules of nature change on the Sabbath day, enabling Israel to rest from its work. Manna, which on any other day would rot, is somehow preserved by the Sabbath's holiness.

This Sabbath legislation gets expanded in the Ten Commandments: "Remember the Sabbath day, and keep it holy. Six days you shall work and do all your work. But the seventh day is a Sabbath to YHWH your God; you shall not do any work—you, your son or your daughter, your male or female slave, your livestock, or the resident alien in your towns. For in six days YHWH made heaven and earth, the sea, and all that is in them, but he rested on the seventh day. Therefore, YHWH blessed the Sabbath day and made it holy" (Exod. 20:8–11; cf. Deut. 5:12–15). This Sabbath legislation is more expansive in stipulating to whom the Sabbath applies: all Israelites. But it also applies to non-Israelite slaves and to resident aliens who reside in Israelite towns. For that matter, even Israelite livestock cannot work. All Israelites and all who reside permanently with them, humans or animals, must observe the Sabbath.

Further, Exodus 20 provides a rationale for Israel's observance of the Sabbath by linking holy time to the creation of the world. God rested on the seventh day of the week after creating heaven and earth: "And on the seventh day God completed the work that he had done. And he rested on the seventh day from all the work that he had done. Therefore, God blessed the seventh day and made it holy, because on it God rested from all the work that he had done in creation" (Gen. 2:2–3).[4] According to the priestly creation narrative, God's primordial activity came to completion, and then God rested on the seventh day. This divine rest, woven into the fabric of the created order, serves as the foundation of the commandment for Israel to rest from its labors every seventh day. God has separated the seventh day from profane time and ontologically distinguished it from the rest of the week. When God commands Israel to sanctify the Sabbath, therefore, God does so because God's own treatment of it has made it inherently holy; Israel's observance of the Sabbath follows the order of creation. This depiction of the Sabbath is indebted to legal essentialism, the belief that a law has authority and power because it reflects the actual nature of things.[5]

Other legislation underlines the holiness of the Sabbath by stipulating the punishment resulting from failure to observe it properly: "You shall observe the Sabbath, because it is holy for you. Everyone who profanes it shall be put to death. Whoever does any work on it shall be cut off from the people. Work shall be done on six days, but the seventh day is a Sabbath of solemn rest, holy to YHWH. Whoever does any work on the Sabbath shall be put to death" (Exod. 31:14–15; cf. 35:2). The punishment for not keeping the Sabbath is the death penalty, a penalty applied to a man who went out to gather wood on the Sabbath while Israel was in the wilderness (Num. 15:32–36). This story provides one further detail about the Sabbath: what sorts of work are prohibited. Though Jewish scriptures are relatively circumspect, giving no systematic statement about what one can and cannot do on the Sabbath, this story condemns the collection of wood for a fire, and Exodus 35:3 explicitly prohibits making a fire on the Sabbath. From the story of the manna in the wilderness, we might conclude that gathering food is also prohibited. And, according to Nehemiah 10:31, the buying or selling of goods was an infringement of Sabbath rest (cf. Neh. 13:15–18; Amos 8:5), while the prophet Jeremiah adds that one is not to bear a burden on the Sabbath (Jer. 17:21). Finally, Trito-Isaiah says,

> If you keep from trampling the Sabbath,
>   from seeking your own interests on my holy day;
> if you call the Sabbath a joy
>   and the holy day of YHWH honorable;

---

4. There is a significant textual issue in Gen. 2:2. The Masoretic Text states that God completed his work on the seventh day and then rested on the seventh day. The LXX, Samaritan Pentateuch, and Syriac of Genesis, on the other hand, read that God completed his work on the sixth day and then rested on the seventh day. Most scholars believe that the Masoretic Text preserves the original reading, since it creates a difficulty in implying that God was still working on the seventh day.

5. See Noam, "Essentialism, Freedom of Choice."

if you honor it by not going in your own ways,
    seeking your own interests, or pursuing your own things;
then you will take joy in Yнwн. (Isa. 58:13–14)

Such an abstract prohibition begs to be filled in with details. What qualifies as seeking one's own interests or things? Even if one were to collect these scattered condemnations of certain activities, one would not have a complete sense of which actions God permits and which actions God prohibits on the Sabbath. Such uncertainties eventually lead, as we shall see, to the creation of lists of types of work prohibited on the Sabbath. After all, if God prohibits working on the Sabbath, should not people who want to honor both God and the Sabbath make sure that they know what constitutes prohibited work? If a chief job of the priests, and ultimately all Israel, was to distinguish between the holy and the profane, then one needed to know which precise actions profaned the Sabbath (Lev. 10:10).

On the other hand, Jewish scriptures also imply that a number of forms of work can occur on the Sabbath without censure. In Genesis 17, for instance, God commands Abraham and his seed to circumcise their sons on the eighth day after their births. Many Jews would have had to circumcise their sons on the Sabbath in order to fulfill this temporal commandment. Priests also worked on the Sabbath day. According to Numbers, the priests were required to offer two lambs, along with grain, oil, and drink offerings every Sabbath (Num. 28:9–10; cf. Ezek. 46:1, 4, 12). Further, Aaron and those who took up his duties were required to place the twelve loaves of the presence before God every Sabbath (Lev. 24:8). And on the Day of Atonement, a day that the priestly writer refers to as a Sabbath of complete rest (16:31), the chief priest was required to perform central rites for the purification of both the sanctuary and the Israelites (16:31–34). These various forms of work show that certain commandments—circumcision and priestly service, at least—take priority over the observance of the Sabbath. Such work does not actually profane this holy day.

Another instance of work on the Sabbath occurs in 2 Kings. Here the priest Jehoiada gives the temple guard the following instructions: "This is what you will do: one-third of you, those who go off duty on the Sabbath and guard the king's house . . . will guard the palace; and your two divisions that come on duty in force on the Sabbath and guard the house of Yнwн will surround the king with weapons in hand. And whoever approaches the guard is to be killed. Be with the king in his coming and going" (11:5–8; cf. 2 Chron. 23:3–11). These instructions require that the guards labor on the Sabbath, carrying weapons, spears, and shields in defense of the newly crowned King Joash. This coronation and military support appear to contravene the Sabbath legislation that prohibits work, and yet neither the Deuteronomistic writer of 2 Kings nor the Chronicler appears bothered by this fact. Nehemiah likewise gives guard duty to the Levites to protect the city gates on the Sabbath, precisely to ensure that people observe the Sabbath properly (Neh. 13:22).

As early as the book of *Jubilees*, we see efforts to systematize all the work prohibited on the Sabbath:

> And (as for) any man who does work on it, or who goes on a journey, or who plows a field either at home or any (other) place, or who kindles a fire, or who rides on any animal, or who travels the sea in a boat, and any man who slaughters or kills anything, or who slashes the throat of cattle or bird, or who snares any beast or bird or fish, or who fasts or makes war on the day of the sabbath, let the man who does any of these on the day of the sabbath die.[6]

And as late as the rabbinic period, we still find efforts to systematize and clarify Sabbath legislation—discussion of Sabbath laws makes up the largest tractate of the Mishnah. This attention derives from the fact that the preceding passages simply do not offer specific enough guidelines for how to keep it correctly.[7] If one were serious about observing the Sabbath rest, then one needed to know what constitutes prohibited work.[8]

But it was precisely here that Jews could disagree with one another. A couple examples will suffice: According to Mishnah *Pesahim*, the men of Jericho held to the legal position that picking up and eating fruit that had fallen off of a tree did not break the Sabbath. Since the fruit was windfall, they concluded that picking it up did not constitute an unlawful act of harvesting. The Sages, though, disagreed with this legal position.[9] The rabbis, in fact, often disagreed with each other about what constituted work. For instance, Rabbi Eliezer argued that it was prohibited to remove honey from a beehive on the Sabbath, whereas the Sages believed that it was permissible.[10] Such disagreement may have occasionally led to heated polemical claims that the person one disagreed with was a lawbreaker and profaned the Sabbath, but such claims are not indicative of the actual attitude or intentions of the person(s) being criticized. Such a person might have be-

---

6. *Jubilees* 50.12–13.

7. H. Weiss, *A Day of Gladness*, 13, and J. Meier, "Historical Jesus," 58–59.

8. Sabbath legislation becomes an integral part of Jewish identity in many works of the Second Temple period. See Grünwaldt, *Exil und Identität*, and Doering, *Schabbat*.

9. Mishnah, *Pesahim* 4.8.

10. Mishnah, *Shevi'it* 10.7; Mishnah, *Uqtzin* 3.10.

lieved that he or she committed no breach of the Sabbath. It is within this context of legal debate that the Sabbath controversies of the Gospels must be read.

In contrast to the topics of the preceding chapters, Sabbath legislation has no simple parallels in the ancient Near East or in the non-Jewish Greco-Roman world. While the concept of sacred time was something with which all cultures of the Mediterranean world would have been familiar, observing a day of rest on the seventh day of the week was something apparently unique to Israelites and Jews. When early readers of the Gospels encountered stories of Sabbath controversies, then, they were entering into a fundamentally Jewish world. To these stories we now turn.

Jesus in the Grainfields

According to Mark, one Sabbath Jesus and his disciples were traveling through a grainfield when the disciples began to pluck heads of grain (Mark 2:23–28).[11] Upon noticing this behavior, the Pharisees ask Jesus why his disciples are doing what is unlawful on the Sabbath. Mark's narrative distances Jesus both from the actions and from the accusation; it is Jesus's disciples, not Jesus, who pluck grain. In their rewriting of Mark, Matthew and Luke similarly focus on the disciples' behavior (Matt. 12:1–8; Luke 6:1–5), although in Luke's narrative the Pharisees might include Jesus in their accusation: "Why are *you* [plural] doing what is unlawful on the Sabbath?" (Luke 6:2).[12]

Jesus's response to this accusation shows that he thinks their actions are legally defensible.[13] But what the disciples are doing on the Sabbath, plucking grain, would have been considered work. While not a blatant infraction of Sabbath observance as mandated by Sabbath legislation (such as Exod. 20:10 and 34:21), their behavior certainly transgressed common contemporary interpretations of what such observance entailed (perhaps based on Exod. 34:21, which requires people to observe the Sabbath even at harvest time). The Qumran *Damascus Document* describes numerous requirements

11. The act of walking through the grainfields itself does not necessarily infringe upon Sabbath observance. As Lutz Doering says, "We know from various sources that fields were as close to dwellings as to allow for reaching them without transgressing the Sabbath limit. Therefore, the story as it stands does not point to an infringement of the Sabbath by walking a forbidden distance" ("Much Ado about Nothing?," 214).

12. But see Daube, "Responsibilities of Master and Disciples."

13. Jesus's *legal response* to the charge of the Pharisees shows that Mark's Jesus is anything but indifferent toward this accusation, contrary to Holmén, *Jesus and Jewish Covenant Thinking*, 102.

of Sabbath observance[14] and contains judgments that are relevant to this story: "A person may not eat anything on the Sabbath day except food already prepared."[15] It is possible, therefore, that the Qumran community would have found the disciples' act of plucking grain and removing the husk (Luke 6:1) a desecration of the Sabbath. In the early first century CE, Philo claims that the Sabbath "extends also to every kind of tree and plant; for it is not permitted to cut any shoot or branch, or even a leaf, or to pluck any fruit whatsoever."[16] The third transgressor of the Sabbath, according to later rabbinic interpretation, is the one who reaps.[17] The rabbis flesh out what this category of work entails in the Tosefta—it includes the plucking of grain as a subset of reaping.[18] This different literary evidence demonstrates how widespread the view was that plucking grain or harvesting other foods was a breach of the Sabbath.

How does Mark's Jesus respond? First, Jesus acknowledges that his disciples *are* working on the Sabbath by plucking grain. In other words, Jesus also shares in common with the *Damascus Document*, Philo, and the early rabbis the belief that, as a rule, harvesting food is prohibited on the Sabbath. But then he mounts a legal defense of their actions by pointing to the example of David and his men, who ate the bread of the presence out of hunger even though it was prohibited for them to do so (1 Sam. 21:1–6). It is clear that David's actions in this story went against the law, which stated that the bread of the presence was only for Aaron and his sons—that is, the priests (cf. Lev. 24:9). Jesus's argument in Mark proceeds in the following manner:

Proposition 1: Scripture shows that because of their hunger and need, David and his men ate bread not permitted to them.

Conclusion: Jesus's disciples can pluck grain on the Sabbath.

Mark's narration of the story weakens his argument. While he stresses that David and his men were able to eat prohibited bread because their hunger and need took precedence over the law of the bread of the presence, Mark fails to inform his readers that Jesus's disciples were hungry. An integral piece of his argument, then, is lacking:

14. *Damascus Document* X, 14–XI, 18.
15. *Damascus Document* X, 22.
16. Philo, *On the Life of Moses* 2.22, translation slightly modified from the Loeb Classical Library.
17. Mishnah, *Shabbat* 7.2.
18. Tosefta, *Shabbat* 9.17.

Proposition 2: Jesus's disciples were hungry and in need on the Sabbath.

Only once Proposition 2 is combined with Proposition 1 does the conclusion become potentially compelling as a legal argument. Further, Mark fails to mention that the disciples actually *ate* what they plucked. As a result, one might again conclude that there was no pressing need that drove the disciples to pluck grain. Had Mark mentioned that the disciples ate the grain, his argument would appear stronger yet:

> Proposition 1: Scripture shows that because of their hunger and need, David and his men ate bread not permitted to them.
>
> Proposition 2: Jesus's disciples were hungry and in need on the Sabbath.
>
> Conclusion: Jesus's disciples are able to pluck grain on the Sabbath in order to eat it to meet their physical needs.

Further, Mark identifies the high priest as Abiathar in the story of David and his men. Here he appears to have confused Abiathar with Abiathar's father, Ahimelech, who was the priest with whom David had dealings, according to the story of 1 Samuel 21:1–6. On the basis of this mistake, John Meier concludes, "This Marcan Jesus is not only ignorant but also reckless, foolishly challenging Scripture experts to a public debate about the proper reading of a specific text—only to prove immediately to both his disciples and his opponents how ignorant he is of the text that he himself has put forward for discussion."[19] In other words, within a story aimed at demonstrating Jesus's legal expertise, Mark accidentally depicts Jesus mistaking one priest for another.

Finally, and perhaps most fatally, Mark leaves unstated one important step in the logic of Jesus's argument. Revising the argument detailed above, Jesus's legal reasoning in Mark appears to be the following:

> Assumed Premise: Hunger and need > temple/tabernacle laws
>
> Evidence: First Samuel 21:1–6 shows that David and his men were able to eat bread not permitted to them by temple laws because of their hunger and need.
>
> Conclusion: Jesus's disciples can pluck grain to meet their physical needs on the Sabbath.

19. J. Meier, *A Marginal Jew*, 4:278. At least some of Mark's first readers, including Matthew and Luke (as well as manuscripts D and W), were aware of how this undermined Mark's portrayal of Jesus and attempted to correct the Markan Jesus's argument. For a helpful treatment of some of these difficulties, see Botner, "Has Jesus Read What David Did?"

Maxim 1: Sabbath was made for humanity not humanity for the Sabbath (Mark 2:27).[20]

= Humanity > Sabbath

Maxim 2: The Son of Man is lord over the Sabbath (Mark 2:28).

= Son of Man > Sabbath

On the basis of this form of the argument, scholars have claimed that the example of David does not fit well the argument Jesus is here trying to make, since nothing about 1 Samuel 21 actually relates to the Sabbath.[21] In fact, Stephen Westerholm argues that in this story "satisfaction is taken and an argument built on the very fact that David's action was unlawful; he ate 'what is unlawful to eat' (v. 26). His action is not brought in line with Torah, but cited as a biblical example where the letter of Torah is broken. No Pharisaic argument, this."[22] I would suggest, in contrast, that Mark fails to make explicit a significantly fuller legal logic that undergirds Jesus's words. If hunger and need precede the temple service, then hunger and need (of both humanity and the Son of Man) must precede Sabbath observance.[23] This is the implicit shape of Jesus's argument in Mark:

Assumed Premise 1: Hunger and need > temple/tabernacle laws

Evidence: First Samuel 21:1–6 shows that David and his men were able to eat bread, which temple laws prohibited to them, because of their hunger and need.

Assumed Premise 2: Temple/tabernacle > Sabbath

Assumed Evidence: Legislation that *requires* offerings be made on the Sabbath (Lev. 24:8; Num. 28:9; Ezek. 46:1, 4, 12)

---

20. The *Mekilta* connects a similar pronouncement to Rabbi Simon ben Menasiah: "The Sabbath is given to you but you are not surrendered to the Sabbath" (*Mekilta of Rabbi Ishmael, Shabbata* 1, trans. Lauterbach, 3:198). Likewise, Babylonian Talmud, *Yoma* 85b preserves a saying of Rabbi Yosé, son of Rabbi Judah: "*Only ye shall keep My Sabbaths*; one might assume under all circumstances, therefore the text reads: '*Only*' viz., allowing for exceptions. R. Jonathan b. Joseph said: *For it is holy unto you*; i.e. it [the Sabbath] is committed to your hands, not you to its hands" (emphasis original). Cf. *2 Baruch* 14.18: "Humanity was not created for the world, but the world for humanity."

21. E.g., Dunn, *Jesus, Paul and the Law*, 22.

22. Westerholm, *Jesus and Scribal Authority*, 98. In contrast, N. Collins demonstrates the remarkable similarities between Jesus's arguments in Sabbath controversy stories and later rabbinic argumentation, although I am unconvinced by her conclusion that Jesus's followers have merely taken these arguments from their Jewish contemporaries in order to provide Jesus with credibility (*Jesus, the Sabbath and the Jewish Debate*).

23. So too N. Collins, *Jesus, the Sabbath and the Jewish Debate*, 54.

Conclusion: Hunger and need > Sabbath

Maxim 1: Sabbath given to humans

Maxim 2: Son of Man is lord of the Sabbath

Although I have suggested that Mark has not made explicit his second premise, that temple service takes precedence over Sabbath observance, it is possible that he assumes his readers will know enough to supply this step of the argument. In fact, the very scriptural example he provides, 1 Samuel 21:1–6, might bring this premise to mind, since the story of David's prohibited consumption of the bread of the presence not only shows that human hunger and need take precedence over the temple cult but also forges a connection to the Sabbath. The same text that prohibits nonpriests from consuming this bread also requires the priests to work on the Sabbath in order to set out the bread of the presence (Lev. 24:8–9). This connection between the bread of the presence and priestly work on the Sabbath is something that later rabbinic texts note in connection with 1 Samuel 21—the rabbis not only emphasize David's legal infraction but also heighten it by noting that it occurred *on* the Sabbath.[24] This addition to the story of 1 Samuel 21 is eminently logical. Either Ahimelech enters into the tabernacle at the wrong time in order to provide for the needs of David and his men, thus further demonstrating that human need takes precedence over the tabernacle/temple cult, or he enters the tabernacle on the Sabbath and thereby does work on the Sabbath by bringing something out of sacred space in order to meet human needs.[25]

Additionally, Mark's Jesus claims that the Sabbath was given to humanity, not humanity to the Sabbath. We see a parallel claim in rabbinic literature.[26] Such a sentiment once again is legal in nature. Both Jesus and the rabbis depend upon scriptural texts for this conclusion. For instance, in talking about the collection of manna, Moses claims that God has given the Sabbath *to* Israel (Exod. 16:29). Similarly, Ezekiel portrays God saying, "My Sabbaths I gave *to* them" (Ezek. 20:12, emphasis mine). On the basis of these and other texts, both Jesus and later rabbis aver that Sabbath observance cannot take precedence over the preservation of life; God gave the Sabbath to Israel, not Israel to the Sabbath.

24. Cf. Babylonian Talmud, *Menahot* 95b; *Yalqut Shimoni* on 1 Sam. 21:5.

25. Cf. 1 Chron 9:32; Josephus, *Jewish Antiquities* 3.255–56; Mishnah, *Sukkah* 5.7–8; Mishnah, *Menahot* 11.7. See Casey, *Aramaic Sources of Mark's Gospel*, 155–57.

26. *Mekilta of Rabbi Ishmael, Shabbata* 1, on Exod. 31:14.

Matthew's Rewriting of Mark's Story

Confirmation that this is the correct way to read Mark's narrative and that this is the underlying logic of Jesus's argument comes in the form of one of the very first rereadings of it (Matt. 12). In numerous ways, Matthew strengthens the form of the argument that the Markan Jesus makes, demonstrating his concern to provide a legal defense of Jesus and his disciples. He removes Mark's mistaken claim about Abiathar, makes clear that Jesus's disciples were hungry, claims that they plucked grain in order to eat it, and fills in the key link in Jesus's legal argument that is at best implied in Mark's account. It is this final improvement that I want to focus on here.

Matthew's Jesus asks, "Or have you not read in the law that on the Sabbath the priests in the temple profane the Sabbath and yet are blameless?" (Matt. 12:5). Jesus rightly observes that there is a hierarchy in law observance and that there will be times when a person must obey one law even as it involves the breaking of another law. When priests work on the Sabbath, they are not guilty, even though they fail to keep the Sabbath, since temple service is superior to Sabbath observance. Matthew makes explicit, then, what Mark implies. And Mark could assume his readers would supply this missing step of the argument because the belief that temple service was superior to Sabbath observance was probably universally held. For instance, two centuries before Mark writes his Gospel, the author of *Jubilees* plainly states that there is only one type of work that can occur on the Sabbath:

> For great is the honor which the LORD gave to Israel to eat and to drink and to be satisfied on this day of festival and to rest in it from all work of the occupations of the children of men except to offer incense and to bring gifts and sacrifices before the LORD for the days and the sabbaths. This work alone shall be done on the day of the sabbath in the sanctuary of the LORD your God so that they might atone for Israel (with) continual gift day by day for an acceptable memorial before the LORD. And so that he might accept them forever, day by day, just as he commanded you.[27]

Later rabbinic pronouncements note this same legal hierarchy: "Temple service overrides Sabbath."[28] Both *Jubilees* and later rabbis acknowledge that priests who perform temple service can *legally* "break" the Sabbath. Were either the author of *Jubilees* or the rabbis to become convinced that there

---

27. *Jubilees* 50.10–11. My intuition is that the author would also have made an exception for the rite of circumcision, which he elsewhere emphasizes, in accordance with Gen. 17:12–14 and Lev. 12:3, which state it *must* occur on the eighth day after birth (see *Jubilees* 15).

28. E.g., Mishnah, *Temurah* 2.1; *Sifre Numbers* 144; Babylonian Talmud, *Yoma* 85b.

was something that took precedence over temple service, they would need to conclude that whatever this thing was, it too took legal precedence over the Sabbath.   X as Temple

Mark assumes this logic; Matthew makes it overt. Matthew's Jesus argues that there is something now here that is even greater than the temple, so it must take precedence over the Sabbath. He acknowledges that his disciples work on the Sabbath, yet they are, in his mind, compelled to do so in a way that compares to the priestly obligation to work on the Sabbath. Neither form of work actually profanes the Sabbath. What this greater thing is, Matthew does not make explicit,[29] although his quotation of Hosea 6:6 LXX ("I [God] desire mercy more than sacrifice") suggests that another hierarchy exists, one that prioritizes mercy over sacrifice—that is, the temple service.[30] Matthew's Jesus has already stressed this verse (Matt. 9:13) to defend his practice of associating with sinners and tax collectors. And toward the end of Matthew's Gospel, Jesus again emphasizes this same hierarchical order as the way to proper law observance; tithing herbs, while valuable, is not equivalent to the weighty aspects of the law, such as justice, mercy, and faithfulness (23:23).

In other words, mercy takes precedence even over temple service and sacrifice. What is this mercy? While Matthew does not say, the following story, which Matthew inherits from Mark and which we shall look at in more depth shortly, illustrates at least part of what this mercy entails: healing and restoring human life (Matt. 12:9–14; cf. Mark 3:1–6; Luke 6:6–11). Here, perhaps contrary to modern Christian perceptions, Matthew's Jesus says nothing remarkable. In the first half of the second century CE, for instance, Rabbi Simeon ben Azzai refers to minor laws,[31] while in the third century CE, Rabbi Yehudah ha-Nasi distinguishes between minor and major commandments.[32] Building on this logic, the Tosefta contains the anonymous legal opinion that "charity and righteous deeds outweigh all other commandments in the Torah."[33] Such a legal opinion dates to the first century BCE, since the house of Shammai and the house of Hillel (according to Rabban Simeon ben Gamaliel) argued over how best to observe the law.[34] The house of Shammai prioritized

New Creation

---

29. So too Luz, *Matthew 8–20*, 181–82, and Doering, "Sabbath Laws," 223. William R. G. Loader argues that this something is Jesus, the Messiah (*Jesus' Attitude towards the Law*, 202–4), while Daniel J. Harrington suggests that Jesus, the kingdom of God, and the community of followers are all in mind (*Gospel of Matthew*, 172).

30. See Kruse, "Die 'dialektische Negation,'" which argues that this construction does not intend to negate "sacrifice" but to prioritize mercy.

31. Mishnah, *Avot* 4.2.

32. Mishnah, *Avot* 2.1.

33. Tosefta, *Pe'ah* 4.19; cf. Mishnah, *Avot* 1.2.

34. Tosefta, *Shabbat* 16.22.

Sabbath over deeds of charity or prayer for the sick, while Hillel prioritized deeds of charity and prayer for the sick over the Sabbath. Similarly, according to the Talmud, the first-century CE Rabbi Eleazar ruled, "One may determine charity [grants] to the poor on the Sabbath."[35] As a rule, financial calculations cannot take place on the Sabbath, but when it comes to the work of charity, such actions are permissible because charity (that is, mercy) is a legal requirement weightier than observing the Sabbath.[36] When Matthew's Jesus prioritizes mercy/charity over temple service (and consequently Sabbath), he is not some lone voice calling out in a supposed wilderness of inhumane Jewish legalism; rather, he is one of many Jewish voices who have come to the conclusion that mercy and charity take legal precedence even over such crucial things as temple service and Sabbath.

The Sabbath: For Life or Death?

Immediately after the story of the plucking of the grain, Mark introduces a story in which Jesus heals on the Sabbath—presumably showing what kind of work takes precedence over the Sabbath. Mark 3:1–6, then, demonstrates *how* or *why* the Sabbath was given to humanity and *how* the Son of Man is lord over even the Sabbath.

> And again [Jesus] entered into the synagogue. And there was there a man who had a dried-up hand. And they were watching him to see whether he would heal on the Sabbath, in order that they might reproach him. And [Jesus] said to the man who had the dried-up hand, "Stand up in the center." And he said to them, "Is it lawful to do good or to do evil on the Sabbath, to save life or to kill?" But they were silent. And looking around at them with wrath, and grieving at the hardness of their hearts, he said to the man, "Stretch out your hand!" And [the man] stretched out his hand and it was restored. And going out, the Pharisees immediately conspired with the Herodians against Jesus as to how they might kill him. (Mark 3:1–6; cf. Matt. 12:9–14; Luke 6:6–11)

Since this is the second deed of power that Jesus performs on the Sabbath, it appears that Mark envisages the exorcism that Jesus performed in Mark 1 to have led to subsequent concerns among at least some of Jesus's

---

35. Babylonian Talmud, *Shabbat* 150a.

36. On the central place of charity in rabbinic thought, see Gray, "Redemptive Almsgiving and the Rabbis"; Gray, *Charity in Rabbinic Judaism*; Wilfand, *Poverty, Charity, and the Poor*; and Gardner, *Origins of Organized Charity*. On the topic of charity (and its identification with mercy) in the Gospel of Matthew, see Eubank, *Wages of Cross-Bearing*; for Luke, see Giambrone, *Sacramental Charity*.

contemporaries. Consequently, when Jesus enters into a synagogue on another Sabbath, some Pharisees watch to see whether he will heal yet again. At least as Mark narrates it, these Pharisees appear to be using the man with the dried-up hand as bait to see if they can draw Jesus's suspected Sabbath disregard out into the open. Instead of furtively healing the man, Jesus calls the entire synagogue's attention to the man, telling him to stand up in their midst. Using the man with the dried-up hand as an object lesson, he asks his opponents two questions:

Is it lawful to do good or to do evil on the Sabbath?
Is it lawful to save life or to kill on the Sabbath?

Both questions, in Mark's mind, provide a rationale for Jesus's custom of healing on the Sabbath.

The latter question, whether it is lawful to save life or to kill, needs to be understood in light of contemporary Jewish debates, which reflect concerns over the impracticalities of observing the Sabbath in warfare. Already in the fourth century BCE, the Macedonian Ptolemy I Soter was able to capture Jerusalem because he entered it on the Sabbath.[37] Then in the second century BCE, the Seleucid Antiochus IV Epiphanes killed many Jews on the Sabbath, since they piously refused to profane the Sabbath by defending themselves.[38] Instead of finding this type of Sabbath observance praiseworthy, Mattathias, a priest from Modin who instigated the rebellion against the Syrians, argued that Jews should fight on the Sabbath in order to prevent such slaughter from ever happening again. This decision was strikingly practical, given the fact that he was himself a zealous defender of the Jewish law. Mattathias's rationale is the following: "If we all do what our brothers did and do not wage war against the gentiles [on the Sabbath] for our lives and for our ordinances, then they will wipe us out from the land."[39] For Mattathias, preserving life was a greater law than observing the Sabbath rest. Yet there were limits to this work: "Let us wage war against any man who comes upon us for war on the Sabbath day" (1 Macc. 2:41). Only if directly attacked on the Sabbath would Mattathias and his warriors respond. Military defense was legally permissible; military aggression was not.[40]

In contrast to both Mattathias's commonsense approach and later rabbinic argumentation, the book of *Jubilees* condemns any military activity on the

37. Josephus, *Jewish Antiquities* 12.4.
38. 1 Macc. 2:35–38; cf. Josephus, *Jewish Antiquities* 12.274.
39. 1 Macc. 2:40; cf. Josephus, *Jewish Antiquities* 12.276.
40. See Doering, *Schabbat*, 201–4, 232–35.

Sabbath. At the very end of a discussion of the Sabbath, the author declares that making war is one of the prohibited forms of work on the Sabbath.[41] Without exception, for the author of *Jubilees* at least, the waging of war on the Sabbath would result in the death penalty. As Meier concludes, the fact that this reference to war concludes the author's discussion of the Sabbath suggests that this issue was contentious when he wrote it.[42] And a fragmentary text from Qumran might also support the position of *Jubilees*, since it appears to prohibit going out to meet an attacking enemy.[43] Nonetheless, it was the just-war theory that Mattathias articulated that prevailed among Jews in the latter half of the Second Temple period.[44] Josephus himself, though, voices two different legal positions regarding war and the Sabbath, putting the following words on the lips of Herod Agrippa II, who attempts to persuade his fellow Jews not to revolt against Rome:

> Consider, too, the difficulty of preserving your religious rules from contamination [in war], even were you engaging a less formidable foe; and how, if compelled to transgress the very principles on which you chiefly build your hopes of God's assistance, you will alienate Him from you. If you observe your Sabbath customs and refuse to take any action on that day, you will undoubtedly be easily defeated, as were your forefathers by Pompey, when the besieged remained inactive; if, on the contrary, you transgress the law of your ancestors, I fail to see what further object you will have for hostilities, since your one aim is to preserve inviolate all the institutions of your fathers. How could you invoke the aid of the Deity, after deliberately omitting to pay Him the service which you owe Him?[45]

The position of Mattathias, on the other hand, is rooted in the belief that the safeguarding of life is more important than Sabbath observance, a belief that one can see preserved in later rabbinic literature: "Any matter of doubt pertaining to the saving of life supersedes the Sabbath."[46] This text cites a number of cases in which a person's life *might* be at risk. For instance, if a person has a ravenous hunger, one can feed him anything, even impure food, in order to save his life; a person bitten by a rabid dog should be, according to some, fed part of the dog's liver even though it is not kosher; and a person

---

41. *Jubilees* 50.12.
42. J. Meier, *A Marginal Jew*, 4:34.
43. *Community Rule* (4Q264ᵃ) 3 8.
44. Cf. Josephus, *Jewish Antiquities* 13.12; 14.64; 14.226; Josephus, *Jewish War* 1.146; 2.517; Frontinus, *Strategems* 2.1.18.
45. Josephus, *Jewish War* 2.390–93.
46. Mishnah, *Yoma* 8.6; cf. Babylonian Talmud, *Yoma* 83a, 84b.

who has a sore throat should be given medicine even on the Sabbath. Later rabbinic tradition refers to this legal principle as *piqquaḥ nefesh*: the legal-religious duty to save life.[47]

Nonetheless, Qumranic legal materials suggest that others believed that the Sabbath outweighed human life—something that would be consonant with the prohibition of war on the Sabbath found in *Jubilees* and 4Q264. For instance, the *Damascus Document* states,

> And any living person who falls into a place of water or a place
> of [. . .]
> Let no one bring him up with a ladder, or a rope, or a tool.[48]

On the other hand, another Qumran text stipulates that one can use the garment one is wearing to help the person out of the pit but cannot go to one's house to retrieve some other object to help the person in distress.[49]

It is within this context of Jewish legal debate that we must read the controversies about Jesus's actions on the Sabbath. Jesus's own words in Mark 3 fit within a stream of tradition that emphasizes the preservation of life over the observance of Sabbath, although Jesus's contrast between saving life and killing might also be a pointed criticism of waging war on the Sabbath.[50] If Jesus's opponents answer that it is permissible to save life on the Sabbath, then they concede that his actions are legally defensible. By refusing to answer, Jesus's opponents implicitly choose death over life, thereby demonstrating their hardness of heart.[51] This preference of Jesus's opponents for killing over giving life resurfaces at the end of the story; Mark depicts the Pharisees and Herodians departing the synagogue in order to plot the death of Jesus. Confirming that they have chosen death over life, doing evil over doing good, *they* become guilty of desecrating the Sabbath by doing the work of plotting to create both moral and corpse impurity. As Joel Marcus puts it, "Contrary, then, to the Pharisees' principle of saving life on the Sabbath and their professed concern for the day's sanctity, they themselves desecrate the

---

47. See also Tosefta, *Shabbat* 9.22; 15.11. *Mekilta of Rabbi Ishmael*, Nezikin 4: "R. Simon b. Menasya says: The duty of saving life should supersede the Sabbath laws, and the following reasoning favors it: If the punishing of murder sets aside the Temple service, how much the more should the duty of saving life, which likewise sets aside the Temple service, supersede the Sabbath law" (Lauterbach, 3:40).

48. *Damascus Document* XI, 16–17.

49. 4Q265 6 5–8.

50. See here, Casey, *Aramaic Sources of Mark's Gospel*, 173–92.

51. So Bolt, *Jesus' Defeat of Death*, 118. As Bolt notes, some later scribes pick up on this preference for death over life and modify "hardness [*pōrōsis*] of heart" to "dead [*nekrōsis*] of heart."

Sabbath by using it to plot Jesus' murder."[52] In fact, those who subscribed to the legal position of Qumran or *Jubilees* would have deemed the plotting of the Pharisees and Herodians to be an impermissible breach of the Sabbath, since this position prohibits the discussion of work on the Sabbath, something that presumably would have included the plotting of someone's death.[53] The Qumran work known as 4Q264[a] seems to expand upon this prohibition:

> No one shall reckon [with his mouth]
> [to pursue his affairs on the Sabbath. He shall not speak] about any
>   matters or working or property or [buying]
> [and selling or traveling] on the next d[a]y. He may only sp[eak w]ords
>   of [holy] matters [as is customary and he may spe]ak to bless
>   God. Yet, one may speak [of things] with regard to eating and
>   drinking [ ]
> [. . . and with regard to any] delight on the Sa[bbath . . .].[54]

The legal position poorly preserved in this text suggests that any conversation that does not pertain to the delights of the Sabbath legally breaches the Sabbath's sanctity. Consequently, anyone holding this position would deem the macabre discussion of the Pharisees and Herodians to be unlawful. Given the arguments of the preceding chapters, it is noteworthy that Mark and Matthew (but not Luke) depict the Pharisees and Herodians using sacred time to plot a way to create corpse impurity. Mark's story aims to demonstrate that it is the Pharisees and Herodians who break the Sabbath and in so doing increase ritual impurity.

Unlike the Pharisees and Herodians in this story, "Jesus literally *does nothing*. He simply issues two brief, simple commands to the afflicted man."[55] The words that Jesus speaks, in contrast to the words of the Pharisees and Herodians, pertain to the delight of the Sabbath. Surely both the afflicted man and those present at the synagogue experienced joy over the healed hand. But in contrast to this story, elsewhere Jesus does heal others through touch on the Sabbath (e.g., Mark 1:31; John 9:14).

---

52. Marcus, *Mark 1–8*, 253–54.

53. *Jubilees* 50.8; *Damascus Document* X, 19.

54. 4Q264[a] 1 I, 5–2 II, 1. I reproduce here the reconstruction of 4Q264[a] fragment 1 and 4Q241 fragments 2, 8, and 13 found in Noam and Qimron, "Qumran Composition of Sabbath Laws."

55. J. Meier, *A Marginal Jew*, 4:254. As Tertullian recognized long ago, "For when it says of the Sabbath day, No work of thine shalt thou do in it, by saying thine it has made a ruling concerning that human work which any man performs by his craft or business, not divine work. But the work of healing or of rescue is not properly man's work but God's." *Against Marcion* 4.12.10.

Jesus may be doing good on the Sabbath in healing the man, but how can the Gospel writers justify the implication that Jesus is saving life on the Sabbath (Mark 3:4; cf. Matt. 12:12; Luke 6:9) when he heals those who suffer from non-life-threatening illnesses? After all, a man who has had a withered hand for an undefined period of time is unlikely to drop dead because of it. Matthew, at least, conforms Jesus's question to his action of healing the man: "Is it lawful to heal on the Sabbath?" (12:10). But what about Mark and Luke? A partial answer might be found in ancient Jewish thinking surrounding illness, which Jon Levenson suggests differs from modern conceptions of illness.[56] Especially in light of modern medical advances, we view illness in the following way:

$$\text{Life} \rightarrow \text{Illness} \parallel \text{Death}$$

That is, there is a sharp distinction in modern thinking between life, whether healthy or sick, and death. On the other hand, ancient Jewish thought associated illness more closely with death:

$$\text{Life} \parallel \text{Illness} \rightarrow \text{Death}$$

If sickness is closely connected to death, then the healing of illnesses, of whatever sort, is an effort to move someone across the barrier that separates life from death and illness. Such thinking would also provide a conceptual connection between Jesus's numerous healings of people with a variety of illnesses and his related but more specific healings of those who suffer conditions that create ritual impurity. Since ritual impurity represents mortality or death, and since illness also can be associated with death, all of these various deeds of power depict a Jesus who has power over death and can liberate those oppressed by the forces of death.

Additionally, a withered hand would likely be a paralyzed hand and could therefore be associated with the death-dealing activities of the demonic. For instance, though written later, the *Testament of Solomon* associates the paralysis of limbs with the destructive activity of a demon named Sphandor.[57] And dried-up body parts were considered lifeless or dead in Greco-Roman medical thought.[58] A dried-up limb was a dead limb. To restore that limb was to transfer one body part (and perhaps the whole body) from death to life.

---

56. Levenson, *Resurrection and the Restoration of Israel*, 35–66.
57. *Testament of Solomon* 18.11.
58. See Plato, *Timaeus* 88D; Hippocrates, according to Aretaeus, *De causis* 1.7.2. See here Bolt, *Jesus' Defeat of Death*, 119–21. On ancient understandings of paralysis more generally, see pp. 104–15.

As in the story of Jesus and his disciples in the grainfields, Matthew supplements Mark's story by adding another legal argument to the discussion: "Suppose one of you has only one sheep and it falls into a pit on the Sabbath; will you not lay hold of it and lift it out? How much more valuable is a human being than a sheep! So it is lawful to do good on the Sabbath" (Matt. 12:11–12). While Luke follows Mark's account quite closely, elsewhere he adds a similar legal claim in relation to the healing of a man with dropsy: "If one of you has a son or an ox that had fallen into a well, would you not immediately pull him out on the day of the Sabbath?" (Luke 14:5).[59] In regard to this latter story, at least one ancient writer, Diogenes Laertius, would have viewed dropsy (*hydrōpikos*) as potentially life-threatening since it hastened the death of a man.[60] Luke, however, does not make explicit any such belief.

In adding this material to Mark's controversy stories, both Matthew and Luke provide legal defenses for Jesus's proclivity for Sabbath healings. Jesus's argument in both of these stories presupposes that his audience will answer yes to his question; they would indeed save their animals on the Sabbath. And given this assumed agreement, how much more should one save human life? The logic of the statement proceeds in the following manner:

Stated Premise: The life of one's animals > Sabbath

Assumed Premise: Human life > animal life

Conclusion: Human life > Sabbath

But some have argued that Jesus's assumption that his audience would agree that one should or would set aside Sabbath rest to rescue an animal from a pit is unfounded, since the few texts that address this possibility suggest otherwise. For instance, the *Damascus Document* asserts that

> no one should help an animal give birth on the day of the Sabbath; and if it falls into a well or a pit, no one may lift it out on the Sabbath. . . .

59. Many manuscripts read "son or ox"; a number of manuscripts read "donkey or ox"; others read "donkey, son, or ox"; and still others read "sheep or ox." The latter reading probably results from the influence of Matt. 12:11–12 on Luke 14:5. The third reading is probably an attempt to conflate the first two readings. Given the early manuscript support for "son or ox" (e.g., P[45], P[75], A, B, W, Δ, 28) and the fact that it is a slightly odd combination (a human and an animal in comparison to two animals), the first reading is preferable.

60. Diogenes Laertius, *Lives of Eminent Philosophers* 4.27. As pointed out by Oliver, *Torah Praxis*, 140.

> And any living person who falls into a place of water or a place of [. . .]
> Let no one bring him up with a ladder, or a rope, or a tool.[61]

This work concludes that one can do no work to preserve an animal's life on the Sabbath. Its author and those who subscribed to its position would have disagreed with Jesus's stated premise in this story. In fact, they also thought that Sabbath observance was more important than preserving a person's life. A related text, 4Q265, contains a slightly different legal position: "Let no one lift up an animal that has fallen into the water on the day of the Sabbath. But if it is a living person who falls into the water [on] the [day] of the Sabbath, one shall extend his garment to him to lift him out with it, but he shall not carry a tool [on the day of] the Sabbath."[62] Here the text again suggests that one cannot work on the Sabbath in order to save the life of an animal. In contrast with the *Damascus Document*, though, it makes one vital concession with regard to human life: one can use what one is wearing to save another person's life but cannot go home and bring back any implement to help that distressed person. Both of these works, then, wrestle with how to order (potentially) competing aspects of the Jewish law: the need to preserve life and the need to observe the Sabbath rest.

We see a similar effort to prioritize competing laws in later rabbinic literature. For instance, according to the Tosefta, Rabban Simeon ben Gamaliel concluded that on the Sabbath one can feed an animal that has fallen into a pit, but one cannot pull it out of the pit until after the Sabbath has ended.[63] The Talmud preserves a saying attributed to the third-century CE Rav:

> If an animal falls into a dyke, one brings pillows and bedding and places [them] under it, and if it ascends it ascends. An objection is raised: If an animal falls into a dyke, provisions are made for it where it lies so that it should not perish. Thus, only provisions, but not pillows and bedding?—There is no difficulty: here it means where provisions are possible; there, where provisions are impossible. If provisions are possible, well and good; but if not, one brings pillows and bedding and places them under it. But he robs a utensil of its readiness [for use]?—[The avoidance of] suffering of dumb animals is a Biblical [law], so the Biblical law comes and supersedes the [interdict] of the Rabbis.[64]

These texts demonstrate that Jews debated to what degree they could alleviate the discomfort of animals on the Sabbath. While their various authors differ

---

61. *Damascus Document* XI, 13–14, 16–17.
62. 4Q265 6 5–8.
63. Tosefta, *Shabbat* 14.3.
64. Babylonian Talmud, *Shabbat* 128b.

in the answers they provide, none of them suggest that one can lift an animal out of a pit on the Sabbath.[65] Perhaps Jesus's statement reflects non-Qumranic and non-rabbinic (or non-Pharisaic) practices here.[66]

And one could make a scriptural case for Jesus's assumption. As the final statement of the Talmudic passage quoted above notes, Jewish scriptures require that Israelites relieve the suffering of animals, even animals that hate their owners or that belong to one's enemy (Exod. 23:5; Deut. 22:4).[67] What happens when this law and the law of the Sabbath come into conflict? Again, recall the words of the Roman politician and lawyer Cicero: "One should compare the laws by considering which one deals with the most important matters, that is, the most expedient, honourable or necessary. The conclusion from this is that if two laws (or whatever number there may be if more than two) cannot be kept because they are at variance, the one is thought to have the greatest claim to be upheld which has reference to the greatest matter."[68] Further, the Sabbath laws expressly require that Israelites permit their domesticated animals to rest on the Sabbath. One could argue that an animal that has fallen into a pit cannot enjoy the Sabbath rest that God intended for it, because it would be distressed, continually seeking to escape its predicament. If one is to give livestock rest on the Sabbath, one may need to rescue them from distress and harm. Such logic might have undergirded Jesus's belief that many of his hearers would find the rescuing of livestock on the Sabbath uncontroversial.

Further, the rabbis also emphasized that one could do whatever was necessary on the Sabbath in order to save the life of a fellow human. For instance, if a person sees a child fall into the sea, one can use a fishing net to pull the child to safety. If one sees a young child trapped behind a closed door, one can open that door to let the child out (even if that child's life is not at risk). And they conclude that if one sees a child fall into a pit, one can break off part of the earth to help the child out again—a close parallel to Jesus's words.[69] And if a building collapses on the Sabbath, one can dig to uncover a living person.[70] Later yet, *Numbers Rabbah* claims that if gentiles or thieves pursue a man on the Sabbath, the man may profane the Sabbath in order to save his life.[71] If such legal positions existed in the first century CE, and presumably they

65. Oliver, *Torah Praxis*, 120.
66. Oliver, *Torah Praxis*, 122–23.
67. Oliver, *Torah Praxis*, 123.
68. Cicero, *On Invention* 2.49.145.
69. Babylonian Talmud, *Yoma* 84b; Jerusalem Talmud, *Shabbat* 14.14.
70. Babylonian Talmud, *Yoma* 85a; cf. Jerusalem Talmud, *Yoma* 8.5.
71. *Numbers Rabbah* 23.1.

did, since Qumran literature demonstrates the existence of such a position by disagreeing with it, then the Gospel writers show the way that Jesus's legal defense coincides with some of his contemporaries' arguments.

The Gospel of John and Jesus's Sabbath Healings

Sabbath controversies occur also in the Gospel of John and demonstrate John's desire to depict Jesus's actions as consistent with Sabbath observance.[72] But John's Jesus makes a different legal argument in support of his Sabbath behavior. After receiving criticism for healing on the Sabbath, Jesus says, "If a man receives circumcision on the Sabbath so that the law of Moses may not be broken, are you upset with me because I healed a man's whole body on the Sabbath?" (John 7:23). Jesus makes use of the fact that circumcision, since it contains a temporal stipulation that it occur on the eighth day after birth (Gen. 17:12, 14; Lev. 12:3), takes precedence over the Sabbath.[73] The work of circumcision, therefore, makes it permissible to "break" the Sabbath. Again, this is no novel argument; we see the same legal position preserved repeatedly in later rabbinic literature. For instance, the Mishnah states, "All that is necessary for circumcision is done on the Sabbath."[74] As the second-century CE Rabbi Yosé puts it, "Great is circumcision, for it supersedes the Sabbath."[75]

Given this legal position, the rabbis extrapolate from circumcision legislation to address how the legal requirement to preserve life supersedes Sabbath observance. This is the argument of Rabbi Eliezer, who lived in the first and second centuries CE: "As to circumcision, on account of which they override the prohibitions of the Sabbath, why is this so? It is because they are liable to extirpation [cf. Gen. 17:14] if it is not done on time. Now lo, the matter yields an argument *a fortiori*: Now if on account of a single limb of a person [i.e., the penis], they override the prohibitions of the Sabbath, is it not logical that one should override the prohibitions of the Sabbath on account of [the saving of] the whole of him?"[76] Frequently the rabbis claim that the rite of

---

72. On this passage, see Derrett, "Circumcision and Perfection," and Pancaro, *Law in the Fourth Gospel*, 164.

73. On the text of Gen. 17:14 and its implications for the timing of circumcision, see Thiessen, "Text of Genesis 17:14."

74. Mishnah, *Shabbat* 18.3; cf. Mishnah, *Shabbat* 19.2–3; Tosefta, *Yom Tov* 1.6.

75. Mishnah, *Nedarim* 3.11.

76. Tosefta, *Shabbat* 15.16, in Neusner, *Tosefta*; cf. *Mekilta of Rabbi Ishmael, Amalek* 3; *Mekilta of Rabbi Ishmael, Shabbata* 1; Babylonian Talmud, *Yoma* 85a–b; Babylonian Talmud, *Shabbat* 132a–b.

circumcision results in bodily wholeness. They make this claim on the basis of Genesis 17:1, where God calls Abram to walk before him and be whole/complete/perfect (Hebrew: *tamim*). For instance, according to the Mishnah, the second-century CE Rabbi Meir taught, "Great is circumcision, for, despite all the commandments that Abraham our father did, he was called complete [*shalom*] only when he had circumcised himself as it is said, Walk before me and be complete [*tamim*]."[77] The legal argument that both Jesus and Rabbi Eliezer ben Azariah make, then, unfolds as follows:

> Premise 1: Circumcision > Sabbath observance
>
> Evidence: Genesis 17:12–14 and Leviticus 12:3, which require that circumcision take place on the eighth day after birth
>
> Premise 2: Circumcision cures the penis of a defect (the foreskin)
>
> Evidence: Genesis 17:1 states that circumcision makes one whole
>
> Premise 3: The entire body > one body part (the penis)[78]
>
> Conclusion: Making the entire body whole > Sabbath observance[79]

Again, Jesus's argument proceeds *legally*. No rejection of the Sabbath occurs here; rather, John's Jesus enters into the debate about ordering the laws in ways that do justice to the weightiest matters of the law first.

The Holy Sabbath: Moving from Impurity to Purity and Holiness

As the Gospel writers portray them, Jesus's actions and his reasoning for acting as he does on the Sabbath fit within a stream of Jewish thought that emphasized the priority of human life (one might be tempted to call this an emphasis on mercy/charity) over Sabbath observance. Consequently, Lutz Doering is correct to conclude that "Jesus took a principle shared by many contemporary Jews (that life saving sets the Sabbath aside) as [a] point of departure and extended its application (Mark 3:4). Disagreement on this legal

77. Mishnah, *Nedarim* 3.11; cf. Babylonian Talmud, *Nedarim* 32a.

78. One can also find legal argumentation that the preservation of life supersedes the requirement to circumcise a male infant eight days after his birth. For instance, both Mishnah, *Shabbat* 19.5 and Babylonian Talmud, *Shabbat* 137a claim that one postpones a sick baby's circumcision in order to preserve the child's life.

79. Given the similarity of Jesus's argument to the argument of Rabbi Eliezer, I find Loader's claim indefensible: "The debate over sabbath law [in John] reflects the stance of an outsider exposing inconsistencies, rather than a serious discussion of its application" (*Jesus' Attitude towards the Law*, 468).

issue must therefore be regarded as about the 'fine points' of the law, not as blunt confrontation or abrogation."[80]

If, as Jacob Milgrom has argued, holiness represents *life*, and impurity represents *death* in the priestly worldview, then when Jesus removes illnesses (whether or not they cause ritual impurities), he is involved in transferring people from the realm of death to the realm of life. In fact, elsewhere Luke's Jesus connects his Sabbath work with deliverance from the ruler of impure *pneumata*—Satan—asking his critics whether a Jewish woman ought to be freed on the Sabbath from her satanic bonds, which make her ill (Luke 13:16; cf. Acts 10:38). For Luke there is no better time than the Sabbath for healing and release from demonic impurity and oppression.[81] In his healings Jesus rescues people and restores them to wholeness of life during holy time, the Sabbath.

Conclusion

All of these various Sabbath controversy stories portray Jesus responding to criticisms of his Sabbath actions with *legal* arguments that would have been recognizable and theoretically acceptable to others.[82] The Jesus of the Gospels is a Jesus who seeks to observe the Jewish law and who provides legal defenses of his actions on the basis of the Jewish law. People may have disagreed with certain aspects of these arguments, whether a premise or a conclusion, but not with the type of arguments he makes. Consequently, these depictions demonstrate that the Gospel writers desired to portray Jesus in a way that proved, to their minds at least, that Jesus was observing the law properly. Central to any law observance (Jewish or otherwise) is the need to properly prioritize the regulations that make a body of laws, so that when two laws appear to conflict, one knows which of the two takes precedence. According to both the Jesus of the Gospels and many rabbis, human life takes precedence over the Sabbath. From this legal position, Jesus concludes that healing is a permissible work on the Sabbath.[83] Such actions are legally justifiable, as Marcus argues,

80. Doering, "Much Ado about Nothing?," 235–36.
81. Mayer-Haas, *"Geschenk aus Gottes,"* 295–96.
82. See also the saying of the *Gospel of Thomas* 27: "If you do not keep the sabbath as sabbath, you shall not see the father." And the D text of Luke 6:5 portrays Jesus saying to a man he sees working on the Sabbath, "Man, if you know what you are doing, you are blessed; but if you do not know, you are accursed and a transgressor of the law!" On these sayings, see Bauckham, "Sabbath and Sunday," 265–66.
83. Similarly, Schaller, "Jesus und der Sabbat."

For Mark's Jesus, the eschatological war is already raging, and on that battle-field every human action either strikes a blow for life or wields one for death; the cautious middle ground, upon which one might wait a few minutes before doing good, has disappeared. And if Jesus is "the holy one of God," whose holiness implies the apocalyptic destruction of demons and disease (cf. 1:24), then his Sabbath-day healing of the man with the paralyzed hand is a fulfillment rather than an infraction of the commandment to "remember the Sabbath day and keep it holy."[84]

I close this chapter with one final rabbinic story already mentioned above. According to the Tosefta, the house of Shammai concluded that one must not pray for or visit the sick on the Sabbath.[85] This legal position may strike some readers as inhumane, but this school of interpretation was convinced that such work broke the Sabbath because the Sabbath was to be a day of gladness,[86] whereas praying for or visiting the sick was not conducive to celebration.

The idea that the Sabbath was a festive day comes from Isaiah 58:13, which calls it a day of "delight" (LXX: *tryphera*), a word that evokes the garden of Eden since Genesis 3:23–24 LXX calls Eden a garden of delight (*tryphē*). Similarly, while the Hebrew of Ezekiel refers to the garden of Eden (Ezek. 28:13; 31:9), the LXX translator renders the Hebrew as "the garden of delight" (*ho paradeisos tēs tryphēs*). Philo calls the feast a symbol of the joy of the soul, using a term that includes and perhaps refers specifically to the Sabbath,[87] a day on which it is fitting to be thankful to God. Elsewhere he says

84. Marcus, *Mark 1–8*, 252–53. Sven-Olav Back also places Mark 2 within the context of the coming of the kingdom of God (*Jesus of Nazareth*, 161–78). Oliver makes similar remarks in connection to the Gospel of Luke:

> The Sabbath finds itself caught in an arena of ongoing *cosmic warfare* between the invasive kingdom of God as proclaimed by Jesus and the opposing forces of Satan. If satanic powers do not cease attacking and oppressing Israel on the Sabbath day, then God's incoming empire cannot and should not resist striking back. Ever since Macca-bean times, certain Jews had acknowledged the necessity of momentarily suspending the Sabbath during times of human warfare. By analogy, we might add that Jesus' healings, which for Luke really just constitute a manifestation of divine power and providence, must also be carried out on the Sabbath. It is a matter of cosmic proportions involving a controversy between good and evil, a story about God's reign overcoming Satan's rule, not just a question of improving human welfare. Luke does not openly draw or develop an analogy between Sabbath halakhah momentarily allowing Jews to engage in warfare and an eschatological theology that involves a cosmic confrontation. Nevertheless, he insinuates at several points through the usage of the passive voice that God is the one acting through Jesus to overcome ailments generated by satanic forces. (*Torah Praxis*, 136)

85. Tosefta, *Shabbat* 16.22; Babylonian Talmud, *Shabbat* 12a.

86. See here H. Weiss, *A Day of Gladness*.

87. Philo, *Migration of Abraham* 92.

that Jews spend the Sabbath cheerfully and in tranquility.[88] This understanding of the Sabbath is also implicit in the widespread prohibition of fasting on the Sabbath that can be found at Qumran,[89] in *Jubilees*,[90] and in later rabbinic literature.[91] While not an explicit prohibition of fasting, the book of Judith portrays its protagonist fasting all the days of her widowhood *except* on the day before the Sabbath, on the Sabbath itself, and on festival days, because these were joyful days (Jdt. 8:6). And according to *Pesiqta Rabbati*, an angel of God calls people out of Sheol so that they can delight in the Sabbath.[92] Any work that takes away from the joy of the Sabbath *must* be a prohibited work.

Perhaps this provides one reason why the Gospel writers depict Mary Magdalene, Mary the mother of James, and Salome coming to the tomb to anoint Jesus's dead body only *after* the Sabbath has ended (Mark 16:1; Matt. 28:1; Luke 23:56 [who explicitly says they rested according to the commandment]).[93] Such a solemn action was unfitting for the day of joy that was the Sabbath. Likewise, Matthew's Jesus tells his hearers to pray that the day of tribulation does not occur on a Sabbath, perhaps because the day would be an unhappy time of fleeing for one's life and not a day of joy (Matt. 24:20).

If such a sentiment were actually a legal principle for assessing what was permissible on the Sabbath, how would someone who holds this position judge Jesus's actions? Simply put, Jesus's actions of healing illnesses are distinctly dissimilar to visiting the sick precisely because the deeds Jesus performs actually increase joy. He does not merely visit the sick; rather, he heals and restores them, making them whole again. He has moved them from the realm of death to the realm of life. *Restorative Joy*

In fact, while one must again exercise caution in using later literature, we see later writers building upon this idea of the Sabbath as a joyful day, claiming that it is in fact a foretaste of the World to Come. For instance, in the Latin *Life of Adam and Eve*, the archangel Michael tells Seth not to mourn at Eve's death for more than six days: "Man of God, do not prolong mourning your dead more than six days, because the seventh day is a sign of the resurrection, the rest of the coming age, and on the seventh day the Lord rested from all his works."[94] Likewise, the Mishnah refers to Psalm 92, which contains a superscription that calls for it to be sung on the Sabbath,

---

88. Philo, *On the Life of Moses* 2.211.
89. *Damascus Document* XI, 4–5.
90. *Jubilees* 50.12.
91. E.g., Babylonian Talmud, *Rosh Hashanah* 19a.
92. *Pesiqta Rabbati* 23.8.
93. Cf. *Gospel of Peter* 27.
94. *Life of Adam and Eve* 51.2.

and rewords the superscription: "On the Sabbath day they did sing, a psalm, a song for the Sabbath day—a psalm, a song for the world to come, which is a perfect Sabbath rest for the life of eternity."[95] In the late third century CE, Rabbi Ḥanina ben Isaac echoes this claim: "The Sabbath is the incomplete form of the next world."[96] And the Talmud preserves the anonymous remark that the Sabbath is a fraction (precisely one-sixtieth!) of the World to Come.[97]

Such connections between the Sabbath and the World to Come coincide perfectly with Jesus's frequent claims that the kingdom of God has broken into this world. For the Gospel writers, the holy one of God has invaded the world and is bringing the life, wholeness, purity, and holiness that constitute the kingdom of God. If Mark, Matthew, and Luke are correct and the kingdom of God has come in Jesus, then what better time for Jesus to heal than the present, especially on the Sabbath, since it serves as a foretaste of all that the kingdom will bring?

95. Mishnah, *Tamid* 7.4.
96. *Genesis Rabbah* 17.5.
97. Babylonian Talmud, *Berakhot* 57b.

Conclusion

Who do people say that I am?

Mark 8:27

[His family] went out to seize him, for people were saying, "He is out of his mind!"

Mark 3:21

And the scribes from Jerusalem said, "He has Beelzebul, and by the ruler of the demons he casts out demons."

Mark 3:22

Peter answered [Jesus]: "You are the Messiah!"

Mark 8:29

Within a larger discussion of the tabernacle camp in the wilderness, God says to Moses, "Command the children of Israel that they send out from the camp every *lepros*, every genital discharger, and everyone who is impure by a corpse—both the male and the female you shall send outside, you shall send them out of the camp so that they do not make impure their camps in the midst of which I dwell" (Num. 5:2–3). Mark portrays Jesus encountering the ritually impure in the same order that is found in Numbers 5.[1] In Mark 1:40–45 he encounters a man suffering *lepra*; in Mark

---

1. Marcus (*Mark 1–8*, 367–68) and Fletcher-Louis ("Jesus as the High Priestly Messiah," 64) note this fact as well.

esus encounters a *zavah*, the female equivalent to the *zav*, who suf-
regular genital discharge; and in Mark 5:35–43 he encounters the
f a young girl. In each case, the ritually impure person leaves Jesus's
presence purified of the source of his or her impurity. I do not think it is a
coincidence that Mark relates stories about these particular ritual impurities;
the person with *lepra*, the woman with an irregular genital discharge, and the
corpse are, according to later rabbinic thought, the most powerful sources of
ritual impurity: "The *zavah* has a stronger impurity than the male with an
irregular genital discharge [and a list of fifteen other lesser sources of ritual
impurity]. . . . The [*lepros*] has a stronger impurity than the *zavah*. . . . A bone
the size of a barley corn has a stronger impurity than the [*lepros*]. . . . The
impurity of the corpse is stronger than all of them."[2] What Mark (and later
Matthew and Luke) conveys to his readers is that Jesus, being the holy one of
God, is so powerful a force of holiness that even the three strongest sources of
impurity (a bone fragment is, of course, part of a corpse) cannot withstand
him. Neither can the demonic forces of impurity that run rampant on earth.

What the narrative arc of Mark's Gospel suggests is that readers must
understand that Jesus is involved in a broadscale purification mission. Mark
portrays Jesus as a mobile power who removes the most stubborn sources
of the impurities he encounters. Jesus not only removes the sources of ritual
impurity, but he also removes moral impurities or sins, explicitly forgiving,
for example, the sins of a paralytic (Mark 2:4).[3] In the midst of a series of
controversy stories, Mark relates a story of Jesus healing a paralytic. After the
paralytic's friends lower him down to Jesus through the roof of a house, Jesus
says to him, "Your sins are forgiven" (2:5). To this remarkable proclamation,
some of the scribes rightly ask, "Why does this one speak in this way?" (2:7).
They accuse him of blasphemy, asking, "Who is able to forgive sins except God
alone?" What Mark's story suggests is that Jesus is interested in removing the
moral impurities of people as well as the sources of their ritual impurities. The
question here, though, unlike with Jesus's healing of the *lepros*, is whether
Jesus is able or powerful enough to remove moral impurities. Mark 1:40–45
demonstrates his ability and willingness to remove *lepra*, and this story proves
his willingness to remove moral impurity. But the scribes rightly stress that
only Israel's God is powerful enough to remove the moral impurity of sins.

Jesus's response, that it is easier to tell people that their sins are forgiven
than it is to tell them to get up and walk, is not entirely satisfying. One cannot disprove a person's claim to forgive someone's sins as easily as one could

---

2. Mishnah, *Kelim* 1.4.
3. E.g., Hägerland, *Jesus and the Forgiveness of Sins*.

disprove that someone has the power to heal a paralytic. Precisely because of the lack of evidence, one cannot be certain that Jesus is able to forgive sins.[4] Nonetheless, the story focuses on Jesus's authority to forgive sins, thus connecting it to a larger theme in Mark's Gospel about Jesus's identity and authority. Already in Jesus's first public act in Mark, the crowds marvel at the authority with which he teaches. Adding to their wonder, Jesus expels an impure *pneuma* from a man (Mark 1:22, 27). But does such authority extend to the removal of moral impurities as well? Mark's answer (and Matthew's and Luke's) is yes.

In his important study on ritual impurity and the historical Jesus, Thomas Kazen suggests that Jesus repeatedly demonstrates laxity toward the Jewish ritual purity system. The reason for this supposed laxity, Kazen concludes, is that "Jesus was part of a moral trajectory which placed relative importance on ethics . . . which did not allow purity rules to intervene with social network, table fellowship and community, [*because*] his eschatological outlook made impurity subordinate to the kingdom."[5] Kazen's conclusion suggests that Jesus and his followers thought that ritual impurity had become, as a result of the in-breaking of God's kingdom, less important than it once was. In contrast, I would argue that ritual impurity remained of fundamental importance for the Gospel writers, but they were convinced that God had introduced something *new* into the world to deal with the sources of these impurities: Jesus. By inserting a new, mobile, and powerfully contagious force of holiness into the world in the person of Jesus, Israel's God has signaled the very coming of the kingdom—a kingdom of holiness and life that throughout the mission of Jesus overwhelms the forces and sources of impurity and death, be they pneumatic, ritual, or moral. Throughout his narrative of Jesus's life, Mark repeatedly depicts Jesus overcoming impurity after impurity. This dramatic story culminates in Jesus facing off with death itself in his crucifixion, taking ritual impurity into his very own body, only once again and with finality to come out victorious when Israel's God raises him from the dead.

How did the Gospel writers understand Jesus in relation to the Jerusalem temple? Simply put, they saw no (or at least no need for) opposition between Jesus and the law or Jesus and the temple or Jesus and the priests.[6]

---

4. Perhaps Mark's Jesus alludes to a belief that we later find preserved in the Talmud: "A sick person does not arise from his sickness until all his sins are forgiven" (Babylonian Talmud, *Nedarim* 41a).

5. Kazen, *Jesus and Purity Halakhah*, 347.

6. Contrary to the claims of scholars such as Jan Lambrecht: "The historical Jesus was in reality both anti-Halachah and anti-Torah" ("Jesus and the Law," 77); and Robert Funk: "[Jesus] was indifferent to the formal practice of religion, he is said to have profaned the temple, the Sabbath, and breached purity regulations of his own legacy" (*Honest to Jesus*, 302).

Fundamentally they are all on the same side in a battle—a battle between Israel's God and the forces of impurity. Further, they are all empowered for this battle by Israel's God, who, as the source of all holiness, is ontologically opposed to any and all impurity.

In Jewish thinking, the Jerusalem temple functioned because God empowered it to function. God dwelled there, and so the temple itself was holy and needed to be protected against impurity. And God created a priestly caste of Israelites who could perform God-given rites to remove impurities that built up in the temple complex. Further, God also gave various purification rites for Israelites whose bodies became impure. Over and over again Exodus, Leviticus, Numbers, and Deuteronomy (as well as a host of other books) emphasize that Israel's laws come from Israel's God. Repeatedly God speaks to Moses, telling him to speak to the people of Israel (e.g., Exod. 30:31; 34:32; Lev. 1:2; 7:23, 29; 9:3; 10:11; 12:2; 15:2). These texts claim that the tabernacle (and temple) cult had its basis in the divine will and was animated by the divine presence. The tabernacle and temple were the divinely given tools to deal with impurities as they arose. But the functions that God gave to the Jerusalem temple and its priests were predominantly *defensive*. They had a divinely ordained limitation: they could not and were never meant to wipe out death itself or cure *lepra* or address the human condition that results in various genital discharges. The temple could not eradicate the *sources* of ritual impurity, but it could eliminate the *aftereffects* once those sources of impurity left a person's body. This remark might sound like a criticism, but it is not. It is, rather, a recognition of what texts like Leviticus and Numbers claim about the efficacy of the temple and its rites; they were inherently and divinely intended to have limitations. Or perhaps better put, the limitation was external to the temple. Humans are mortal, and the earth and all that is in it has been infected with the toxins of death and sin.

The Synoptic Gospel writers, though, would have their readers believe that Israel's God has unleashed a force of holiness in the world that goes on the offense against impurity—Jesus is the holy one of God. A holy power emanates out of Jesus's body and can overcome all sources of impurity. He embodies God's holiness let loose on earth. Whereas the temple apparatus removes the effects of sources of impurity, Jesus addresses the sources of impurity themselves: *lepra* is removed, irregular genital discharges are healed, corpses are revivified, and impure *pneumata* are exorcised and destroyed. Leviticus might not envisage such possibilities, but the Deuteronomistic History does—Elisha cures *lepra*, and both he and Elijah raise the dead.

Nehemia Polen has claimed that priestly literature is perfectly content with the system as it is: "For its part, Leviticus glories in the endless repetition, the day-by-day regularity of one lamb in the morning, one lamb in the evening."[7] Although Leviticus never gives its readers any sense that a different reality is possible or even desirable, I believe it is inaccurate to conclude from this silence that the priestly minds behind it and other literature were content with the state of a world that necessitated regular bathing and offerings, rites (frequently but not always) associated with ritual and moral impurities. The prophet Ezekiel was also a priest, and his writings indicate that one could hope for a different future in which God would permanently address the mortal and immoral condition of his people, creating an ontological change in them. Envisaging this future, Ezekiel depicts God's words to Israel: "I will sprinkle pure water upon you, and you will be purified from all your impurities, and from all your idols I will purify you. A new heart I will give you and a new *ruaḥ* I will place inside of you. And I will remove from your body the heart of stone and give you a heart of flesh. I will put my *ruaḥ* inside of you and make you follow my statutes and be careful to obey all my ordinances" (Ezek. 36:25–27). Ezekiel portrays a time when God would re-create Israel in such a way that it would naturally keep God's law. We see a similar hope in the priestly prophet Jeremiah: "This is the covenant that I will make between the house of Israel after those days, says YHWH: I will place my law into their mind, and upon their hearts I will write them. And I will be their God, and they will be my people" (Jer. 31:33; 38:33 LXX). Christine Hayes aptly describes this divinely created condition in the following way:

> For both of these prophets, it is not the law that will change in the messianic future. The same laws and rules will continue to function as residency requirements for those who would live in Yahweh's land. What will change is *human nature*. Israel will be hardwired to obey Yahweh's will without effort or struggle. The *elimination of human moral freedom* is nothing less than a utopian redesign of human nature, in which the difficulties associated with the exercise of moral freedom are obviated. With perfect knowledge of Yahweh's teaching, obedience to the divine law is automatic, a state we may refer to as "robo-righteousness."[8]

7. Polen, "Leviticus and Hebrews," 224–25.
8. Hayes, *What's Divine about Divine Law?*, 48, emphasis original. Hayes draws a compelling conclusion from such texts that provides a helpful corrective to many Christian misunderstandings of Judaism and the law: "Insofar as Jeremiah and Ezekiel assume that perfect Torah observance will require a future redesign of human nature and elimination of moral freedom that only God can effect, they reinforce the general biblical narrative—perfect Torah obedience is neither expected nor required of human beings as they are" (49).

With regard to moral impurity, Israel's prophets demonstrate the longing for a day when God will fundamentally alter human nature so that humanity can, and naturally will, keep God's law perfectly.

Connected to this hope is the belief that Israel's God will also one day overcome human mortality. We see such hopes in texts like Isaiah and, later, in Daniel. For instance, Isaiah prophesies,

> On this mountain YHWH of hosts will make for all peoples
>> a feast of rich food, a feast of well-aged wines,
>> of rich food filled with marrow, of well-aged wines strained clear.
> And on this mountain he will destroy
>> the shroud that is cast over all peoples,
>> the sheet that is spread over all nations;
>> he will swallow up death forever.
> Then YHWH God will wipe away the tears from all faces,
>> and he will take away the disgrace of his people from all the earth,
>> for YHWH has spoken. (Isa. 25:6–8)

Such a hope implies that the ritual impurity inevitably endured by mortal people will one day come to an end, making the ritual purity laws unnecessary. Later rabbinic texts connect this promise of a deathless future to the messianic era: "In the Messianic future there will be no death at all; as it is stated [in Isa. 25:8]."[9] This deathless future, Isaiah later states, is a return from the dead:

> Your dead will live, their corpses will rise.
>> O those who dwell in the dust, awake and sing for joy!
> For your dew is a glorious dew,
>> and the earth will give birth to those long dead. (Isa. 26:19)

The Psalter, too, appears to envisage a time when God will give unending life to people:

> He asked you for life; you gave it to him—
>> length of days forever and ever. (Ps. 21:4)

Similarly,

> Therefore my heart is glad, and my soul rejoices;
>> my body also rests secure.

9. *Ecclesiastes Rabbah* 1.4.3.

> For you do not give me up to Sheol,
>> or let your faithful one see the Pit. (Ps. 16:9–10)[10]

Finally, in the second century BCE, the book of Daniel also contains this hope of God overcoming death: "Many of those who sleep in the dust of the earth will awake, some to everlasting life, and some to shame and everlasting contempt. Those who are wise will shine like the brightness of the sky, and those who lead many to righteousness, like the stars forever and ever" (Dan. 12:2–3).

All of these texts, and a whole host of other texts from the Second Temple period, attest to a growing interest in and hope for life after death—a life characterized by immortality.[11] These texts envisage a future when God will make redundant the legal requirements pertaining to ritual purity by rewriting human DNA, so to speak. Once humans become immortal, they can no longer become ritually impure: they no longer are marked by sexuality, susceptible to illness, or subject to death. Some readers might be tempted to call such thinking supersessionism, but I think this word inadequately grapples with how widespread the hope was in early Judaism for some form of deathless life to come. If at some future point people no longer die, no longer become sick, and no longer need (or are even able) to reproduce, then the laws pertaining to ritual impurity are not abolished but have become immaterial.

Early Christ followers did not differ from many other Jews in hoping that Israel's God would act in such a way that the mortal and immoral condition of humanity would one day be superseded. If one insists upon using the term *supersessionism*, then we must be precise about what is being superseded. Early Christ followers believed that in Messiah Jesus, the old cosmos was being superseded by a new creation in which Satan and his demons, death, and sin—that is, pneumatic, ritual, and moral impurity—would no longer exist.

The Gospel writers differed from their fellow Jewish contemporaries in that they were convinced that Israel's God had already begun this final battle with death and in fact had dealt it a mortal wound in the person of Jesus. Mark's Jesus epitomizes his mission in the following words: "The time is fulfilled, and the kingdom of God has drawn near! Repent and trust the good news"

---

10. See more fully, Madigan and Levenson, *Resurrection*, and Levenson, *Resurrection and the Restoration of Israel*.

11. See J. Collins, "Apocalyptic Eschatology"; J. Collins, "Root of Immortality"; Nickelsburg, *Resurrection, Immortality, and Eternal Life*; Bauckham, *Fate of the Dead*; and Elledge, *Resurrection of the Dead*.

(Mark 1:15). Matthew depicts both John and Jesus proclaiming the coming of the kingdom of heaven (Matt. 3:2; 4:17), and he links this proclamation of the kingdom of heaven to Jesus's healings precisely because the heavenly realm cannot tolerate the ritual impurities and illnesses associated with the human mortal condition (4:23; 9:35; 10:7–8). Moreover, Matthew's Jesus declares that the very fact that he casts out demons (impure *pneumata*) by God's (holy) *pneuma* demonstrates that the kingdom of heaven has descended upon his hearers (12:28). Luke, too, connects Jesus's proclamation of God's kingdom to his healings and exorcisms (Luke 4:40–44; 8:1–3; 9:2, 11; 10:9; 11:20). Each of these portrayals of Jesus depicts him repeatedly coming into contact with impure people and destroying what makes them impure. And each of these encounters functions as a foretaste of what the authors believed Jesus ultimately brings to those who follow him: the annihilation of all the forces of impurity through the gift of eternal life (Mark 10:30; Matt. 19:29; 25:46; Luke 18:30; cf. John 3:15, etc.).

The Gospel writers portray Jesus first destroying impurities that he encounters, then giving his disciples the power and authority to do what he does, and then personally entering into the source of all impurity: death. Although the Gospels do not dwell at length on what happens in Jesus's death, Matthew depicts the result of Jesus's crucifixion as holy, life-giving power bringing the dead back to life, as I noted in chapter 5. And Luke stresses in Acts that Jesus's death and resurrection caused the destruction of death itself. In the first public declaration after Jesus's disciples receive the holy *pneuma*, Peter says to the people of Jerusalem, "Jesus of Nazareth, a person witnessed to you by God with deeds of power, wonders, and signs that God did through him among you, as you know—this man, handed over to you according to the plan and foreknowledge of God, you crucified and killed by the hands of lawless people. But God raised him up, having freed him from the bonds of death, because it was impossible for him to be held by death" (Acts 2:22–24). These are audacious claims, not least of all because it had become quite clear to Christ followers by the time Luke wrote the Acts of the Apostles that death and sin still exerted authority on the earth. To misquote another Christ follower, death is *not* "no more" (Rev. 21:4), since the apostles continue to address both it and the devil throughout the narrative of Acts.[12] Even after Jesus overcomes the forces of impurity and ultimately death itself on the cross, death persists. If Israel's God were truly at work in Jesus putting death to death, then why does death appear to be so full of life?

12. See Garrett, *Demise of the Devil*.

Simply put, if the Synoptic writers are wrong in their depictions of Jesus, then to follow him would be not only impious but also suicidal. On the other hand, if they are right, if Jesus is the holy one of God, a force of holiness who destroys the forces of death that give rise to ritual impurity, then to follow him would be to follow in the ways of holiness and life.

Εν Χριστον

Sin (moral) └ source
↓
Death (Ritual)
└ symptoms

Appendix

Jesus and the Dietary Laws

> Thus [Jesus] declared all foods clean.
>
> Mark 7:19 NRSV

O r did he? I have argued that the Synoptic Gospel writers portray Jesus in the ways they do in order to demonstrate Jesus's observance of the Jewish law and his concern over the existence of ritual impurity. In the stories I have examined, Jesus systematically destroys the sources of impurity, ritual or pneumatic, suffered by the people he encounters. Such a portrayal of Jesus, though, encounters one final potential obstacle in Mark 7, a passage that many readers interpret as clear evidence that Mark's Jesus rejects the kosher food system that is integral to Jewish identity. After all, according to the NRSV translation, Jesus goes so far as to declare that all foods are clean.[1] In this brief appendix, related but not central to the focus on *ritual* impurity, I reexamine this passage in order to show how it fits within the larger depiction of Jesus that the Synoptic Gospel writers have constructed.

First, Leviticus envisages types of impurity that are distinct but not entirely unrelated. The majority of this book has focused on what most scholars refer

---

1. See Räisänen, "Jesus and the Food Laws"; J. Meier, *A Marginal Jew*, 4:359; Sanders, *Jesus and Judaism*, 264–67; Westerholm, *Jesus and Scribal Authority*, 82; Hübner, *Das Gesetz in der synoptischen Tradition*, 175; N. T. Wright, *Jesus and the Victory of God*, 396–98; and Loader, "Mark 7:1–23 and the Historical Jesus." In a slight variation on this position, Tom Holmén suggests that Jesus here shows his disinterest in the food laws (*Jesus and Jewish Covenant Thinking*, 236).

to as *ritual impurity*, which is associated with only three physical sources: *lepra*, genital discharges of blood and semen, and corpses. Although Leviticus uses the same language of impurity (Hebrew: *tame'*; Greek: *akathartos*) and purity (Hebrew: *tahor*; Greek: *katharos*) for animals, it would be a mistake to include impure animals in the category of the ritually impure, because impure animals are not impure in the same way that *lepra*, genital discharges, or corpses are impure.[2] In contrast to ritual impurity, which can be removed through a combination of time and water (and with corpse impurity, the ashes of a red heifer), nothing can remove the impurity of unclean animals. Nothing a pig does makes it impure, and no one can purify a pig. There is no way to make a pig kosher; it is ontologically, one might say genetically, impure. It is born impure, passes on that impurity to any of its offspring, and then dies impure.

Having said this, impure animals are only *latently* impure when they are alive. Israelites were permitted to own and ride donkeys, horses, and camels (e.g., Deut. 5:14; 17:16; 1 Sam. 27:9; Zech. 9:9), and no rites are prescribed for purifying one's body after touching such an animal, demonstrating that people did not become impure through mere contact with impure animals. Thus, in contrast to ritual impurity, impure animals did not transmit impurity to others through simple physical contact.[3] Only when impure animals died did the impurity lurking within their bodies become a dynamic force; Israelites could not eat the flesh of impure animals or touch the carcass of such animals without becoming impure (Lev. 11:8). As Maimonides states in the twelfth century, "Of all animated creatures there is no species which, while yet alive, contracts and conveys uncleanness except man alone, provided that he is an Israelite."[4]

The impure animals of Leviticus 11 and Deuteronomy 14 simply do not fit within the category of what scholars call ritual impurity.[5] Consequently, even if Mark 7 and its parallel in Matthew demonstrate that Jesus rejected kosher food laws and concluded that all foods were clean, it would not follow that he necessarily rejected the Jewish ritual purity system. Nevertheless, it seems implausible that Mark intended to show that Jesus held to the ritual

---

2. According to Aelian, the third-century BCE Egyptian priest Manetho believed that drinking sow's milk would give a person *lepra* (*On the Nature of Animals* 10.16). Similarly, the late first-century CE Roman philosopher Plutarch claims that all pigs have *lepra* (*Table Talk* 4.5.3). Nothing in Jewish literature suggests any such thinking though.

3. Jonathan Klawans locates food purity laws *between* ritual and moral purity laws (*Impurity and Sin in Ancient Judaism*, 32).

4. Maimonides, *Mishneh Torah*, Corpse Impurity 1.14, in Danby, *Code of Maimonides*.

5. On Lev. 11 and Deut. 14, see Houston, *Purity and Monotheism*, and Rosenblum, *Jewish Dietary Laws*.

purity system while rejecting the laws pertaining to kosher food. Does Mark 7, then, undermine the arguments of the preceding chapters? The answer, yet again, is no.

In his response to the question of why his disciples do not wash their hands prior to eating and instead dine with impure hands (*koinais chersin*), Jesus quotes the prophet Isaiah and concludes, "You abandon the commandments of God and hold to the tradition of humans" (Mark 7:8; cf. Isa. 29:13 LXX).[6] Mark's Jesus goes on to accuse the Pharisees twice more in Mark 7 of prioritizing human traditions at the expense of God's law: "You reject the commandment of God in order to establish your tradition" (7:9); "[You are guilty of] nullifying the word of God by your tradition which you have handed down" (7:13). To demonstrate the veracity of his claims, Jesus provides a specific instance in which the Pharisees supposedly prefer human tradition to the commandments of God: allowing a man to declare his possessions devoted to God upon his death (*korban*). In this way the Pharisees permit a man to avoid using his possessions to care for his parents in their old age and thereby permit him to break God's commandment to honor one's father and mother (Exod. 20:12; Deut. 5:16). Later rabbinic literature also condemns this legal sophistry, and even Origen appears to have knowledge of the practice.[7] According to the Mishnah, Rabbi Eliezer argued that a man's vow should be revoked if keeping it would mean failing to honor his father and mother. In contrast, Rabbi Sadoq argued that if honoring one's parents is important, how much more necessary is it to honor God by keeping one's vows. The Sages ultimately defer to the position of Rabbi Eliezer.[8]

But Jesus's disapproval of the Pharisees' purported preference for human tradition at the cost of divine commands raises a real quandary for those who see in Mark 7 a rejection of the Jewish dietary laws. In a story that, according to traditional interpretations, depicts Jesus's rejection of the Jewish dietary laws, Mark portrays Jesus's condemnation of others who follow human rulings and in so doing disobey God's commandments. How likely is it that Mark would stress obeying God's commandments in a story in which Jesus rejects God's commandments as they pertain to the consumption of impure animals? How rhetorically convincing would this story be if it were advocating the rejection of laws that most, if not all, Jews in the first century CE thought

6. On this contrast between tradition and the commandments of God, see Marcus, "Scripture and Tradition."

7. Origen, *Commentary on Matthew* 11.9–10.

8. Mishnah, *Nedarim* 9.1; cf. Mishnah, *Bava Batra* 8.5, which prohibits oaths that contradict the Torah. Philo, on the other hand, appears to assume that any dedicated property must remain dedicated, even if, for instance, one's wife or son requires it to survive (*Hypothetica* 7.3–6).

were divinely ordained? After all, Leviticus stresses that the dietary laws have their basis in the commandment of Israel's God (Lev. 11:1, 44–45).[9] As Joel Marcus puts it, "Indeed, the antithesis that Mark's Jesus draws in 7,10–11 between what Moses said and what 'you' say could with just as much justice be applied to the Markan Jesus himself, since he sovereignly abrogates the Mosaic distinction between clean and unclean foods. *Jesus* then might easily be accused of substituting human commandments, i.e. his own precepts, for the clear mandates of God, and thus of falling under the judgment of Isa. 29.13—the passage that he himself cites in Mark 7.7."[10]

Such a blatant contradiction between Jesus's accusations against the Pharisees and his alleged rejection of the Jewish dietary laws suggests that traditional readings of Mark 7 have wildly misconstrued the point of the passage. Instead, a careful reading of the story indicates that Mark distinguishes between the traditions of the Pharisees and the actions of Jesus and his disciples in order to show which of the two actually keeps God's commandments. The very introduction of the story makes it clear that the controversy revolves around "the tradition of the elders" (7:3). The question relates, then, to legal positions that these Pharisees and scribes believed Jesus's disciples should be observing. Mark's story stresses, though, that this handwashing tradition was *not* a commandment of God,[11] and therefore Jesus's disciples do not need to observe it.

In this regard, Mark's Jesus does not differ from some Jewish contemporaries, despite Mark's exaggerated claim that *all* the Jews washed their hands prior to eating (7:3).[12] For instance, Josephus claims that the Sadducees did not observe the Pharisaic "traditions of the fathers."[13] And he makes explicit that such traditions differ from the law of Moses. Later, the Tosefta stipulates, "Handwashing must always immediately precede the meal."[14] So committed were the rabbis to the ritual washing of hands before meals that they even excommunicated Eliezer ben Hanokh for casting doubt on the principle.[15]

9. See too Sariola, *Markus und das Gesetz*, 72–73; Crossley, "Mark 7.1–23," 11; and Kazen, "Jesus, Scripture and *Paradosis*."

10. Marcus, "Scripture and Tradition," 183–84. So too Svartvik, *Mark and Mission*, 6.

11. On the question of why the Pharisees were committed to handwashing before meals, see Sanders, *Jewish Law*, 131–254; H. Harrington, "Did Pharisees Eat Ordinary Food?"; Poirier, "Why Did the Pharisees Wash Their Hands?"; and Regev, "Pure Individualism."

12. Westerholm: "Mark exaggerates here (v. 3) in a way typical for him (cf. 1:5, 33, 39; 6:33)" (*Jesus and Scribal Authority*, 73).

13. Josephus, *Jewish Antiquities* 13.297.

14. Tosefta, *Berakhot* 5.26, in Neusner, *Tosefta*.

15. Mishnah, *Eduyyot* 5.6. Other early texts that deal with the washing of hands before meals include Mishnah, *Hagigah* 2.5; Mishnah, *Hullin* 2.5; Mishnah, *Yadayim* 3.2; Tosefta, *Berakhot* 4.8; 5.6; Tosefta, *Demai* 2.11–12.

Elsewhere they claim that when a Jew does not wash his hands before a meal, it can lead to the erroneous conclusion that he is not actually Jewish and therefore result in a multitude of unwitting legal infractions.[16]

Nonetheless, some rabbinic texts suggest that handwashing before meals was not universally viewed, even by the rabbis, as necessary.[17] More pertinent for Mark 7, the rabbis from as late as the Talmud recognized that the washing of hands was not from scripture but was in fact a tradition of the elders: "The washing of hands for secular food is not from the Torah."[18] E. P. Sanders has shown that "in the legal tractates of Mishnah and the Tosefta rabbinic rulings are held to be on a lower level of authority than the words of the Bible itself, and this includes rabbinic traditions which are said to go back to Moses."[19] Such a recognition indicates that Mark 7 does not necessarily intend to depict the Pharisees as claiming that Jesus and his disciples have abandoned the law of Moses; rather, they are curious about Jesus's rationale for not washing hands before eating. They desire to know his legal reasoning for doing something that seems wrong to them.

Mark's Jesus bases his response to the original question about eating with unwashed hands on the shared assumption that the washing of hands is a Pharisaic tradition, *not* a commandment of God, and then goes on to accuse the Pharisees of observing such traditions to the detriment of their observance of God's commandments. And in response to the Pharisaic concern over handwashing, Mark's Jesus enunciates a legal principle about the dynamics of impurity that undermines the practice of handwashing before meals. As Yair Furstenberg puts it, "Jesus contended that these laws, concerned as they were with eating only in a state of ritual purity, were not biblical in origin, but rather were a Pharisaic innovation which reflected a new understanding of ritual contamination, one which changed the focus and significance of ritual purity."[20]

The entire context of the clause of Mark 7:19 ("purifying all foods") situates this statement within a debate about whether one must ritually wash one's hands prior to eating.[21] That is to say, the story simply does not intend

---

16. *Numbers Rabbah* 20.21; cf. *Tanna deve Eliyahu*, *Seder Eliyahu Rabbah* [15] 16. The Talmud even suggests that a particular demon, Sabitha, afflicts those who eat with impure hands (Babylonian Talmud, *Ta'anit* 20b; cf. Babylonian Talmud, *Yoma* 77b).

17. *Numbers Rabbah* 20.21.

18. Babylonian Talmud, *Berakhot* 52b; see Babylonian Talmud, *Yoma* 80b.

19. Sanders, *Jewish Law*, 125. See also A. Baumgarten, "Pharisaic Paradosis."

20. Furstenberg, "Defilement Penetrating the Body," 178. See also VanMaaren, "Does Mark's Jesus Abrogate Torah?"

21. Kazen, *Jesus and Purity Halakhah*, 65: "The most convincing explanations, however, place the saying in a context not of clean and unclean foods (in the sense of Lev. 11:1–23), but

to deal with the question of whether one should eat pork or shellfish; rather, it intends to address the question of whether one can defile kosher food with one's ritually impure hands and then introduce that ritual impurity into one's body by the consumption of that defiled food. According to Mark's Jesus, the answer is no, because of his legal position—that it is not what goes *into* the body (kosher food that has supposedly been defiled by impure hands) that makes something impure but what comes *out* of a body.[22] The question pertains to the dynamics of impurity: Does it move from outside to inside the body, or from inside to outside the body?

In answering this question, Mark's Jesus focuses on the fact that deeds such as sexual immorality, theft, and murder move from inside the body to outside the body. He describes here various sins that defile people, since they are moral impurities. Such moral impurity, though, begins in the heart (Mark 7:21–23; cf. Matt. 15:18–20) and moves outside the body and into actions. Again, such a statement reveals Mark's interest in depicting Jesus in relation to impurity. These claims in no way suggest that ritual impurity does not exist or that it is insignificant, although Jesus, like other Jews of his day, presumably thought moral impurity was of greater consequence than ritual impurity.[23] After all, ritual impurities are not sinful and can be treated relatively easily. Moral impurities, on the other hand, are sinful and not easily removed. The stains caused by such actions are deep set and require a stronger detergent than mere water. We see recognition of this in the Qumran *Community Rule*, which declares that no ritual purification is efficacious when someone does not obey the law: "He will not become pure by the deeds of atonement, nor will he be purified by the purifying waters, or made holy by seas or rivers, nor will he be purified by all the waters of washing. Impure, impure will he be all the days he rejects the decrees of God."[24]

Most if not all Jews of Jesus's day considered sins to be moral impurities, actions that cause a type of pollution that differs from ritual impurity but that exists nonetheless. Already in Leviticus 17–27 one sees sin described as a moral impurity. Scholars usually refer to this section of Leviticus as the Holiness Code, noting how it focuses on moral impurity, which distinguishes it from the focus on ritual impurity in Leviticus 1–16. The Holiness Code

---

of ritual hand-washing, and interpret it in a relative sense." Similarly, Crossley, *Date of Mark's Gospel*, 183–205.

22. Here I disagree with Thomas Kazen, who argues that Jesus's stance was more prophetic than it was halakhic ("A Perhaps Less Halakic Jesus"). See also Kazen, *Scripture, Interpretation, or Authority?*

23. Klawans, *Impurity and Sin*, 146–50.

24. 1QS III, 4–6.

lists a number of moral impurities, stressing various sexual pollutions (Lev. 18; 19:20–22, 29; 20:10–21), idol pollution (19:4), and pollution due to theft, fraud, deception, and injustice (e.g., 19:11–16, 35). Ancient readers, though, would have read Leviticus as a unified work and would have therefore understood this priestly book to emphasize *both* ritual and moral purity. As Jonathan Klawans notes of the list in Mark 7, "What is so striking about these lists is the degree of conceptual correspondence between what Jesus views as defiling and the sins that were generally conceived by ancient Jews to be sources of moral defilement."[25]

Jesus's reference to moral impurities illustrates the way impurity acts in general. Impurities come *out of* the body rather than enter *into* the body. This legal principle applies equally well to ritual impurities; genital discharges, *lepra*, and corpses emit impurity when they come out of the body. And those who contract these impurities wash the outside of their bodies, not the interior. At least one later rabbinic passage concurs, calling ritual impurities "impurities that come out of the body."[26] The Pharisaic tradition implicit in this story, and explicit in later rabbinic literature, offers a different vision of impurity: "The system being opposed is concerned with *food* contaminating *people*. Adopting this line of interpretation, it is reasonable to further suggest that the second limb of the logion, 'the things which come out of a person are what defile him,' defines an alternative conception of ritual purity which *does* fit with the biblical system. Thus each limb of the logion, at least on one level, carries a [legal] meaning. Jesus, according to this interpretation, is contrasting two competing models of ritual purity."[27] According to Leviticus

25. Klawans, *Impurity and Sin*, 148.
26. *Sifra Tazri'a* 12.4 67 (d), my translation. Michelle V. Fletcher rightly notes that readers of Mark 7 almost universally come to it with androcentric assumptions ("What Comes into a Woman"). Were one to think specifically of women's bodies, one could provide an example of something entering a body to make it impure: when a woman has sexual intercourse with a man, semen enters her body, thereby rendering her ritually impure. On the other hand, it is possible that the woman is rendered ritually impure because her body discharges some of the ejaculate after intercourse, and it is this discharge that renders her impure. If so, Jesus's logic still holds—only what comes out of the body, even a woman's body, is what renders that body impure.

Fletcher also notices a potential allusion to Lev. 12. Both Mark and Matthew use the term *aphedrōn* (often translated "latrine"). (The word occurs only one other time in Jewish literature composed or translated into Greek: *Testament of Job* 38.3, where it appears to mean not *latrine* but *bowels*, which separate drink into urine and food into excrement, though Fletcher does not note this.) Lev. 12:2, 5, use the related term *aphedros* to translate the Hebrew *niddah*. I am not sure what to do with this possible allusion, but it is conceivable that the point here is that food goes to the stomach and then to the bowels (and ultimately latrine) and that this process purges or purifies the body of all foods (*katharizōn panta ta brōmata*, Mark 7:19).

27. Furstenberg, "Defilement Penetrating the Body," 194. See also Maccoby, *Ritual and Morality*, 158: "No one ever claimed that the purpose of ritual purity was to prevent impurities

11:39–50 and 17:15, the consumption of clean animals who died on their own or were killed by other animals only renders the exterior of a person impure and requires a ritual bath. The consumption of nonkosher food also does not pollute the inside of the body; while Jews are forbidden to consume swarming creatures—consuming them renders Jews impure—it does not create an *internal* impurity (Lev. 11:41–44).

In sum, Mark's story explicitly situates Jesus's words about impurity (and Mark's own claim about "purifying all foods") within a debate about the Pharisaic tradition of washing hands before meals. Any reading that ignores this specific context and takes Mark 7:19 to refer to all foods (kosher and nonkosher) will likely result in a serious misinterpretation of the passage. Further, Mark's Jesus stresses the necessity of keeping God's commandments. Consequently, any reading of this story that depicts Jesus as rejecting God's commandment to Israel to avoid eating unclean animals results in a Jesus who is irrational at best, and deeply hypocritical at worst.[28] Is Mark so bumbling a narrator that he fails to notice this result?[29]

In fact, Matthew, one of Mark's first readers, understood this story as relating only to handwashing. Matthew follows Mark's account rather closely but makes a number of telling changes. First, he removes Mark's exaggerated claim that all the Jews wash their hands before eating meals. Second, he modifies the claim of Mark's Jesus ("It is the things coming out of the body that pollute, not the things going into the body," Mark 7:15) to a claim that it is not what goes into the mouth that pollutes but what comes out of the mouth (Matt. 15:11). Third, in Matthew's version only the Pharisees take offense at what Jesus says—not, apparently, other Jews, something that would be inconceivable were Jesus to be abandoning food laws (Matt. 15:12). Fourth, he completely omits Mark 7:19 (the phrase "purifying all foods").[30] And fifth, he makes explicit that the evil that comes out of one's heart pollutes,

---

from entering the body. On the contrary, it was held that ritual impurity never penetrates beyond the surface of the body. Even impurities incurred through eating forbidden food do not cause impurity to the interior of the body, only to the exterior." Furstenberg points to Rashi's remarks on Babylonian Talmud, *Shabbat* 13b, and Babylonian Talmud, *Yoma* 80b, that the Torah teaches that food does not pollute the person who eats it ("Defilement Penetrating the Body," 182).

28. Sanders argues that the historical Jesus kept the food laws, or else we would have evidence of an outcry against his nonkosher diet (*Jewish Law*, 23–28). The point is relevant to our discussion; no Gospel story, no matter how one reads Mark 7, indicates that Jesus ever ate or was accused of eating anything nonkosher. And Acts 10 depicts a Peter, years after Jesus's death, who had never before countenanced the idea of eating nonkosher food.

29. See Cohen, "Antipodal Texts."

30. Some interpreters have suggested that Mark 7:19 is the gloss of a later scribe. E.g., Lohmeyer, *Das Evangelium des Markus*, 142. If so, this would explain its absence in the Gospel of Matthew. Nonetheless, there is no manuscript support for this claim.

while eating with unwashed hands does not (Matt. 15:20). One might argue here that Matthew has omitted Mark 7:19 because he disagrees with Mark's conclusion, but it seems more plausible that he omits a potentially confusing phrase and adds the statement of Matthew 15:20 to ensure that readers do not, to his mind, wrongfully extrapolate from Jesus's words in this story to conclude that Jesus has rejected the Jewish dietary laws.

Finally, Luke takes this same story and greatly compresses it (Luke 11:37–41; cf. Matt. 23:25–26). According to him, Jesus dined with a Pharisee but disregarded Pharisaic tradition by not washing his hands before eating. Again, Luke's Jesus addresses only the issue of handwashing, not the separate issue of the dietary laws. And as in Mark and Matthew, Jesus stresses moral purity: all the washing of the outside does not address the moral deficiencies Jesus claims that the Pharisees have. Others have argued that Luke later demonstrates that Christ followers rejected the Jewish dietary laws, since he depicts God telling Peter in a vision to kill and eat nonkosher animals (Acts 10). But this vision,  as Luke painstakingly makes clear, has nothing to do with a change in the Jewish dietary system. Peter does not proceed to eat nonkosher food; rather, he preaches the gospel to the gentile Cornelius and his family. The impure animals, then, function as a coded vision about God's purification movement among those who were formerly impure: the gentiles.[31]

In all three Gospel accounts, Jesus's words about the dynamics of impurity suggest that Jesus has waded into a legal debate about the direction impurity travels. Impurity springs *out of* the body; it does not penetrate the body. Nothing suggests that the Gospel writers intended to portray Jesus rejecting the Jewish dietary laws.

---

31. See Thiessen, *Contesting Conversion*, 124–40.

Bibliography

Akiyama, Kengo. *The Love of Neighbour in Ancient Judaism: The Reception of Leviticus 19:18 in the Hebrew Bible, the Septuagint, the Book of Jubilees, the Dead Sea Scrolls, and the New Testament.* Ancient Judaism and Early Christianity 105. Leiden: Brill, 2018.

Aland, Barbara, Kurt Aland, Johannes Karavidopoulos, Carlo M. Martini, and Bruce M. Metzger, eds. *Novum Testamentum Graece.* 28th ed. Stuttgart: Deutsche Bibelgesellschaft, 2012.

Allison, Dale, Jr. *Constructing Jesus: Memory, Imagination, and History.* Grand Rapids: Baker Academic, 2010.

———. *The End of the Ages Has Come: An Early Interpretation of the Passion and Resurrection of Jesus.* Philadelphia: Fortress, 1985.

Amihay, Aryeh. *Theory and Practice in Essene Law.* Oxford: Oxford University Press, 2016.

Andersen, J. G. "Studies in the Medieval Diagnosis of Leprosy in Denmark." *Danish Medical Bulletin* 16, supplement 9 (1969): 6–142.

Anderson, Gary A. "Celibacy or Consummation in the Garden? Reflections on Early Jewish and Christian Interpretations of the Garden of Eden." *Harvard Theological Review* 82 (1989): 121–48.

Anderson, W. H. P. "Christian Missions and Lepers." *International Review of Mission* 21 (1932): 264–71.

Arnal, William E. *The Symbolic Jesus: Historical Scholarship, Judaism and the Construction of Contemporary Identity.* London: Equinox, 2005.

Assmann, Jan. *Death and Salvation in Ancient Egypt.* Translated by David Lorton. Ithaca, NY: Cornell University Press, 2005.

Back, Sven-Olav. *Jesus of Nazareth and the Sabbath Commandment.* Åbo: Åbo Akademi University Press, 1995.

Baden, Joel S., and Candida R. Moss. "The Origin and Interpretation of ṣāraʿat in Leviticus 13–14." *Journal of Biblical Literature* 130 (2011): 643–62.

Bauckham, Richard. *The Fate of the Dead: Studies on the Jewish and Christian Apocalypses.* Supplements to Novum Testamentum 93. Leiden: Brill, 1998.

———. "Sabbath and Sunday in the Post-apostolic Church." In *From Sabbath to Lord's Day: A Biblical, Historical, and Theological Investigation*, edited by D. A. Carson, 251–98. Grand Rapids: Zondervan, 1982.

———. "The Scrupulous Priest and the Good Samaritan: Jesus' Parabolic Interpretation of the Law of Moses." *New Testament Studies* 44 (1998): 475–89.

Bauernfeind, Otto. *Die Worte der Dämonen im Markusevangelium.* Beiträge zur Wissenschaft vom Alten Testament 44. Stuttgart: Kohlhammer, 1927.

Baumgarten, Albert I. "The Pharisaic Paradosis." *Harvard Theological Review* 80 (1987): 63–77.

Baumgarten, Joseph. "The 4Q Zadokite Fragments on Skin Disease." *Journal of Jewish Studies* 41 (1990): 153–65.

———. "Purification after Childbirth and the Sacred Garden in 4Q265 and Jubilees." In *New Qumran Texts and Studies: Proceedings of the First Meeting of the International Organization for Qumran Studies, Paris 1992*, edited by George J. Brooke with Florentino García Martínez, 3–10. Studies on the Texts of the Desert of Judah 15. Leiden: Brill, 1994.

———. "265. 4QMiscellaneous Rules." In *Qumran Cave 4, XXV: Halakhic Texts*, edited by Joseph Baumgarten et al., 57–78. Discoveries in the Judaean Desert 35. Oxford: Clarendon, 1999.

———. "Zab Impurity in Qumran and Rabbinic Law." *Journal of Jewish Studies* 45 (1994): 273–77.

Beck, Richard. *Unclean: Meditations on Purity, Hospitality, and Mortality.* Eugene, OR: Cascade Books, 2011.

Beckman, Gary. *Hittite Birth Rituals.* 2nd rev. ed. Studien zu den Bogazköy-Texten 29. Wiesbaden: Harrassowitz, 1983.

Berlejung, Angelika. "Variabilität und Konstanz eines Reinigungsrituals nach der Berührung eines Toten in Num. 19 und Qumran: Überlegungen zur Dynamik der Ritualtransformation." *Theologische Zeitung* 65 (2009): 289–331.

Bernier, Jonathan. *The Quest for the Historical Jesus after the Demise of Authenticity: Toward a Critical Realist Philosophy of History in Jesus Studies.* The Library of New Testament Studies 540. London: Bloomsbury T&T Clark, 2016.

Berthelot, Katell. "La place des infirmes et des 'lépreux' dans les texts de Qumrân et les Évangiles." *Revue biblique* 113 (2006): 211–41.

Betz, Hans Dieter, ed. *The Greek Magical Papyri in Translation, Including the Demotic Spells: Volume One Texts.* 2nd ed. Chicago: University of Chicago Press, 1992.

Bhishagratna, Kaviraj Kunja Lal. *The Sushruta Samhita*. 3 vols. Varanasi: Chowkhamba, 1963.

Biggs, Robert, and Marten Stol, eds. *Babylonisch—assyrische Medizin in Texten und Untersuchungen*. 10 vols. Berlin: de Gruyter, 1963–2018.

Bock, Darrell. *Luke 1:1–9:50*. Baker Exegetical New Testament Commentary 3. Grand Rapids: Baker, 1994.

Bolt, Peter. "Jesus, the Daimons and the Dead." In *The Unseen World: Christian Reflections on Angels, Demons and the Heavenly Realm*, edited by Anthony N. S. Lane, 75–102. Grand Rapids: Baker, 1996.

———. *Jesus' Defeat of Death: Persuading Mark's Early Readers*. Society for New Testament Studies Monograph Series 125. Cambridge: Cambridge University Press, 2003.

Borg, Marcus. *Conflict, Holiness, and Politics in the Teachings of Jesus*. Harrisburg, PA: Trinity Press International, 1998.

———. *Jesus in Contemporary Scholarship*. Valley Forge, PA: Trinity Press International, 1994.

———. *Meeting Jesus Again for the First Time: The Historical Jesus and the Heart of Contemporary Faith*. San Francisco: HarperSanFrancisco, 1994.

Boring, M. Eugene. *Mark: A Commentary*. New Testament Library. Louisville: Westminster John Knox, 2006.

Botner, Max. "Has Jesus Read What David Did? Probing Problems in Mark 2:25–26." *Journal of Theological Studies* 69 (2018): 484–99.

Bovon, François. *A Commentary on the Gospel of Luke 1:1–9:50*. Hermeneia. Minneapolis: Fortress, 2002.

Boyce, Mary, ed. and trans. *Textual Sources for the Study of Zoroastrianism*. Textual Sources for the Study of Religion. Chicago: University of Chicago Press, 1990.

Bradshaw, Paul, ed. *The Canons of Hippolytus*. Translated by Carol Bebawi. Grove Liturgical Study 50. Bramcote, Nottingham: Grove Books, 1987.

Braude, William G., trans. *Pesikta Rabbati: Discourses for Feasts, Fasts, and Special Sabbaths*. 2 vols. Yale Judaica Series 18. New Haven: Yale University Press, 1968.

Braude, William G., and Israel J. Kapstein, trans. *Pesikta de-Rab Kahana: R. Kahana's Compilation of Discourses for Sabbaths and Festal Days*. Philadelphia: Jewish Publication Society of America, 2002.

———. *Tanna Debe Eliyyahu: The Lore of the School of Elijah*. Philadelphia: Jewish Publication Society of America, 1981.

Brodhead, Edwin K. "Christology as Polemic and Apologetic: The Priestly Portrait of Jesus in the Gospel of Mark." *Journal for the Study of the New Testament* 15 (1992): 21–34.

Brown, Raymond E. *The Birth of the Messiah: A Commentary on the Infancy Narratives in the Gospels of Matthew and Luke.* New and updated ed. New York: Doubleday, 1993.

———. "The Presentation of Jesus (Luke 2:22–40)." *Worship* 51 (1977): 2–11.

Bruners, Wilhelm. *Die Reinigung der zehn Aussätzigen und die Heilung des Samariters, Lk 17,11–19 Ein Beitrag zur lukanischen Interpretation der Reinigung von Aussatzigen.* Forschung zur Bibel 23. Stuttgart: Katholisches Bibelwerk, 1977.

Büchler, Adolph. "Family Purity and Family Impurity in Jerusalem before the Year 70 C.E." In *Studies in Jewish History: The Büchler Memorial Volume*, edited by Israel Brodie and Joseph Rabbinowitz, 64–98. London: Oxford University Press, 1956.

Burkert, Walter. *Homo Necans: The Anthropology of Ancient Greek Sacrificial Ritual and Myth.* Translated by Peter Bing. Berkeley: University of California Press, 1983.

Burridge, Richard. *What Are the Gospels? A Comparison with Graeco-Roman Biography.* 25th anniv. ed. Waco: Baylor University Press, 2018.

Caird, G. B. *The Gospel of St. Luke.* Pelican New Testament Commentaries. Harmondsworth: Penguin, 1963.

Carmichael, Calum. "Death and Sexuality among Priests (Leviticus 21)." In *The Book of Leviticus: Composition and Reception*, edited by Rolf Rendtorff and Robert A. Kugler with Sarah Smith Bartel, 225–44. Supplements to Vetus Testamentum 93. Leiden: Brill, 2003.

Carroll, John. *Luke: A Commentary.* New Testament Library. Louisville: Westminster John Knox, 2012.

Carson, Anne. "Dirt and Desire: The Phenomenology of Female Pollution in Antiquity." In *Constructions of the Classical Body*, edited by James I. Porter, 77–100. The Body, In Theory: Histories of Cultural Materialism. Ann Arbor: University of Michigan Press, 1999.

Casey, Maurice. *Aramaic Sources of Mark's Gospel.* Society for New Testament Studies Monograph Series 102. Cambridge: Cambridge University Press, 1998.

Censorinus. *The Birthday Book.* Translated by Holt N. Parker. Chicago: University of Chicago Press, 2007.

Charlesworth, James H., ed. *The Old Testament Pseudepigrapha.* 2 vols. Garden City, NY: Doubleday, 1983–85.

Choksy, Jamsheed K. *Purity and Pollution in Zoroastrianism: Triumph over Evil.* Austin: University of Texas Press, 1989.

Cochrane, R. G. *Biblical Leprosy: A Suggested Interpretation.* 2nd ed. London: Tyndale, 1963.

Cohen, Shaye J. D. "Antipodal Texts: B. Eruvin 21b–22a and Mark 7:1–23 on the Tradition of the Elders and the Commandment of God." In vol. 2 of *Envisioning Judaism: Studies in Honor of Peter Schäfer on the Occasion of his Seventieth Birthday*, edited by Ra'anan S. Boustan et al., 965–83. Tübingen: Mohr Siebeck, 2013.

————. "Menstruants and the Sacred in Judaism and Christianity." In *Women's History and Ancient History*, edited by Sarah B. Pomeroy, 273–99. Chapel Hill: University of North Carolina Press, 1991.

Cole, Susan Guettel. "*Gynaiki ou Themis*: Gender Difference in the Greek *Leges Sacrae*." *Helios* 19 (1992): 104–22.

Coleman-Norton, P. R. *The Twelve Tables*. Princeton: Princeton University, Department of Classics, 1960.

Collins, Adela Yarbro. *Mark: A Commentary*. Hermeneia. Minneapolis: Fortress, 2007.

Collins, John J. "Apocalyptic Eschatology as the Transcendence of Death." *Catholic Biblical Quarterly* 36 (1974): 21–43.

————. "The Root of Immortality: Death in the Context of Jewish Wisdom." *Harvard Theological Review* 71 (1978): 177–92.

Collins, Nina L. *Jesus, the Sabbath and the Jewish Debate: Healing on the Sabbath in the 1st and 2nd Centuries CE*. The Library of New Testament Studies 474. London: Bloomsbury, 2014.

Cranz, Isabel. "Priests, Pollution and the Demonic: Evaluating Impurity in the Hebrew Bible in Light of Assyro-Babylonian Texts." *Journal of Ancient Near Eastern Religions* 14 (2014): 68–86.

Crossan, John Dominic. *The Historical Jesus: The Life of a Mediterranean Jewish Peasant*. San Francisco: HarperSanFrancisco, 1991.

————. *Jesus: A Revolutionary Biography*. San Francisco: HarperSanFrancisco, 1994.

Crossley, James G. *The Date of Mark's Gospel: Insight from the Law in Earliest Christianity*. Journal for the Study of the New Testament Supplement Series 266. London: T&T Clark, 2004.

————. "Mark 7.1–23: Revisiting the Question of 'All Foods Clean.'" In *The Torah in the New Testament: Papers Delivered at the Manchester-Lausanne Seminar of June 2008*, edited by Peter Oakes and Michael Tait, 8–20. The Library of New Testament Studies 401. London: T&T Clark, 2009.

————. "The Multicultural Christ: Jesus the Jew and the New Perspective on Paul in an Age of Neoliberalism." *Bible and Critical Theory* 7 (2011): 8–16.

Danby, Herbert. *The Code of Maimonides, Book Ten: The Book of Cleanness*. Yale Judaica Series 8. New Haven: Yale University Press, 1954.

————. *The Mishnah: Translated from the Hebrew with Introduction and Brief Explanatory Notes*. Oxford: Oxford University Press, 1933.

D'Angelo, Mary Rose. "Gender and Power in the Gospel of Mark: The Daughter of Jairus and the Woman with the Flow of Blood." In *Miracles in Jewish and Christian Antiquity: Imagining the Truth*, edited by John C. Cavadini, 83–109. Notre Dame Studies in Theology 3. Notre Dame: University of Notre Dame Press, 1999.

Darmesteter, James, and Lawrence Heyworth Mills, trans. *The Zend-Avesta*. 3 vols. Sacred Books of the East. Oxford: Clarendon, 1880–87.

Daube, David. "Responsibilities of Master and Disciples in the Gospels." *New Testament Studies* 19 (1972–73): 1–15.

Dean-Jones, Lesley. "Menstrual Bleeding according to the Hippocratics and Aristotle." *Transactions of the American Philological Association* 119 (1989): 177–92.

———. *Women's Bodies in Classical Greek Science*. Oxford: Clarendon, 1994.

Denaux, Adelbert, ed. *John and the Synoptics*. Bibliotheca Ephemeridum Theologicarum Lovaniensium 101. Leuven: Leuven University Press, 1992.

Derrett, J. Duncan. "Circumcision and Perfection: A Johannine Equation (John 7:22–23)." *Evangelical Quarterly* 63 (1991): 211–24.

De Vries, Simon. *1 and 2 Chronicles*. Forms of the Old Testament Literature 11. Grand Rapids: Eerdmans, 1989.

Dietrich, Manfried, Oswald Loretz, and Joaquín Sanmartín, eds. *Die keilalphabetischen Texte aus Ugarit*. 3rd enl. ed. Münster: Ugarit-Verlag, 2013.

Dirven, Lucinda. "The Author of *De Dea Syria* and His Cultural Heritage." *Numen* 44 (1997): 153–79.

Doering, Lutz. "Much Ado about Nothing? Jesus' Sabbath Healings and Their Halakhic Implications Revisited." In *Judaistik und Neutestamentliche Wissenschaft: Standorte–Grenzen–Beziehungen*, edited by Lutz Doering, Hans-Günther Waubke, and Florian Wilk, 217–41. Forschungen zur Religion und Literatur des Alten und Neuen Testaments 226. Göttingen: Vandenhoeck & Ruprecht, 2008.

———. "Sabbath Laws in the New Testament Gospels." In *The New Testament and Rabbinic Literature*, edited by Reimund Bieringer et al., 207–54. Journal for the Study of Judaism in the Persian, Hellenistic, and Roman Periods Supplement Series 136. Leiden: Brill, 2010.

———. *Schabbat: Sabbathalacha und -praxis im antiken Judentum und Urchristentum*. Texte und Studien zum antiken Judentum 78. Tübingen: Mohr Siebeck, 1999.

Douglas, Mary. *In the Wilderness: The Doctrine of Defilement in the Book of Numbers*. Journal for the Study of the Old Testament Supplement Series 158. Sheffield: JSOT Press, 1993.

———. *Jacob's Tears: The Priestly Work of Reconciliation*. Oxford: Oxford University Press, 2004.

———. *Leviticus as Literature*. Oxford: Oxford University Press, 1999.

———. *Purity and Danger: An Analysis of Concepts of Pollution and Taboo*. London: Routledge, 1966.

Dunn, James D. G. *Jesus, Paul and the Law: Studies in Mark and Galatians*. Louisville: Westminster John Knox, 1990.

———. "Jesus and Purity: An Ongoing Debate." *New Testament Studies* 48 (2002): 449–67.

Dzierzykray-Rogalski, T. "Paleopathology of the Ptolemaic Inhabitants of Dakhleh Oasis (Egypt)." *Journal of Human Evolution* 9 (1980): 71–74.

Ebbell, Bendix. *The Papyrus Ebers: The Greatest Egyptian Medical Document*. Copenhagen: Levin & Munksgaard, 1937.

Edwards, Catharine. *Death in Ancient Rome*. New Haven: Yale University Press, 2007.

Ego, Beate. "Heilige Zeit—heiliger Raum—heiliger Mensch: Beobachtungen zur Struktur der Gesetzesbegründung in der Schöpfungs- und Paradiesgeschichte des Jubiläenbuchs." In *Studies in the Book of Jubilees*, edited by Matthias Albani, Jörg Frey, and Armin Lange, 207–19. Texte und Studien zum antiken Judentum 65. Tübingen: Mohr Siebeck, 1997.

Ehrman, Bart. *The Orthodox Corruption of Scripture: The Effect of Early Christological Controversies on the Text of the New Testament*. Updated ed. Oxford: Oxford University Press, 2011.

———. "Text and Interpretation: The Exegetical Significance of the 'Original' Text." *TC: A Journal of Biblical Textual Criticism* 5 (2000), http://rosetta.reltech.org/TC/v05/Ehrman2000a.html.

Elledge, C. D. *Resurrection of the Dead in Early Judaism, 200 BCE–CE 200*. New York: Oxford University Press, 2017.

Elliger, Karl. *Leviticus*. Handbuch zum Alten Testament 4. Tübingen: Mohr Siebeck, 1966.

Elliger, K., and W. Rudolph, eds. *Biblia Hebraica Stuttgartensia*. Stuttgart: Deutsche Bibelgesellschaft, 1967–77.

Ellis, E. Earle. *The Gospel of Luke*. Rev. ed. London: Oliphants, 1974.

Epstein, Isidore, ed. *The Babylonian Talmud: Translated into English with Notes, Glossary and Indices*. 18 vols. London: Soncino, 1935–52.

Eubank, Nathan. *Wages of Cross-Bearing and Debt of Sin: The Economy of Heaven in Matthew's Gospel*. Beihefte zur Zeitschrift für die neutestamentliche Wissenschaft 196. Berlin: de Gruyter, 2013.

Evans, C. F. *Saint Luke*. TPI New Testament Commentaries. Philadelphia: Trinity Press International, 1990.

Evans, Craig A. *Luke*. New International Biblical Commentary on the New Testament 3. Peabody, MA: Hendrickson, 1990.

———. "Luke's Use of the Elijah/Elisha Narratives and the Ethics of Election." *Journal of Biblical Literature* 106 (1987): 75–83.

———. "'Who Touched Me?': Jesus and the Ritually Impure." In *Jesus in Context: Temple, Purity, and Restoration*, edited by Bruce Chilton and Craig A. Evans, 353–76. Arbeiten zur Geschichte des antiken Judentums und des Urchristentums 39. Leiden: Brill, 1997.

Feder, Yitzhaq. "Contagion and Cognition: Bodily Experience and the Conceptualization of Pollution (*tum'ah*) in the Hebrew Bible." *Journal of Near Eastern Studies* 72 (2013): 151–67.

———. "The Polemic regarding Skin Disease in *4QMMT*." *Dead Sea Discoveries* 19 (2012): 55–70.

Feinstein, Eve Levavi. *Sexual Pollution in the Hebrew Bible*. Oxford: Oxford University Press, 2013.

Ferguson, Everett. *Demonology of the Early Christian World*. New York: Edwin Mellen, 1984.

Fitzmyer, Joseph A. *The Gospel according to Luke I–IX: Introduction, Translation, and Notes*. Anchor Bible 28. Garden City, NY: Doubleday, 1981.

Flemming, Rebecca. *Medicine and the Making of Roman Women: Gender, Nature, and Authority from Celsus to Galen*. Oxford: Oxford University Press, 2000.

Fletcher, Michelle V. "What Comes into a Woman and What Comes out of a Woman: Feminist Textual Intervention and Mark 7:14–23." *Journal of Feminist Studies in Religion* 30 (2014): 25–41.

Fletcher-Louis, Crispin. "Jesus as the High Priestly Messiah: Part 2." *Journal for the Study of the Historical Jesus* 5 (2007): 57–79.

Fong, Albert F. de. "Purity and Pollution in Ancient Zoroastrianism." In *Purity and the Forming of Religious Traditions in the Ancient Mediterranean World and Ancient Judaism*, edited by Christian Frevel and Christophe Nihan, 183–94. Dynamics in the History of Religion 3. Leiden: Brill, 2013.

Fonrobert, Charlotte Elisheva. *Menstrual Purity: Rabbinic and Christian Reconstructions of Biblical Gender*. Contraversions. Stanford, CA: Stanford University Press, 2000.

France, R. T. *The Gospel of Mark: A Commentary on the Greek Text*. New International Greek Testament Commentary. Grand Rapids: Eerdmans, 2002.

Frandsen, Paul John. "The Menstrual 'Taboo' in Ancient Egypt." *Journal of Near Eastern Studies* 66 (2007): 81–105.

Fredriksen, Paula. "Compassion Is to Purity As Fish Is to Bicycle and Other Reflections on Constructions of 'Judaism' in Current Work on the Historical Jesus." In *Apocalypticism, Anti-Semitism and the Historical Jesus: Subtexts in Criticism*, edited by John S. Kloppenborg and John W. Marshall, 55–67. Journal for the Study of the New Testament Supplement Series 275. London: T&T Clark, 2005.

———. "Did Jesus Oppose the Purity Laws?" *Bible Review* 11 (1995): 18–25, 42–47.

———. "Mandatory Retirement: Ideas in the Study of Christian Origins Whose Time Has Come to Go." *Studies in Religion* 35 (2006): 231–46.

———. *Sin: The Early History of an Idea*. Princeton: Princeton University Press, 2012.

———. "What You See Is What You Get: Context and Content in Current Research on the Historical Jesus." *Theology Today* 52 (1995): 75–97.

Freedman, H., and Maurice Simon, eds. *Midrash Rabbah*. 10 vols. London: Soncino, 1939.

Frevel, Christian. "Purity Conceptions in the Book of Numbers in Context." In *Purity and the Forming of Religious Traditions in the Ancient Mediterranean World and Ancient Judaism*, edited by Christian Frevel and Christophe Nihan, 369–411. Dynamics in the History of Religion 3. Leiden: Brill, 2013.

Frevel, Christian, and Christophe Nihan, eds. *Purity and the Forming of Religious Traditions in the Ancient Mediterranean World and Ancient Judaism*. Dynamics in the History of Religion 3. Leiden: Brill, 2013.

Friedlander, Gerald. *Pirke de Rabbi Eliezer [The chapters of Rabbi Eliezer the Great] according to the Text of the Manuscript Belonging to Abraham Epstein of Vienna.* 2nd ed. New York: Hermon, 1965.

Frymer-Kensky, Tikva. "Pollution, Purification and Purgation in Biblical Israel." In *The Word of the Lord Shall Go Forth: Essays in Honor of David Noel Freedman in Celebration of His Sixtieth Birthday*, edited by Carol L. Meyers and M. O'Connor, 399–404. Winona Lake, IN: Eisenbrauns, 1983.

Funk, Robert. *Honest to Jesus*. San Francisco: HarperSanFrancisco, 1996.

Furstenberg, Yair. "Defilement Penetrating the Body: A New Understanding of Contamination in Mark 7.15." *New Testament Studies* 54 (2008): 176–200.

Gall, August Freiherrn von, ed. *Der Hebräische Pentateuch der Samaritaner*. Giessen: Töpelmann, 1914–18.

Gardner, Gregg. *The Origins of Organized Charity in Rabbinic Judaism*. Cambridge: Cambridge University Press, 2015.

Gardner-Smith, Percival. *St. John and the Synoptic Gospels*. Cambridge: Cambridge University Press, 1938.

Garland, David E. *Reading Matthew: A Literary and Theological Commentary*. Macon, GA: Smyth & Helwys, 2001.

Garland, Robert. *The Greek Way of Death*. Ithaca, NY: Cornell University Press, 1985.

Garrett, Susan R. *The Demise of the Devil: Magic and the Demonic in Luke's Writings*. Minneapolis: Fortress, 1989.

Geller, Markham. *Evil Demons: Canonical Utukkū Lemnūtu Incantations; Introduction, Cuneiform Text, and Transliteration with a Translation and Glossary*. State Archives of Assyria Cuneiform Texts 5. Helsinki: Neo-Assyrian Text Corpus Project, 2007.

———. *Forerunners to Udug-Hul: Sumerian Exorcistic Incantations*. Stuttgart: Steiner, 1985.

Giambrone, Anthony. *Sacramental Charity, Creditor Christology, and the Economy of Salvation in Luke's Gospel*. Wissenschaftliche Untersuchungen zum Neuen Testament 2/439. Tübingen: Mohr Siebeck, 2017.

Gnilka, Joachim. *Das Evangelium nach Markus*. 2 vols. Evangelisch-katholischer Kommentar zum Neuen Testament 2. Neukirchen-Vluyn: Neukirchener Verlag, 1978–79.

Goodacre, Mark. *The Case against Q: Studies in Markan Priority and the Synoptic Problem*. London: T&T Clark, 2002.

Gorman, Frank, Jr. *The Ideology of Ritual: Space, Time and Status in the Priestly Theology*. Journal for the Study of the Old Testament Supplement Series 91. Sheffield: Sheffield Academic, 1990.

Grappe, Christian. "Jesus et l'impureté." *Revue d'histoire et de philosophie religieuses* 84 (2004): 393–417.

Gray, Alyssa. "Redemptive Almsgiving and the Rabbis of Late Antiquity." *Jewish Studies Quarterly* 18 (2011): 144–84.

———. *Charity in Rabbinic Judaism: Atonement, Rewards, and Righteousness*. Routledge Jewish Studies Series. London: Routledge, 2019.

Grmek, Mirko D. *Diseases in the Ancient Greek World*. Baltimore: Johns Hopkins University Press, 1989.

Grünwaldt, Klaus. *Exil und Identität: Beschneidung, Passa und Sabbat in der Priesterschrift*. Bonner biblische Beiträge 85. Frankfurt am Main: Anton Hain, 1992.

Guichard, Michaël, and Lionel Marti. "Purity in Ancient Mesopotamia: The Paleo-Babylonian and Neo-Assyrian Periods." In *Purity and the Forming of Religious Traditions in the Ancient Mediterranean World and Ancient Judaism*, edited by Christian Frevel and Christophe Nihan, 47–113. Dynamics in the History of Religion 3. Leiden: Brill, 2013.

Gundry, Robert H. *Mark: A Commentary on His Apology for the Cross*. Grand Rapids: Eerdmans, 1983.

Haber, Susan. "A Woman's Touch: Feminist Encounters with the Hemorrhaging Woman in Mark 5.24–34." *Journal for the Study of the New Testament* 26 (2003): 171–92.

Hägerland, Tobias. *Jesus and the Forgiveness of Sins: An Aspect of His Prophetic Mission*. Society for New Testament Studies Monograph Series 150. Cambridge: Cambridge University Press, 2011.

Hallo, William W., ed. *The Context of Scripture*. 3 vols. Leiden: Brill, 1997–2002.

Hammer, Reuven. *Sifre: A Tannaitic Commentary on the Book of Deuteronomy*. Yale Judaica Series 24. New Haven: Yale University Press, 1986.

Harnack, Adolf von. *What Is Christianity?* Translated by Thomas Bailey Saunders. Philadelphia: Fortress, 1957.

Harrington, Daniel J. *The Gospel of Matthew*. Sacra Pagina 1. Collegeville, MN: Liturgical Press, 1991.

Harrington, Hannah K. "Did Pharisees Eat Ordinary Food in a State of Ritual Purity?" *Journal for the Study of Judaism in the Persian, Hellenistic, and Roman Periods* 26 (1995): 42–54.

———. *The Purity Texts*. Companion to the Qumran Scrolls 5. London: T&T Clark, 2004.

Hatch, W. H. P. "The Text of Luke 2:22." *Harvard Theological Review* 14 (1921): 377–81.

Haupt, Paul. "Asmodeus." *Journal of Biblical Literature* 40 (1921): 174–78.

Hayes, Christine E. *Gentile Impurities and Jewish Identities: Intermarriage and Conversion from the Bible to the Talmud*. New York: Oxford University Press, 2002.

———. *What's So Divine about Divine Law: Early Perspectives*. Princeton: Princeton University Press, 2015.

Hayward, C. T. R. "The Figure of Adam in Pseudo-Philo's Biblical Antiquities." *Journal for the Study of Judaism in the Persian, Hellenistic, and Roman Periods* 23 (1992): 1–20.

Herzer, Jens. "Riddle of the Holy Ones in Matthew 27:51b–53." In *The Synoptic Gospels*, vol. 1 of *"What Does the Scripture Say?" Studies in the Function of Scripture in Early Judaism and Christianity*, edited by Craig A. Evans and H. Daniel Zacharias, 142–57. The Library of New Testament Studies 470. London: T&T Clark, 2012.

Himmelfarb, Martha. "Impurity and Sin in 4QD, 1QS, and 4Q512." *Dead Sea Discoveries* 8 (2001): 9–37.

Hodges, Horace Jeffrey, and John C. Poirier. "Jesus as the Holy One of God: The Healing of the Zavah in Mark 5.24b–34." *Journal of Greco-Roman Christianity and Judaism* 8 (2011–12): 151–84.

Holmén, Tom. *Jesus and Jewish Covenant Thinking*. Biblical Interpretation Series 55. Leiden: Brill, 2001.

———. "Jesus' Inverse Strategy of Ritual (Im)purity and the Ritual Purity of Early Christians." In *Anthropology in the New Testament and Its Ancient Context: Papers from the EABS-Meeting in Piliscsaba/Budapest*, edited by Michael Labahn and Outi Lehtipuu, 15–32. Contributions to Biblical Exegesis and Theology 54. Leuven: Peeters, 2010.

Horsley, Greg H. R., and Stephen Llewelyn, eds. *New Documents Illustrating Early Christianity*. 10 vols. North Ryde, New South Wales: Ancient History Documentary Research Centre, Macquarie University, 1981–.

Houston, Walter. *Purity and Monotheism: Clean and Unclean Animals in Biblical Law*. Journal for the Study of the Old Testament Supplement Series 140. Sheffield: JSOT Press, 1993.

Hübner, Hans. *Das Gesetz in der synoptischen Tradition: Studien zur These einer progressiven Qumranisierung und Judaisierung innerhalb der synoptischen Tradition*. Göttingen: Vandenhoeck & Ruprecht, 1986.

Hude, C., ed. *Corpus Medicorum Graecorum II*. 2nd ed. Berlin: de Gruyter, 1958.

Hulse, E. V. "The Nature of Biblical 'Leprosy' and the Use of Alternative Medical Terms in Modern Translations of the Bible." *Palestine Exploration Quarterly* 107 (1975): 87–105.

Insler, Stanley. *The Gāthās of Zarathustra*. Acta Iranica 8. Leiden: Brill, 1975.

Jacobsen, Thorkild. *Treasures of Darkness: A History of Mesopotamian Religion*. New Haven: Yale University Press, 1976.

Jervell, Jacob. *Luke and the People of God: A New Look at Luke-Acts*. Minneapolis: Augsburg, 1972.

———. *The Unknown Paul: Essays on Luke-Acts and Early Christian History*. Translated by Roy A. Harrisville. Minneapolis: Augsburg, 1984.

Johnson, Nathan C. "Anger Issues: Mark 1.41 in Ephrem the Syrian, the Old Latin Gospels and Codex Bezae." *New Testament Studies* 63 (2017): 183–202.

Joseph, Simon J. *Jesus and the Temple: The Crucifixion in Its Jewish Context*. Society for New Testament Studies Monograph Series 165. Cambridge: Cambridge University Press, 2016.

Josephus. *Josephus*. Translated by H. St. J. Thackeray et al. 10 vols. Loeb Classical Library. Cambridge, MA: Harvard University Press, 1926–65.

Kampen, John. *Matthew within Sectarian Judaism*. New Haven: Yale University Press, 2019.

Kaufmann, Yehezkel. *The Religion of Israel: From Its Beginning to the Babylonian Exile*. Translated by Moshe Greenberg. New York: Schocken, 1960.

Kazen, Thomas. *Emotions in Biblical Law: A Cognitive Science Approach*. Hebrew Bible Monographs 36. Sheffield: Sheffield Phoenix, 2011.

———. *Issues of Impurity in Early Judaism*. Coniectanea Biblica: New Testament Series 45. Winona Lake, IN: Eisenbrauns, 2010.

———. "Jesus, Scripture and *Paradosis*: Response to Friedrich Avemarie." In *The New Testament and Rabbinic Literature*, edited by Peter Tomson et al., 281–88. Journal for the Study of Judaism in the Persian, Hellenistic, and Roman Periods Supplement Series 136. Leiden: Brill, 2010.

———. *Jesus and Purity Halakhah: Was Jesus Indifferent to Impurity?* Coniectanea Biblica: New Testament Series 38. Stockholm: Almqvist & Wiksell, 2002.

———. "A Perhaps Less Halakic Jesus and Purity: On Prophetic Criticism, Halakic Innovation, and Rabbinic Anachronism." *Journal for the Study of the Historical Jesus* 14 (2016): 120–36.

———. *Scripture, Interpretation, or Authority? Motives and Arguments in Jesus' Halakic Conflicts*. Wissenschaftliche Untersuchungen zum Neuen Testament 320. Tübingen: Mohr Siebeck, 2013.

Kee, Howard Clark. "The Terminology of Mark's Exorcism Stories." *New Testament Studies* 14 (1967–68): 232–46.

Keith, Chris. "'If John Knew Mark': Critical Inheritance and Johannine Disagreements with Mark." In *John's Transformation of Mark*, edited by Eve-Marie Becker, Helen K. Bond, and Catrin Williams. London: T&T Clark, 2020.

Keith, Chris, and Anthony Le Donne, eds. *Jesus, Criteria, and the Demise of Authenticity*. London: T&T Clark, 2012.

Kellenbach, Katharina von. *Anti-Judaism in Feminist Religious Writings*. American Academy of Religion Classics in Religious Studies. Oxford: Oxford University Press, 1994.

King, Helen. *Hippocrates' Woman: Reading the Female Body in Ancient Greece*. London: Routledge, 1998.

Kinnier Wilson, James. "Organic Disease in Ancient Mesopotamia." In *Diseases in Antiquity: A Survey of the Diseases, Injuries, and Surgery of Early Populations*, edited by D. R. Brothwell and A. T. Sandison, 281–88. Springfield, IL: Charles C. Thomas, 1967.

Klawans, Jonathan. *Impurity and Sin in Ancient Judaism*. New York: Oxford University Press, 2000.

Klein, Ralph W. *1 Chronicles*. Hermeneia. Minneapolis: Fortress, 2006.

Klinghardt, Matthias. *Gesetz und Volk Gottes: Das lukanische Verständnis des Gesetzes nach Herkunft, Funktion und seinem Ort in der Geschichte des Urchristentums*. Wissenschaftliche Untersuchungen zum Neuen Testament 32. Tübingen: Mohr Siebeck, 1988.

Kloppenborg, John, and Joseph Verheyden, eds. *The Elijah-Elisha Narrative in the Composition of Luke*. The Library of New Testament Studies 493. London: Bloomsbury, 2014.

Klostermann, Erich. *Das Lukasevangelium*. 3rd ed. Handbuch zum Neuen Testament 5. Tübingen: Mohr Siebeck, 1975.

Kraemer, Ross Shepard, and Mary Rose D'Angelo, eds. *Women and Christian Origins*. New York: Oxford University Press, 1999.

Kruse, Heinz. "Die 'dialektische Negation' als semitisches Idiom." *Vetus Testamentum* 4 (1954): 385–400.

Kümmel, Werner Georg. *Introduction to the New Testament*. Rev. ed. Translated by Howard Clark Kee. London: SCM, 1975.

Lambert, W. G. "A Middle Assyrian Medical Text." *Iraq* 31 (1969): 28–39.

Lambrecht, Jan. "Jesus and the Law: An Investigation of Mk 7,1–23." *Ephemerides Theologicae Lovanienses* 53 (1977): 24–79.

Lane, William L. *The Gospel of Mark*. New International Commentary on the New Testament. Grand Rapids: Eerdmans, 1974.

Lange, Armin. "Considerations concerning the 'Spirit of Impurity' in Zech 13:2." In Lange, Lichtenberger, and Römheld, *Die Dämonen—Demons*, 254–68.

Lange, Armin, Hermann Lichtenberger, and K. F. Diethard Römheld, eds. *Die Dämonen—Demons: Die Dämonologie der israelitisch-jüdischen und frühchristlichen Literatur im Kontext ihrer Umwelt—The Demonology of Israelite-Jewish and Early Christian Literature in the Context of Their Environment.* Tübingen: Mohr Siebeck, 2003.

Laroche, Emmanuel. *Catalogue des textes hittites.* Paris: Klincksieck, 1971.

Lauterbach, Jacob Z., ed. and trans. *Mekilta de-Rabbi Ishmael.* 3 vols. Philadelphia: Jewish Publication Society of America, 1933–35.

Lemos, Tracy M. "The Universal and the Particular: Mary Douglas and the Politics of Impurity." *Journal of Religion* 89 (2009): 236–51.

———. "Where There Is Dirt, Is There System? Revisiting Biblical Purity Constructions." *Journal for the Study of the Old Testament* 37 (2013): 265–94.

Lennon, Jack J. "Menstrual Blood in Ancient Rome: An Unspeakable Impurity?" *Classica et Mediaevalia* 61 (2010): 71–87.

———. *Pollution and Religion in Ancient Rome.* Cambridge: Cambridge University Press, 2014.

Levenson, Jon D. *Resurrection and the Restoration of Israel: The Ultimate Victory of the God of Life.* New Haven: Yale University Press, 2006.

Levine, Amy-Jill. "Discharging Responsibility: Matthean Jesus, Biblical Law, and Hemorrhaging Woman." In *Treasures New and Old: Contributions to Matthean Studies,* edited by David Bauer and Mark Allan Powell, 379–97. Symposium Series 1. Atlanta: Scholars Press, 1996.

———. *The Misunderstood Jew: The Church and the Scandal of the Jewish Jesus.* San Francisco: HarperSanFrancisco, 2006.

———. *Short Stories by Jesus: The Enigmatic Parables of a Controversial Rabbi.* New York: HarperOne, 2014.

Levine, Baruch. *Leviticus = Va-yikra: The Traditional Hebrew Text with the New JPS Translation.* JPS Torah Commentary. Philadelphia: Jewish Publication Society of America, 1989.

Lewis, C. S. *The Lion, the Witch and the Wardrobe.* New York: HarperTrophy, 1950.

Lilly, Ingrid. "Conceptualizing Spirit: Supernatural Meteorology and Winds of Distress in the Hebrew Bible and the Ancient Near East." In *Sibyls, Scriptures, and Scrolls: John Collins at Seventy,* edited by Joel Baden, Hindy Najman, and Eibert J. C. Tigchelaar, 826–44. Journal for the Study of Judaism in the Persian, Hellenistic, and Roman Periods Supplement Series 175. Leiden: Brill, 2016.

Lindsay, Hugh. "Death-Pollution and Funerals in the City of Rome." In *Death and Disease in the Ancient City,* edited by Valerie M. Hope and Eireann Marshall, 152–74. Routledge Classical Monographs. London: Routledge, 1998.

Loader, William. "Challenged at the Boundaries: A Conservative Jesus in Mark's Tradition." *Journal for the Study of the New Testament* 63 (1996): 45–61.

————. *Jesus' Attitude towards the Law: A Study of the Gospels.* Wissenschaftliche Untersuchungen zum Neuen Testament 2/97. Tübingen: Mohr Siebeck, 1997.

————. "Mark 7:1–23 and the Historical Jesus." *Colloquium* 30 (1998): 123–51.

Lohmeyer, Ernst. *Das Evangelium des Markus.* Kritisch-exegetischer Kommentar über das Neue Testament 1/2. Göttingen: Vandenhoeck & Ruprecht, 1953.

Lonie, I. M. *The Hippocratic Treatises "On Generation," "On the Nature of the Child," "Diseases IV": A Commentary.* Ars Medica 7. Berlin: de Gruyter, 1981.

Love, Stuart L. "Jesus Heals the Hemorrhaging Woman." In *The Social Setting of Jesus and the Gospels,* edited by Wolfgang Stegemann, Bruce J. Malina, and Gerd Theissen, 85–101. Minneapolis: Fortress, 2002.

Lührmann, Dieter. *Das Markusevangelium.* Handbuch zum Neuen Testament 3. Tübingen: Mohr Siebeck, 1987.

Luz, Ulrich. *Matthew 8–20: A Commentary.* Translated by James E. Crouch. Hermeneia. Minneapolis: Fortress, 2001.

Maccoby, Hyam. *Ritual and Morality: The Ritual Purity System and Its Place in Judaism.* Cambridge: Cambridge University Press, 1999.

Machiela, Daniel A. "Luke 13:10–13: 'Woman, You Have Been Set Free from Your Ailment'—Illness, Demon Possession, and Laying on Hands in Light of Second Temple Period Jewish Literature." In *The Gospels in First-Century Judaea: Proceedings of the Inaugural Conference of Nyack College's Graduate Program in Ancient Judaism and Christian Origins, August 29th, 2013,* edited by R. Steven Notley and Jeffrey P. García, 122–35. Jewish and Christian Perspectives 29. Leiden: Brill, 2016.

Macht, Daniel I. "A Scientific Appreciation of Leviticus 12:1–5." *Journal of Biblical Literature* 52 (1933): 253–60.

Madigan, Kevin J., and Jon D. Levenson. *Resurrection: The Power of God for Christians and Jews.* New Haven: Yale University Press, 2008.

Magonet, Jonathan. "'But If It Is a Girl, She Is Unclean for Twice Seven Days . . .': The Riddle of Leviticus 12:5." In *Reading Leviticus: A Conversation with Mary Douglas,* edited by John F. A. Sawyer, 144–52. Journal for the Study of the Old Testament Supplement Series 227. Sheffield: Sheffield Academic, 1996.

Malina, Bruce J. *The New Testament World: Insights from Cultural Anthropology.* 3rd ed. Louisville: Westminster John Knox, 2001.

Mann, Jacob. "Jesus and the Sadducean Priests: Luke 10.25–37." *Jewish Quarterly Review* 6 (1915–16): 415–22.

————. "Rabbinic Studies in the Synoptic Gospels, II: The Redemption of a First-Born Son and the Pilgrimages to Jerusalem." *Hebrew Union College Annual* 1 (1924): 323–55.

Manus, Chris U., and Bolaji O. Bateye. "The Plight of HIV and AIDS Persons in West Africa: A Contextual Re-reading of Mk 1:40–45 and Parallels." *Asian Journal of Theology* 20 (2006): 155–69.

Marcus, Joel. "Entering into the Kingly Power of God." *Journal of Biblical Literature* 107 (1988): 663–75.

———. *John the Baptist in History and Theology.* Studies on Personalities of the New Testament. Columbia: University of South Carolina Press, 2018.

———. *Mark 1–8: A New Translation with Introduction and Commentary.* Anchor Bible 27. New York: Doubleday, 2000.

———. *Mark 8–16: A New Translation with Introduction and Commentary.* Anchor Bible 27A. New Haven: Yale University Press, 2009.

———. *The Mystery of the Kingdom of God.* Society of Biblical Literature Dissertation Series 90. Atlanta: Scholars Press, 1986.

———. "Scripture and Tradition in Mark 7." In *The Scriptures in the Gospels*, edited by Christopher M. Tuckett, 145–63. Bibliotheca Ephemeridum Theologicarum Lovaniensium 131. Leuven: Leuven University Press, 1997.

Mark, Samuel. "Alexander the Great, Seafaring, and the Spread of Leprosy." *Journal of the History of Medicine and Allied Sciences* 57 (2002): 285–311.

Marshall, I. Howard. *The Gospel of Luke: A Commentary on the Greek Text.* New International Greek Testament Commentary. Grand Rapids: Eerdmans, 1978.

Martin, Dale B. *Inventing Superstition: From the Hippocratics to the Christians.* Cambridge, MA: Harvard University Press, 2004.

Martínez, Florentino García, and Eibert J. C. Tigchelaar, eds. *The Dead Sea Scrolls: Study Edition.* 2 vols. Leiden: Brill, 1997–98.

Matheson, Carney D., Kim K. Vernon, Arlene Lahti, Renee Fratpietro, Mark Spigelman, Shimon Gibson, Charles L. Greenblatt, and Helen D. Donoghue. "Molecular Exploration of the First-Century Tomb of the Shroud in Akeldama, Jerusalem." *PLoS ONE* 4 (2009). http://www.plosone.org/article/info%3Adoi%2F10.1371%2F journal.pone.0008319.

Mayer-Haas, Andreas J. *"Geschenk aus Gottes" (bSchab 10b): Jesus und der Sabbat im Spiegel der neutestamentlichen Schriften.* Neutestamentliche Abhandlungen 43. Aschendorff: Aschendorff Verlag, 2003.

Meier, John P. "The Historical Jesus and the Historical Law: Some Problems with the Problem." *Catholic Biblical Quarterly* 65 (2003): 52–79.

———. *A Marginal Jew: Rethinking the Historical Jesus.* 5 vols. Anchor Yale Bible Reference Library. New Haven: Yale University Press, 1991–2009.

Meier, Sam. "House Fungus: Mesopotamia and Israel (Lev. 14:33–53)." *Revue biblique* 96 (1989): 184–92.

Meinel, Fabian. *Pollution and Crisis in Greek Tragedy.* Cambridge: Cambridge University Press, 2015.

Metzger, Bruce. *A Textual Commentary on the Greek New Testament.* 2nd ed. Stuttgart: Deutsche Bibelgesellschaft, 1994.

Meyer, Nicholas A. *Adam's Dust and Adam's Glory in the Hodayot and the Letters of Paul: Rethinking Anthropogony and Theology.* Novum Testamentum Supplements 168. Leiden: Brill, 2016.

Milgrom, Jacob. "The Dynamics of Purity in the Priestly System." In *Purity and Holiness: The Heritage of Leviticus,* edited by Marcel J. H. M. Poorthuis and Joshua Schwartz, 29–32. Jewish and Christian Perspectives Series 2. Leiden: Brill, 2000.

———. "First Day Ablutions in Qumran." In *The Madrid Qumran Congress: Proceedings of the International Congress on the Dead Sea Scrolls. Madrid 18–21 March, 1991,* edited by J. Trebolle Barrera and L. Vegas Montaner, 561–70. Studies on the Texts of the Desert of Judah 11/2. Leiden: Brill, 1992.

———. "Israel's Sanctuary: The Priestly 'Picture of Dorian Gray.'" *Revue biblique* 83 (1976): 390–99.

———. *Leviticus: A Book of Ritual and Ethics.* Continental Commentary. Minneapolis: Fortress, 2004.

———. *Leviticus 1–16: A New Translation with Introduction and Commentary.* Anchor Bible 3. New York: Doubleday, 1991.

———. *Leviticus 17–22: A New Translation with Introduction and Commentary.* Anchor Bible 3A. New York: Doubleday, 2000.

———. *Leviticus 23–27: A New Translation with Introduction and Commentary.* Anchor Bible 3B. New York: Doubleday, 2001.

———. *Numbers = BeMidbar: The Traditional Hebrew Text with the New JPS Translation.* JPS Torah Commentary. Philadelphia: Jewish Publication Society of America, 1990.

———. "The Paradox of the Red Cow (Num. XIX)." *Vetus Testamentum* 31 (1981): 62–72.

———. "The Rationale for Biblical Impurity." *Journal of the Ancient Near Eastern Society of Columbia University* 22 (1993): 107–11.

———. *Studies in Levitical Terminology, I: The Encroacher and the Levite; The Term 'Aboda.* University of California Publications, Near Eastern Studies 14. Berkeley: University of California Press, 1970.

Miller, Stuart S. *At the Intersection of Texts and Material Finds: Stepped Pools, Stone Vessels, and Ritual Purity among the Jews of Roman Galilee.* Journal of Ancient Judaism Supplement 16. Göttingen: Vandenhoeck & Ruprecht, 2015.

Moller, Hilda Brekke. *The Vermes Quest: The Significance of Geza Vermes.* The Library of New Testament Studies 576. London: Bloomsbury, 2017.

Møller-Christensen, V. "Evidence of Leprosy in Earlier Peoples." In *Diseases in Antiquity: A Survey of the Diseases, Injuries, and Surgery of Early Populations,* edited by D. R. Brothwell and A. T. Sandison, 295–305. Springfield, IL: Charles C. Thomas, 1967.

Moss, Candida R. "The Man with the Flow of Power: Porous Bodies in Mark 5:25–34." *Journal of Biblical Literature* 129 (2010): 507–19.

Munck, Johannes. *The Acts of the Apostles: Introduction, Translation, and Notes.* Anchor Bible 31. Garden City, NY: Doubleday, 1967.

Myers, Ched. *Binding the Strong Man: A Political Reading of Mark's Story of Jesus.* Maryknoll, NY: Orbis Books, 1988.

Neusner, Jacob. *The Tosefta: Translated from Hebrew with a New Introduction.* 2 vols. Peabody, MA: Hendrickson, 2002.

Neyrey, Jerome. "The Idea of Purity in Mark's Gospel." *Semeia* 35 (1986): 91–128.

———. "The Symbolic Universe of Luke-Acts: 'They Turn the World Upside Down.'" In *The Social World of Luke-Acts: Models for Interpretation*, edited by Jerome H. Neyrey, 271–304. Peabody, MA: Hendrickson, 1991.

Nickelsburg, George W. E. *Resurrection, Immortality, and Eternal Life in Intertestamental Judaism.* Harvard Theological Studies 26. Cambridge, MA: Harvard University Press, 1972.

Nihan, Christophe. "Forms and Functions of Purity in Leviticus." In *Purity and the Forming of Religious Traditions in the Ancient Mediterranean World and Ancient Judaism*, edited by Christian Frevel and Christophe Nihan, 311–67. Dynamics in the History of Religion 3. Leiden: Brill, 2013.

Nilsson, Martin P. *Geschichte der Griechischen Religion.* 2 vols. Munich: Beck, 1961–67.

Noam, Vered. "Essentialism, Freedom of Choice, and the Calendar: Contradictory Trends in Rabbinic Halakhah." *Dine Israel* 30 (2015): 121–37.

———. "Josephus and Early Halakhah: The Exclusion of the Impure Persons from Holy Precincts." In *"Go Out and Study the Land" (Judges 18:2): Archaeological, Historical and Textual Studies in Honor of Hanan Eshel*, edited by Aren M. Maeir, Jodi Magness, and Lawrence H. Schiffman, 133–46. Journal for the Study of Judaism in the Persian, Hellenistic, and Roman Periods Supplement Series 148. Leiden: Brill, 2011.

Noam, Vered, and Elisha Qimron. "A Qumran Composition of Sabbath Laws and Its Contribution to the Study of Early Halakah." *Dead Sea Discoveries* 16 (2009): 55–96.

Nolland, John. *Luke 1:1–9:20.* Word Biblical Commentary 35A. Dallas: Word, 1989.

Novakovic, Lidija. *Messiah, the Healer of the Sick: A Study of Jesus as the Son of David in the Gospel of Matthew.* Wissenschaftliche Untersuchungen zum Neuen Testament 2/170. Tübingen: Mohr Siebeck, 2003.

Novenson, Matthew V. *The Grammar of Messianism: An Ancient Jewish Political Idiom and Its Users.* New York: Oxford University Press, 2017.

Öhler, Markus. *Elia im Neuen Testament: Untersuchungen zur Bedeutung des alttestamentlichen Propheten im frühen Christentum.* Beihefte zur Zeitschrift für die neutestamentliche Wissenschaft 88. Berlin: de Gruyter, 1997.

Oliver, Isaac W. *Torah Praxis after 70 CE: Reading Matthew and Luke-Acts as Jewish Texts.* Wissenschaftliche Untersuchungen zum Neuen Testament 2/355. Tübingen: Mohr Siebeck, 2013.

Olyan, Saul M. *Rites and Rank: Hierarchy in Biblical Representations of Cult.* Princeton: Princeton University Press, 2000.

Oppenheim, A. Leo. *Letters from Mesopotamia: Official, Business, and Private Letters on Clay Tablets from Two Millennia.* Chicago: University of Chicago Press, 1967.

Origen. *Contra Celsum.* Translated by Henry Chadwick. Cambridge: Cambridge University Press, 1953.

———. *Homilies 1–14 on Ezekiel.* Translated by Thomas P. Scheck. Ancient Christian Writers 62. New York: Newman, 2010.

———. *Homilies on Leviticus.* Translated by Gary Wayne Barkley. Fathers of the Church 83. Washington, DC: Catholic University of America Press, 1990.

———. *Homilies on Luke.* Translated by Joseph T. Lienhard. Fathers of the Church 94. Washington, DC: Catholic University of America Press, 1996.

Orlov, Andrei. *Dark Mirrors: Azazel and Satanael in Early Jewish Demonology.* Albany: State University of New York Press, 2011.

Owens, J. Edward. "Asmodeus: A Less than Minor Character in the Book of Tobit: A Narrative-Critical Study." In *Angels: The Concept of Celestial Beings—Origins, Development and Reception,* edited by Friedrich V. Reiterer, Tobias Nicklas, and Karin Schöpflin, 277–90. Deuterocanonical and Cognate Literature Yearbook 2007. Berlin: de Gruyter, 2007.

Pancaro, Severino. *The Law in the Fourth Gospel: The Torah and the Gospel, Moses and Jesus, Judaism and Christianity according to John.* Supplements to Novum Testamentum 42. Leiden: Brill, 1975.

Parker, Robert. *Miasma: Pollution and Purification in Early Greek Religion.* Oxford: Clarendon, 1983.

Paschen, Wilfried. *Rein und Unrein: Untersuchung zur biblischen Wortgeschichte.* Studien zum Alten und Neuen Testaments 24. Munich: Kösel, 1970.

Pelling, Christopher. "Childhood and Personality in Greek Biography." In *Characterization and Individuality in Greek Literature,* edited by Christopher Pelling, 213–44. Oxford: Oxford University Press, 1990.

Penney, Douglas L., and Michael O. Wise. "By the Power of Beelzebub: An Aramaic Incantation Formula from Qumran." *Journal of Biblical Literature* 113 (1994): 627–50.

Pervo, Richard I. *Dating Acts: Between the Evangelists and the Apologists.* Santa Rosa, CA: Polebridge, 2006.

Pesch, Rudolf. *Das Markusevangelium*. 2 vols. Herders Theologischer Kommentar zum Neuen Testament 2. Basel: Herder, 1976.

Petersen, Anders Klostergaard. "The Notion of Demon: Open Questions to a Diffuse Concept." In Lange, Lichtenberger, and Römheld, *Die Dämonen—Demons*, 23–41.

Philip, Tarja S. "Gender Matters: Priestly Writing on Impurity." In *Embroidered Garments: Priests and Gender in Biblical Israel*, edited by Deborah W. Rooke, 40–59. Hebrew Bible Monographs 25. Sheffield: Sheffield Phoenix, 2009.

Philo. Translated by F. H. Colson, G. H. Whitaker, and Ralph Marcus. 12 vols. Loeb Classical Library. Cambridge, MA: Harvard University Press, 1929–62.

Pilch, John J. *Healing in the New Testament: Insights from Medical and Mediterranean Anthropology*. Minneapolis: Fortress, 2000.

Plaskow, Judith. "Feminist Anti-Judaism and the Christian God." *Journal of Feminist Studies in Religion* 7 (1991): 99–108.

Plummer, Alfred. *A Critical and Exegetical Commentary on the Gospel according to S. Luke*. 5th ed. International Critical Commentary. Edinburgh: T&T Clark, 1922.

Poirier, John C. "Why Did the Pharisees Wash Their Hands?" *Journal of Jewish Studies* 47 (1996): 217–33.

Poirier, John, and Jeffrey Peterson, eds. *Markan Priority without Q: Explorations in the Farrer Hypothesis*. The Library of New Testament Studies 455. London: Bloomsbury, 2015.

Polen, Nehemia. "Leviticus and Hebrews . . . and Leviticus." In *The Epistle to the Hebrews and Christian Theology*, edited by Richard Bauckham, Daniel R. Driver, Trevor A. Hart, and Nathan MacDonald, 213–25. Grand Rapids: Eerdmans, 2009.

Preuss, Julius. *Biblical and Talmudic Medicine*. Edited and translated by Fred Rosner. New York: Sanhedrin, 1978.

Puech, Émile. "11QPsAp^a: Un Rituel d'exorcismes: Essai de reconstruction." *Revue de Qumran* 14 (1990): 377–408.

―――. "Les deux derniers psaumes davidiques du ritual d'exorcisme 11QPsAp^a IV 4—V 14." In *The Dead Sea Scrolls: Forty Years of Research*, edited by Devorah Dimant and Uriel Rappaport, 64–89. Studies on the Texts of the Desert of Judah 10. Leiden: Brill, 1992.

Rahlfs, Alfred, ed. *Septuaginta: Id est Vetus Testamentum Graece iuxta LXX interpretes*. 9th ed. Stuttgart: Württembergische Bibelanstalt Stuttgart, 1971.

Räisänen, Heikki. *Die Mutter Jesu im Neuen Testament*. Annales Academiae Scientiarum Fennicae 247. Helsinki: Suomalainen Tiedeakatemia, 1989.

―――. "Jesus and the Food Laws: Reflections on Mark 7:15." *Journal for the Study of the New Testament* 16 (1982): 79–100.

Regev, Eyal. "Pure Individualism: The Idea of Non-priestly Purity in Ancient Judaism." *Journal for the Study of Judaism in the Persian, Hellenistic, and Roman Periods* 31 (2000): 176–202.

Reiner, Erica. *Šurpu: A Collection of Sumerian and Akkadian Incantations*. Archiv für Orientforschung 11. Graz: Im Selbstverlage des Herausgebers, 1958.

Rhoads, David. "Social Criticism: Crossing Boundaries." In *Mark and Method: New Approaches in Biblical Studies*, edited by Janice Capel Anderson and Stephen D. Moore, 135–61. Minneapolis: Fortress, 1992.

Rhodes, P. J., and Robin Osborne, eds. *Greek Historical Inscriptions 404–323 BC*. New York: Oxford University Press, 2003.

Roberts, Alexander, and James Donaldson, eds. *The Ante-Nicene Fathers*. 10 vols. Peabody, MA: Hendrickson, 1994.

Robertson, Noel. "The Concept of Purity in Greek Sacred Laws." In *Purity and the Forming of Religious Traditions in the Ancient Mediterranean World and Ancient Judaism*, edited by Christian Frevel and Christophe Nihan, 195–243. Dynamics in the History of Religion 3. Leiden: Brill, 2013.

Robertson, Paul. "De-spiritualizing *Pneuma*: Modernity, Religion, and Anachronism in the Study of Paul." *Method and Theory in the Study of Religion* 26 (2014): 365–83.

Robinson, James M., ed. *The Nag Hammadi Library in English*. 3rd ed. San Francisco: Harper & Row, 1988.

Rodríguez, Rafael. *Structuring Early Christian Memory: Jesus in Tradition, Performance, and Text*. The Library of New Testament Studies 407. London: T&T Clark, 2010.

Ronis, Sara. "'Do Not Go Out Alone at Night': Law and Demonic Discourse in the Babylonian Talmud." PhD diss., Yale University, 2015.

Rordorf, Willy. *Sunday: The History of the Day of Rest and Worship in the Earliest Centuries of the Christian Church*. Translated by A. A. K. Graham. Philadelphia: Westminster, 1968.

Rosenblum, Jordan. *The Jewish Dietary Laws in the Ancient World*. Cambridge: Cambridge University Press, 2016.

Rosen-Zvi, Ishay. *Demonic Desires: "Yetzer Hara" and the Problem of Evil in Late Antiquity*. Divinations. Philadelphia: University of Pennsylvania Press, 2011.

Roth, Martha T., trans. *Law Collections from Mesopotamia and Asia Minor*. 2nd ed. Writings of the Ancient World 6. Atlanta: Scholars Press, 1997.

Runesson, Anders. *Divine Wrath and Salvation in Matthew: The Narrative World of the First Gospel*. Minneapolis: Fortress, 2016.

Ryan, Jordan J. *The Role of the Synagogue in the Aims of Jesus*. Minneapolis: Fortress, 2017.

Salmon, Marilyn. "Insider or Outsider? Luke's Relationship with Judaism." In *Luke-Acts and the People of God*, edited by Joseph B. Tyson, 76–82. Minneapolis: Augsburg Fortress, 1988.

Sanders, E. P. *Jesus and Judaism*. London: SCM, 1985.

———. *Jewish Law from Jesus to the Mishnah: Five Studies*. London: SCM, 1990.

———. *Judaism: Practice and Belief, 63 BCE–66 CE*. London: SCM, 1992.

Sariola, Heikki. *Markus und das Gesetz: Eine redaktionskritische Untersuchung.* Annales Academiae Scientiarum Fennicae 56. Helsinki: Suomalainen Tiedeakatemia, 1990.

Sawyer, John F. A., ed. *Reading Leviticus: A Conversation with Mary Douglas.* Journal for the Study of the Old Testament Supplement Series 227. Sheffield: Sheffield Academic, 1996.

Schaller, Berndt. "Jesus und der Sabbat." In *Fundamenta Judaica: Studien zum antiken Judentum und zum Neuen Testament*, edited by Lutz Doering and Annette Steudel, 125–47. Studien zur Umwelt des Neuen Testaments 25. Göttingen: Vandenhoeck & Ruprecht, 2001.

Schams, Christine. *Jewish Scribes in the Second-Temple Period*. Journal for the Study of the Old Testament Supplement Series 291. Sheffield: Sheffield Academic, 1998.

Schiffman, Lawrence H. "The Impurity of the Dead in the *Temple Scroll*." In *Archaeology and History in the Dead Sea Scrolls: The New York University Conference in Memory of Yigael Yadin*, edited by Lawrence H. Schiffman, 135–56. Journal for the Study of the Pseudepigrapha Supplement Series 8. Sheffield: JSOT Press, 1990.

Schmithals, Walter. *Das Evangelium nach Lukas*. Zürcher Bibelkommentare 3/1. Zurich: Theologischer, 1980.

Schneemelcher, Wilhelm, ed. *Gospels and Related Writings*. Vol. 1 of *New Testament Apocrypha*, translated by R. McL. Wilson. Rev. ed. Louisville: Westminster John Knox, 1991.

Schneider, Gerhard. *Das Evangelium nach Lukas, Kapitel 1–10.* Ökumenischer Taschenbuch-Kommentar 3/1. Gütersloh: Gütersloher Verlagshaus, 1992.

Schuller, Eileen M. "Women at Qumran." In vol. 2 of *The Dead Sea Scrolls after Fifty Years: A Comprehensive Assessment*, edited by Peter W. Flint and James C. Vanderkam, 117–44. Leiden: Brill, 1999.

———. "Women in the Dead Sea Scrolls: Research in the Past Decade and Future Directions." In *The Dead Sea Scrolls and Contemporary Culture: Proceedings of the International Conference Held at the Israel Museum, Jerusalem (July 6–8, 2008)*, edited by Adolfo D. Roitman, Lawrence H. Schiffman, and Shani Tzoref, 571–88. Studies on the Texts of the Desert of Judah 93. Leiden: Brill, 2010.

Schultz, Jennifer. "Doctors, Philosophers, and Christian Fathers on Menstrual Blood." In *Wholly Woman, Holy Blood: A Feminist Critique of Purity and Impurity*, edited by Kristen De Troyer, Judith A. Herbert, Judith Ann Johnson, and Anne-Marie Korte, 97–116. Studies in Antiquity and Christianity. Harrisburg, PA: Trinity Press International, 2003.

Schwartz, Daniel R. "On Two Aspects of a Priestly View of Descent at Qumran." In *Archaeology and History in the Dead Sea Scrolls: The New York University Conference in Memory of Yigael Yadin*, edited by Lawrence H. Schiffman, 157–79.

Journal for the Study of the Pseudepigrapha Supplement Series 8. Sheffield: JSOT Press, 1990.

————. *Studies in the Jewish Background of Christianity.* Wissenschaftliche Untersuchungen zum Neuen Testament 60. Tübingen: Mohr Siebeck, 1992.

Schweitzer, Albert. *The Quest of the Historical Jesus: A Critical Study of Its Progress from Reimarus to Wrede.* Translated by W. Montgomery. New York: Macmillan, 1968.

Schweizer, Eduard. *The Good News according to Mark.* Translated by Donald H. Madvig. Richmond: John Knox, 1970.

Selvidge, Marla. "Mark 5:25–34 and Leviticus 15:19–20: A Reaction to Restrictive Purity Regulations." *Journal of Biblical Literature* 103 (1984): 619–23.

————. *Woman, Cult and Miracle Recital: A Redactional Critical Investigation on Mark 5:24–34.* Lewisburg, PA: Bucknell University Press, 1990.

Slenczka, Notger. "Die Kirche und das Alte Testament." *Das Alte Testament in der Theologie,* edited by Elisabeth Gräb-Schmidt, 83–119. Marburger Theologische Studien 119. Leipzig: Evangelische Verlagsanstalt, 2013.

Smith, G. Elliot, and Warren R. Dawson. *Egyptian Mummies.* London: G. Allen and Unwin, 1924.

Sommer, Benjamin. *The Bodies of God and the World of Ancient Israel.* Cambridge: Cambridge University Press, 2011.

————. *Revelation and Authority: Sinai in Jewish Scripture and Tradition.* New Haven: Yale University Press, 2015.

Soranus. *Soranus' Gynecology.* Translated by Owsei Temkin, Nicholson J. Eastman, Ludwig Edelstein, and Alan F. Guttmacher. Baltimore: Johns Hopkins University Press, 1956.

Sorenson, Eric. *Possession and Exorcism in the New Testament and Early Christianity.* Wissenschaftliche Untersuchungen zum Neuen Testament 2/157. Tübingen: Mohr Siebeck, 2002.

Stanley, Andy. "Aftermath, Part 3: Not Difficult." Published April 30, 2018. YouTube video, 39:44. https://www.youtube.com/watch?v=pShxFTNRCWI.

Stein, Robert H. *Luke.* New American Commentary 24. Nashville: Broadman, 1992.

Sterling, Gregory. *Historiography and Self-Definition: Josephos, Luke-Acts and Apologetic Historiography.* Supplements to Novum Testamentum 64. Leiden: Brill, 1992.

Stol, Marten. *Birth in Babylonia and the Bible: Its Mediterranean Setting.* Cuneiform Monographs 14. Groningen: Styx, 2000.

Strawn, Brent. *The Old Testament Is Dying: A Diagnosis and Recommended Treatment.* Grand Rapids: Baker Academic, 2017.

Strelan, Rick. *Luke the Priest: The Authority of the Author of the Third Gospel.* Aldershot: Ashgate, 2008.

Stuckenbruck, Loren. "The 'Angels' and 'Giants' of Genesis 6:1–4 in Second and Third Century BCE Jewish Interpretation: Reflections on the Posture of Early Apocalyptic Traditions." *Dead Sea Discoveries* 7 (2000): 354–77.

———. "Giant Mythology and Demonology: From the Ancient Near East to the Dead Sea Scrolls." In Lange, Lichtenberger, and Römheld, *Die Dämonen—Demons*, 318–38.

———. "Satan and Demons." In *Jesus among Friends and Enemies: A Historical and Literary Introduction to Jesus in the Gospels*, edited by Chris Keith and Larry W. Hurtado, 173–97. Grand Rapids: Baker Academic, 2011.

Svartvik, Jesper M. *Mark and Mission: Mark 7:1–23 in Its Narrative and Historical Contexts*. Coniectanea Biblica: New Testament Series 32. Stockholm: Almqvist & Wiksell, 2000.

Taylor, Joan. *The Immerser: John the Baptist within Second Temple Judaism*. Grand Rapids: Eerdmans, 1997.

Te Riele, Gérard-Jean. "Une Nouvelle Loi Sacreé en Arcadie." *Bulletin de correspondance hellénique* 102 (1978): 325–31.

Tertullian. *Adversus Marcionem*. Translated by Ernest Evans. 2 vols. Oxford Early Christian Texts. Oxford: Clarendon, 1972.

Tervanotko, Hanna. "Members of the Levite Family and Ideal Marriages in Aramaic Levi Document, Visions of Amram, and Jubilees." *Revue de Qumran* 106 (2015): 155–76.

Thiessen, Matthew. "Abolishers of the Law in Early Judaism and Matthew 5,17–20." *Biblica* 93 (2012): 543–56.

———. *Contesting Conversion: Genealogy, Circumcision, and Identity in Ancient Judaism and Christianity*. New York: Oxford University Press, 2011.

———. "The Legislation of Leviticus 12 in Light of Ancient Embryology." *Vetus Testamentum* 68 (2018): 297–319.

———. "Luke 2:22, Leviticus 12, and Parturient Impurity." *Novum Testamentum* 54 (2012): 16–29.

———. *Paul and the Gentile Problem*. New York: Oxford University Press, 2016.

———. "The Text of Genesis 17:14." *Journal of Biblical Literature* 128 (2009): 625–42.

Toorn, Karel van der. "The Theology of Demons in Mesopotamia and Israel: Popular Belief and Scholarly Speculation." In Lange, Lichtenberger, and Römheld, *Die Dämonen—Demons*, 61–83.

Trummer, Peter. *Die blutende Frau: Wunderheilung im neuen Testament*. Freiburg: Herder, 1991.

Tyson, Joseph B. *Marcion and Luke-Acts: A Defining Struggle*. Columbia: University of South Carolina Press, 2006.

VanderKam, James C., trans. *The Book of Jubilees: A Critical Edition.* Corpus Scriptorum Christianorum Orientalium 511. Leuven: Peeters, 1989.

———. "The Demons in the Book of *Jubilees.*" In Lange, Lichtenberger, and Römheld, *Die Dämonen—Demons,* 339–64.

VanMaaren, John. "Does Mark's Jesus Abrogate Torah? Jesus' Purity Logion and Its Illustration in Mark 7:15–23." *Journal of the Jesus Movement in Its Jewish Setting* 4 (2017): 21–41.

———. "The Gospel of Mark within Judaism: Reading the Second Gospel in Its Ethnic Landscape." PhD diss., McMaster University, 2019.

Vermes, Geza. *Jesus the Jew: A Historian's Reading of the Gospels.* New York: Macmillan, 1973.

———. *The Religion of Jesus the Jew.* London: SCM, 1993.

Voorwinde, Stephen. *Jesus' Emotions in the Gospels.* The Library of New Testament Studies 284. London: T&T Clark, 2011.

Wächter, Theodor. *Reinheitsvorschriften im griechischen Kult.* Giessen: Töpelmann, 1910.

Wahlen, Clinton. *Jesus and the Impurity of Spirits in the Synoptic Gospels.* Wissenschaftliche Untersuchungen zum Neuen Testament 2/185. Tübingen: Mohr Siebeck, 2004.

Wardle, Timothy. "Resurrection and the Holy City: Matthew's Use of Isaiah in 27:51–53." *Catholic Biblical Quarterly* 78 (2016): 666–81.

Wassen, Cecilia. "The Impurity of the Impure Spirits in the Gospels." In *Healing and Exorcism in Second Temple Judaism and Early Christianity,* edited by Mikael Tellbe and Tommy Wasserman, 40–61. Wissenschaftliche Untersuchungen zum Neuen Testament 2/511. Tübingen: Mohr Siebeck, 2019.

———. "Jesus and the Hemorrhaging Woman in Mark 5:24–34: Insights from Purity Laws from Qumran." In *Scripture in Transition: Essays on Septuagint, Hebrew Bible, and Dead Sea Scrolls in Honour of Raija Sollamo,* edited by Anssi Voitila and Jutta Jokiranta, 641–60. Journal for the Study of Judaism in the Persian, Hellenistic, and Roman Periods Supplement Series 126. Leiden: Brill, 2008.

———. "Jesus' Table Fellowship with 'Toll Collectors and Sinners': Questioning the Alleged Purity Implications." *Journal for the Study of the Historical Jesus* 14 (2016): 137–57.

———. "Jesus' Work as a Healer in Light of Jewish Purity Laws." In *Bridging between Sister Religions: Studies of Jewish and Christian Scriptures in Honor of Prof. John T. Townsend,* edited by Isaac Kalimi, 87–104. Brill Reference Library of Judaism 51. Leiden: Brill, 2016.

———. "The Jewishness of Jesus and Ritual Purity." *Scripta Instituti Donneriani Aboensis* 27 (2016): 11–36.

———. "The Use of the Dead Sea Scrolls for Interpreting Jesus' Action in the Temple." *Dead Sea Discoveries* 23 (2016): 280–303.

———. "What Do Angels Have against the Blind and the Deaf? Rules of Exclusion in the Dead Sea Scrolls." In *Common Judaism, Explorations in Second-Temple Judaism*, edited by Wayne O. McCready and Adele Reinhartz, 115–29. Minneapolis: Fortress, 2008.

———. *Women in the Damascus Document*. Academia Biblica 21. Leiden: Brill, 2005.

Watts, James W. *Ritual and Rhetoric in Leviticus: From Sacrifice to Scripture*. Cambridge: Cambridge University Press, 2007.

Webb, Robert L. "Jesus Heals a Leper: Mark 1.40–45 and Egerton Gospel 35–47." *Journal for the Study of the Historical Jesus* 4 (2006): 177–202.

Weiss, Herold. *A Day of Gladness: The Sabbath among Jews and Christians in Antiquity*. Columbia: University of South Carolina Press, 2003.

Weiss, Johannes. *Jesus' Proclamation of the Kingdom of God*. Translated by Richard Hyde Hiers and David Larrimore Holland. Philadelphia: Fortress, 1971.

Weissenrieder, Annette. "The Plague of Uncleanness? The Ancient Illness Construct 'Issue of Blood' in Luke 8:43–48." In *The Social Setting of Jesus and the Gospels*, edited by Wolfgang Stegemann, Bruce J. Malina, and Gerd Theissen, 207–22. Minneapolis: Fortress, 2002.

Wenham, Gordon J. *The Book of Leviticus*. New International Commentary on the Old Testament. Grand Rapids: Eerdmans, 1979.

Werrett, Ian C. *Ritual Purity and the Dead Sea Scrolls*. Studies on the Texts of the Desert of Judah 72. Leiden: Brill, 2005.

Westerholm, Stephen. *Jesus and Scribal Authority*. Coniectanea Biblica: New Testament Series 10. Lund: Gleerup, 1978.

Wevers, John William, ed. *Leviticus*. Septuaginta: Vetus Testamentum Graecum 2/2. Göttingen: Vandenhoeck & Ruprecht, 1986.

Whitekettle, Richard. "Leviticus 12 and the Israelite Woman: Ritual Process, Liminality, and the Womb." *Zeitschrift für die alttestamentliche Wissenschaft* 107 (1995): 393–408.

Wilfand, Yael. *Poverty, Charity, and the Poor in Rabbinic Texts from the Land of Israel*. Sheffield: Sheffield Phoenix, 2014.

Wilfong, Terry G. "Menstrual Synchrony and the 'Place of Women' in Ancient Egypt (OIM 13512)." In *Gold of Praise: Studies on Ancient Egypt in Honor of Edward F. Wente*, edited by E. Teeter and J. A. Larson, 419–34. Studies in Ancient Oriental Civilizations 58. Chicago: University of Chicago Press, 1999.

Williams, Frank. *The Panarion of Epiphanius of Salamis*. 2nd ed. 2 vols. Nag Hammadi and Manichaean Studies 63 and 79. Leiden: Brill, 2009–13.

Williams, Peter J. "An Examination of Ehrman's Case for ὀργισθείς in Mark 1:41." *Novum Testamentum* 54 (2012): 1–12.

Wright, David P. *The Disposal of Impurity: Elimination Rites in the Bible and in Hittite and Mesopotamian Literature*. Society of Biblical Literature Dissertation Series 101. Atlanta: Scholars Press, 1987.

———. "Unclean and Clean (OT)." In vol. 6 of *The Anchor Bible Dictionary*, edited by David Noel Freedman, 729–41. New York: Doubleday, 1992.

Wright, N. T. *Jesus and the Victory of God*. Minneapolis: Fortress, 1997.

Yang, Yong-Eui. *Jesus and the Sabbath in Matthew's Gospel*. Journal for the Study of the New Testament Supplement Series 139. Sheffield: Sheffield Academic, 1997.

Zucconi, Laura M. "Aramean Skin Care: A New Perspective on Naaman's Leprosy." In *Sacred History, Sacred Literature: Essays on Ancient Israel, the Bible, and Religion in Honor of R. E. Friedman on His Sixtieth Birthday*, edited by Shawna Dolansky, 169–77. Winona Lake, IN: Eisenbrauns, 2008.

Author Index

Scripture and Ancient Writings Index

Subject Index

Made in the USA
Las Vegas, NV
26 March 2021